Louise M. Coffman

Abner's Story
By Louise M. Coffman

(Telling why some Pennsylvania Dutch left Germany in the 1730's and moved to what later became York County, Pennsylvania, and featuring some of their customs, food, superstitions and language.)

E. may

ISBN: 0-75964-824-7

This book is printed on acid free paper.

1stBooks – rev. 7/30/01

Preface

In the summer of 1998, I read in the local newspaper that more than 92% of the people who live in the borough of West York, adjacent to York, Pennsylvania, were born and raised there. Furthermore, in some of the small towns in York County the rate was even higher. Also, there are a number of farms that are owned by the descendants of the original settlers who came in the 1730's, and 1740's, more than two hundred fifty years ago. I began to wonder why their forefathers had ever left Germany, considering that over the years most of them choose to remain in the same locality, refusing to move even a few miles. It occurred to me that something cataclysmic must have taken place back in the 1700's for them to even consider moving. I began asking persons of Pennsylvania Dutch ancestry why their ancestors had left the old country and most of them did not know.

On Labor Day weekend, I stopped at a roadside stand near Hellam that was operated by Myron Dietz. He was dressed in bib overalls and had a long white beard. I asked him my standard question, and he proved to be a gold mine of information. He had taught history at Lancaster County Mennonite High School for more than forty years. He said that some early settlers came for cheap land, but many, mostly the Anabaptists, came because of religious persecution. He explained that Anabaptists include the Amish, Mennonites, Brethren and others, and do not consider themselves to be Protestants but another branch of Christianity altogether. Then came the shocker! He informed me that the persecutors of the Anabaptists were Protestants, members of the Lutheran and Reformed churches. There was more to the story than I thought.

Later I ran into Holly Brillhart Kurtz whose roots are deep in York County. She said that one of her ancestors, an Anabaptist, was dragged behind a horse until he died because he refused to recant his beliefs. Kim Brenneman Martin told me that one of her ancestors was arrested for religious reasons and spent time in prison before he was released and allowed to come to America. Gradually, my story grew. I learned that by the time the "troubles" were over, not one single member of the Brethren Church, remained in what is now Germany. They had all been driven out or massacred. This group is also known as the Dunkards.

I realized that no story of the Pennsylvania Dutch would be complete without including examples of various superstitions that are believed and practiced by many, even into the twenty-first century. One of these practices is a type of faith healing called powwowing. I asked a number of my friends and family if as a child, they had ever been powwowed-for [sic] to be cured of any sickness or ailment, such as warts or poison ivy. A surprising number had been, even younger ones. Powwowing is a combination of prayers, spells and mystical incantations for healing, as described in a book called *Lang Verborgne Freund (Long Lost Friend,)* by John George Hohman, published in Reading, Pennsylvania, in 1820. The person who performed the ritual is called a powwow doctor or powwower. The German word is b*raucher,* which means healer. How the word changed to what is now considered by most to be an Indian term, is anyone's guess, but the term 'powwow' is used throughout this area.

A powwower, who could be a man or woman, always told patients that they must believe or the powwowing would not work. Without belief nothing could be done. There was a different treatment for each disease. For example, to cure erysipelas, a streptococcal infection that was common before antibiotics, three strands of red wool or silk were wound around the patient's body and a shovelful of hot coals was carried around him three times.

One did not joke around about powwowing because behind it was the supernatural. Superstitious people believed that powwow doctors, and those who owned a copy of *The Long Lost Friend,* had the power to put curses or hexes on persons, animals and crops. Many believed that these hexes could make a person sick, a woman or an animal unable to conceive or if pregnant to miscarry, crops to fail, and other calamities. The powwow doctor was also familiar with the healing properties of plants and herbs.

Betty Stambaugh, who was born in the 1930's, said that when she was little, she cried all the time. Her mother took her to a powwow doctor who said that she had bladders in her eyes, and he assured her mother that he could heal her. He performed the string and egg ritual that the grandmother uses in this book. Mrs. Stambaugh said that she remembers it well, and feels that it helped some, but admits that she still cries easily. She was a great source of general knowledge about the culture and superstitions of the Pennsylvania Dutch, as were Phyllis and Leroy Bechtel, and Dean Artz.

My husband's grandmother, Charlotte Menchey Coffman, has been gone for many years, but I still remember things that she told me about powwowing and other superstitions. For example, if someone dropped a knife, a male visitor was coming; a fork, a woman; a spoon, a child. Dropping a dishrag on the floor was a sure sign of a coming calamity. Grandma Coffman's sister, Iowa "Ovie" Menchey Fuhrman, was a powwow doctor. Grandma said that in order to become a powwow doctor one had to have a certain spirituality or gift for it, and be taught by an older person of the opposite sex. Aunt Ovie gave it up in her later years because she said that it took too much out of her. I do not know if she passed it on to the next generation, but I do not know of anyone who does it now. It seems as if the practice has virtually died out, although I do know of only one person who owns a copy of *The Long Lost Friend*, and there are many superstitious people.

I have lived in this Pennsylvania Dutch Country for more than fifty years, but I was born and raised in California. My husband, Dean, who was born in Hanover, Pennsylvania, and graduated from West York High School, was stationed in California during World War II. We married in 1945 and moved to Abbottstown, Pennsylvania, three years later. It was a small town in Adams County just over the York County line, and as Dutch as Dutch could be. It was a real culture shock for me and I had a difficult time adjusting. I wanted to go home to California; but Dean would not leave Pennsylvania once he got back. He, like most of his people, insisted on staying put.

As far as we know, Dean's earliest ancestors to come to America were Jacob Altland and his wife, Mary Sybilla Altland. They arrived in Philadelphia in 1739 on the *Princess Augusta*, and acquired land near Bigmount, which northwest of York, halfway between Dover and East Berlin. That land stayed in the family until just recently. I used Jacob Altland's name to honor him, but this is not his story. I don't know much about him except that he or his son gave land for Altland's Meeting House. All characters and place names are fictitious. However, I endeavored to make the story historically and culturally accurate using surnames names that are common to York County.

York County is in the south central part of Pennsylvania just north of the Manson-Dixon line between Gettysburg and Lancaster.

* * * * *

This book is dedicated to Doug Ward who got me started and encouraged me to do something I didn't think I could do. Thanks to members of "Write Stuff," a writing group affiliated with the American Association of University Women: Karen Julian, Laura Hess and Dorothy Bruno. Special thanks to my son, Dane and his wife, Sara, for helping me to learn to use the computer while trying to write my first book; and to my daughters, Nancy and Janet, because without their love and encouragement this book would not have been written. It is also dedicated to Dean, always Dean. Without him, I would never have known these "Dutchers."

* * * * *

Scripture is from the King James Version of the with the exception of one or two verses.

PROLOGUE

Ten-year-old Freddie Hartzell and his great grandpa, Abner Hartzell, were sitting together on the porch of the native stone house where they lived in the rolling hills of York County, Pennsylvania. Looking up at the elderly gentleman, Freddie said, "Grandpa Abner, you often say, 'Forget not the reason.' It wonders me,* why do you say that? What reason daresn't* I forget?"

Abner Hartzell, a spry, bright-eyed eighty-year old with a long white beard, looked at his great grandson in surprise, but before he could answer, Freddie continued, "It wonders me, too, why did you leave the old country? Why did you and your family get on a boat and come across the big ocean to Pennsylvania? Why did you keep on coming until you got to York County? Why for did you do that? What for was the reason?"

Grandpa Abner smiled at his great grandson, rubbed his chin and said, "We get old so fast and smart so late, and years go by before you know it. I forgot that I had never told you why we left there and came here."

Freddie looked up expectantly, and asked, "Could you tell me now? I really want to know."

Grandpa Abner took a deep breath and began, "There were many reasons for leaving there and never going back, but the main one was so that in the old country our people couldn't worship God in the way we felt He wanted us to. William Penn offered the persecuted people and the poor people of Europe a chance to go to this new place where no king could tell them what church to go to, or tax them to support a church sponsored by the government. You take all that for granted in this new country that we call the United States of America. Can you imagine what it would be like if soldiers came and took your papa away and made him work for the king? Can you

---

* It wonders me.: I wonder.
* daresn't : we dare not; we should not

vii

imagine what it would be like if soldiers moved into your house, ate up your food, slept in your bed, paid you no rent and refused to move out? Can you imagine what it would be like if suddenly, many of your neighbors turned on you and tried to kill you?"

Freddie's eyes grew wide as he shook his head in disbelief. "No, Grandpa Abner, I can't."

The old man got a faraway look on his face as he recalled those days more than seventy years before.

"It was the week before my tenth birthday," he said, "and what a week that was! My mother's cousin, Jake Altland, who was a land agent for the William Penn Company, had come back from America and was over at the square telling the villagers about Pennsylvania. My friend, Schotzy, you remember Herr Schotzenberger, don't you? Well, Schotzy and I decided that we wanted to go to Pennsylvania when we grew up, but we hadn't figured on going so soon. If I tell you the whole story, will you promise that you will remember? Will you promise that you will tell your children and your grandchildren so that they, too, will know why I say, 'Forget not the reason!' It is important for everyone to remember because many lives were lost and many sacrifices were made. We are here only by the goodness and mercy of God."

ACKNOWLEDGMENTS

Dean Artz
Dean Coffman
Phyllis Bechtel
Katie Dempsey
Myron Dietz
Gary Geiselman

Nancy Hildreth
Holly Brillhart Kurtz
Carol Mann
Betty Stambaugh
David Wenger
Dr. Michael Zittle

ABNER'S STORY

By Louise M. Coffman

"Grandpa, I need to know everything," cried Abner breathlessly as he ran to the workshop at the back of his grandparent's old stone house in the village of Rittendorf, in what is now south central Germany. It was a perfect spring day, crisp and cool in the shade or away from buildings, and warm on the sunny side out of the wind. The door to the workshop was open and Grandpa was busy at his workbench.

"Ach, vell, little fella, what brought this on?" Grandpa looked up from the wooden peg he was carving.

Abner started excitedly, "Herr Jacob Altland just got back from America and he was at the square. He says that there is a place in America called Pennsylvania. An Englisher* owns it. And guess what? He sent Herr Altland to our country to tell people about it to try to get them to move there."

Grandpa raised his bushy gray eyebrows and looked interested. "Herr Altland is your mother's cousin. He went to America before you were born, probably around 1725. So that's ten years he's been gone. What's that got to do with your needing to know everything?" Grandpa smiled at the idea and his eyes twinkled with humor.

"I'm going to go to Pennsylvania as soon as I can," answered Abner, very seriously. "Herr Altland says the houses there be dear* and that's why and I need to know how to build one."

"America is far across the ocean, Abner. What does your mother think about your going to Pennsylvania?" asked Grandpa, leaning forward and putting down the peg.

"I haven't told her yet. I don't know what she'll say about it, be-ins* Papa's gone. Maybe I'd better wait to tell her until Papa gets

---

* Englisher: A person from England
* be dear: are expensive

home, but then again, it might be a long time." He stopped and thought a bit and added, "Ya,* and it might take awhile before I know everything. When I do, I'll go to America and build a house. Do you think it will take me long to learn everything?"

Grandpa looked at Abner with a great deal of love in his dark brown eyes and tried not to smile. He was saved from answering when Abner continued, "I forgot to tell you. Schotzy is going with me and I came over here to ask if you…"

Just then Schotzy came running around the corner to the workshop and interrupted. "Greetings, Herr Hartzell, did Abner tell you we're going to Pennsylvania? Did he ask you to teach us how to build a house? I'm so excited I can't wait! We need to get there quick before Pennsylvania gets filled up with people. Are you going to teach us?"

Abner gave Schotzy a dirty look and said, "Now you've done it! You dumkopf!* I haven't even asked him yet." Abner gave Schotzy a shove and Schotzy shoved him back.

"Boys!" said Grandpa sternly. "We'll have none of that around here."

"I'm sorry," both of the boys said at once.

Grandpa looked at the two of them: his grandson, tall for his age, dark and sturdily built; and Schotzy, shorter and thin, with light skin, freckles, and a mass of strublig* blond hair that looked like it hadn't been combed forever. They had been friends since they were babies.

"We'll be good if you teach us," said Abner. "Won't we, Schotzy?"

Schotzy nodded his head seriously. "Ya, Herr Hartzell," he said. "We'll be good. We'll be really, really good if you will teach us. I cross my heart and I know it's terrible bad luck to cross your heart and not keep your word." With a very dirty hand, he crossed his heart.

(..continued)
* be-ins: due to the fact that
* ya: yes
* dumkopf: dumb-head, stupid person
* strublig: windblown or uncombed

2

Grandpa's cat, Princess, a large tiger, got up from her nap in the sun and rubbed against Abner's leg. He reached down, petted her and scratched her ears.

"Ach vell, anyhow," said Grandpa, "sit down awhile." He motioned to an old wooden bench outside in the sunshine. "Abner is telling me about America and some place else over there. What is the name of it again?" The boys sat down and Princess jumped up onto Abner's lap.

"I can't play with you now, Princess," he said, stroking her gently. "I have to tell Grandpa all about Pennsylvania."

Princess settled herself and looked at him as if to say, "Whatever," and began to purr loudly.

"So the name of the place is Pennsylvania, but who is this Englisher and what does he want?" asked Grandpa.

"William Penn he is." explained Abner. "The Englisher's king owed him money, a lot of money, but the king had no way to pay, so he gave William Penn land in America instead."

"Except another king before him may have given some of the same land to someone else," interrupted Schotzy. "And it's good land, real good land. Herr Altland says you can raise anything on it. He says it is some of the best farm land he's ever seen."

"Ya," interrupted Abner. "Now people from that place, I believe so half* it's called Maryland. Anyway, whatever it's called, they are moving onto William Penn's land."

"There is no clear boundary," put in Schotzy, "so the lord who owns Maryland, is trying to claim as much land as he can."

"So the Englisher has a problem," said Grandpa. "What has that got to do with you?"

"Herr Altland says that William Penn will sell the land cheap and he wants good, godly people to move there. He said a lot of other things, but I don't remember everything, do you, Schotzy?"

"Ya, I remember some things," said Schotzy, scratching his head again, "but I can't talk about it now. It's almost suppertime; and if I don't help make it, I don't eat." He stood up, gave Princess a pat,

---

* believe so half: think so, but not completely sure

and hurried up the cobblestone street and across the bridge toward his house.

Looking seriously at Abner, Grandpa said, "So you want me to teach you. I know you can read some, but you need to get better at it. How about Schotzy?"

"He can't read much, only the alphabet and whatever else I've taught him, but he is better than me at numbers."

"Your numbers, Abner, you must get good at them. If you don't, you will have a crooked house." Grandpa laughed and held his hands this way and that.

Abner didn't like to be laughed at and hung his head, saying, "Numbers are hard for me."

"Lots of things are hard for most people, but they keep at them anyway. If you don't know your numbers people could cheat you and you wouldn't even know it. You wouldn't want that, would you?"

Abner shook his head and replied, "Grandpa, if you will teach us, I will really try, and I know Schotzy will, too. If you won't teach us, who will? My papa would teach me if he were here, but he's not, and Schotzy's grandfather hardly ever says a word. He is grouchy all of the time. Schotzy is like a brother to me. What's going to happen to us, but especially him, unless someone helps us? He has no mother or father. And me, I need to know a lot more than I know now. I need to be taught, too."

Grandpa thought a bit and then said, "Walter Schotzenberger just isn't the same since his wife died and the tree fell on his son. I think he blames himself for the accident, even though it wasn't his fault. You said he was grouchy, but I would call him sad. He takes care of his grandson the best he knows, I'm sure. What do you think it's like for an old man to suddenly be without his wife and son, and have to take care of a motherless grandson?"

"I never thought about that."

"It's best if you think before you talk, Grandson, because what you say and what you do have consequences, but you are right about one thing. Schotzy's grandfather can't teach him very much. All he knows is how to cut and chop wood, although I must say he was a tricky fellow when he was young. I doubt that he's been back to the forest since his son was killed."

"Grandpa, I promise you that if you teach Schotzy and me, we will work hard and make you proud." Grandpa sat and thought, and while he thought, he stroked his bearded chin.

Abner wondered what he was thinking. He could not sit still. He rutched* around and the bench began to squeak. He had no rest in his britches so he stood up and Princess jumped off his lap. Abner knew that Grandpa did not like to be disturbed when he was thinking.

After what seemed to be a long time, Grandpa said, "Tomorrow morning I am going to Widow Schneider's to repair her back porch. That's why I am carving these pegs. I am also going to replace the stone steps at the back of her house. The ones there are so old and worn down, I'm afraid she will hurt herself going down them. I imagine her house is about five hundred years old. Steps made of that kind of stone usually aren't that badly worn down unless they are that old or used hard. I gathered and prepared the replacement stones last week."

Abner looked at the pegs Grandpa had been carving and saw that they were pieces of a small branch from which Grandpa had stripped off the bark and sawed into lengths about as long and as thick as Abner's little finger. Seeing that Abner was interested, Grandpa explained to him how pegs were used. "First you drill the hole, then you pound the peg into the hole with a mallet," he said. "You saw it off underneath and on top, and then you smooth it off with a pumice rock. The peg must be hard wood, harder than the wood that you are pounding it into."

"Why are you using pegs instead of nails?" asked Abner, "I thought that you used pegs only on fine furniture."

"I have run out of nails and I can't get any more because the king has taken all of the nails in the kingdom to use on his new palace. That's why." Grandpa looked disgusted.

"We don't have a very good king, do we?" asked Abner.

---

* rutch: wiggle or squirm (rhymes with butch)

5

"Ssshhh." Grandpa said, looking startled. He put his finger to his lips, and whispered, "The walls have ears."

Abner raised his eyebrows in question. "What do you mean?"

"I mean we live in dangerous times, and although we feel safe in our own homes, there are some things that are best not said."

Abner nodded his head. As young as he was, he understood.

"Now about tomorrow," Grandpa continued, "if your mother will allow you, and Schotzy's grandfather will allow him; you may both come along and help. I will have to talk to Herr Schotzenberger before I say anything to Schotzy about teaching him. The boy is his responsibility so it is up to him to decide. You must understand that I cannot teach him for free."

"But you will teach him if it is all right with his grandfather, and something can be worked out. Not?"

Grandpa smiled and nodded his head.

Abner jumped up and down, almost stepping on the cat. He hugged his grandpa as hard as he could. "Thank you! Thank you! Thank you! I promise you that you'll never be sorry that you decided to do this. I don't know what we'd do without you."

Grandpa hugged him back and mussed up his hair. "You're both good boys. Oh, and another thing, I see no reason to tell your grandmother about your plans to go to America. We wouldn't want to get her all fussed up* would we? It will be a while before you know everything you need to know in order to build a house and to get along in a new country. We'll tell her when the time comes. What do you think?"

Abner nodded his head in agreement. He knew how excitable Grandma was lately and how she could worry about the least little thing. "You are right, sir, and maybe I won't tell my mama because I wouldn't want her all fussed up either."

"Good idea, that's wisdom, and now I think it's time for you to go home. Go in and greet your grandmother, and don't forget to wipe your feet."

---

* fussed up: nervous and worried

The cat tried to go in, too, but Grandpa pushed her away with his foot, saying, "Kitty, you are a barn cat, and you are not allowed in the house."

Abner and Grandpa both wiped their feet on the mat, and Grandma met him at the back door saying, "Make yourself in. It's good to see you." He hadn't even got inside the door before she had hugged him and kissed him twice.

"Ach, Grandma, I'm getting too big for all that schmutzig."[*]

"You are my only grandbaby and I will hug you and schmutz[*] you every chance I get." She laughed, ignoring his protest completely. "I made some little cakes[*] this afternoon."

"I knew that's what I smelled. Do they ever smell good!"

"Here," she said, handing him a small basketful. She carefully covered it with a napkin and added, "I made a nice sized batch, and I thought you might like to take some home for supper."

"Thank you, Grandma," said Abner. "Little cakes are my favorite and you make the best ones in the world." Forgetting that he had just told her he was too big for all that schmutzig stuff, he gave her a big hug. She was soft and round and wonderful to hug, and she always smelled like spice and good things cooking or baking in the kitchen.

"You are a good boy and so handsome, too," she said, patting him on the cheek. "Come back tomorrow and I will give you some more. Those are the first ones. There are more in the oven."

"Wunderbar,"[*] Abner said with a smile, as he headed toward the front door.

"Ach, no. No! No! No!" Grandma cried out in a fearful voice. "You know you must always go out the same door you came in! You know it's very bad luck to go out the front door when you come in the back. You leave your luck behind when you do that, and you need all the luck you can get. Remember now! Always go out the

---

[*] schmutzig: kissing or smearing; slobbery kisses; anything smeared such as cake icing (rhymes with puts pig)
[*] schmutz: kiss (rhymes with puts)
[*] little cakes: soft cookies
[*] wunderbar: wonderful (pronounced voonderbar)

same door you came in. I've told you before." Grandma was so excited that she knocked a knife onto the floor. "Now look at that! That means a man or a boy is coming to visit."

Grandpa had followed Abner into the house. "Now, Bertl," he scolded. "Don't fill his head with all that superstitious nonsense."

Abner had heard them argue before about superstition, and he left quickly out the back door, calling, "Goodnight, I hope I see you in the morning."

CHAPTER TWO

As Abner walked home, he looked at his village of Rittendorf as if he had never seen it before. It was a small village where the hills met the mountains and there were no other villages higher up. However, there was a difficult pass that people came through occasionally when they were trying to escape from places to the south. The pass was closed in the winter and dangerous in the springtime because of avalanches. Abner could not see the pass, but he had heard avalanches several times and the idea of going through the pass in the springtime was frightening.

As he looked around, he could see beautiful hills with rows of grapevines climbing their sides and steep mountains beyond. Most of the trees and vines were just budding or still bare, except for the very dark evergreens, and the golden willows, showing off their early spring color. The sun was setting and the sky was a deep blue with pinkish-purple clouds in the west. A fast running stream cut through the middle of the village to a lake below. Around and beyond the lake was a meadow that was just beginning to turn green and the lake glistened with the reflected colors of the setting sun. Way down in the valley he could see the spires of two churches, and in the far distance a castle that could be seen only on very clear days. Abner thought to himself, *It wonders me what Pennsylvania looks like. Could it be as beautiful as this?*

Just then Abner saw his friend coming towards him. "Hey, Schotzy, just the one I want to see. You sure fressed[*] your supper down fast."

"Ya well, all we had was some cabbage soup that Pappaw[*] warmed up from yesterday. It didn't take long to eat it," he said, ignoring the insult. "What fer do you want me?"

---

[*] fress: to gobble, eat like an animal,
[*] Pappaw: grandfather

9

"Grandpa's going to work on Widow Schneider's house in the morning. He says we can come along and help. I'm going if my mother will let me. Wanta come?"

"Sure, if my pappaw will let me. I think he will, but you never know." Schotzy eyed the basket. "What fer stuff you got?" he asked. "It smells awful good."

"Little cakes. Would you like one?" Abner offered him the basket.

Schotzy reached in, took one, and gobbled it down.

The way Schotzy ate, Abner could tell he was still hungry.

"Would you like another?"

"Ya," he answered as he promptly reached in.

Never before had it ever occurred to Abner that Schotzy might not have enough to eat. There was always more than enough to eat on his table and on his grandparents' table. In fact, sometimes he became upset when his mother tried to make him eat more than he wanted.

"Here," he said, handing Schotzy four more. "Give a cuppy[*] to your pappaw. He probably likes them, too. Grandma said she'll give me more tomorrow."

"Gee thanks," said Schotzy in surprise. "It's long already[*] that we had any little cakes, way before my grandma died. Pappaw will be glad to have some, too. Thank you very much."

"That's all right," answered Abner, "I'm glad to share." He was embarrassed and didn't quite know what to say. "Here, take some more, take them all."

"Ach, no. That wouldn't be right. Thanks anyways," said Schotzy, as he started walking home. Abner watched him all the way across the bridge and back to his house. He noticed that his clothes were too small for him; worn out and dirty, filthy dirty, and he was thin, really thin. *No wonder,* thought Abner, *that Schotzy couldn't keep up like he used to. He doesn't get enough to eat. And*

---

[*] cuppy: couple
[*] long already: a long time

10

his hands were absolutely filthy when he reached in for the little cake!

"This is terrible," Abner said aloud to himself. "Something must be done about this. I gotta think on it." Without realizing it, he stroked his chin just the way Grandpa did when he was thinking.

When Abner got home, he was surprised to see Herr Altland and his mother sitting on the wooden bench in front of their house. He was surprised for two reasons: Herr Altland was at his house, and his mother was sitting down, doing nothing. His mother never sat down and did nothing; never, except in church, and then she was worshipping. She was always busy from early morning until late at night.

"Herr Altland, good evening. How good to see you again! What brings you here this evening?" greeted Abner, a little surprised at how grown-up he sounded.

Herr Altland stood and shook his hand, "So you're Abner, Rachel's and Matthias' son. I didn't know that when I saw you at the square this afternoon, but I should have known. You favor your father."

"That's what they tell me, sir," he answered politely.

"Herr Altland is my cousin," said his mother. "I was an Altland before I married your father. His father and my father were brothers. You may call him Cousin Jake. Did you know that Jake introduced me to your father?"

"Is that a fact?" said Abner, smiling. "No, I didn't know that before."

"Ya, it's true," Cousin Jake laughed, "I'll tell you all about it sometime." His face lit up and the lines around his eyes crinkled with the remembrance.

"It wasn't all that funny," said his mother, looking somewhat embarrassed, "and you don't have to tell him about it."

Cousin Jake laughed all the harder. "But I do. I do! Of course, I do!"

Except that Cousin Jake laughed a lot more easily that his mother, Abner could see a strong family resemblance. He was taller

11

and heavier set than she, but they both had fair skin and very black hair. Hers was thick and pulled back into a bun, with just a few gray hairs; his was cut off just above his collar and getting thin on top. He had some gray at the temples, but still, it was the same color. Their noses were long, thin and pointed; their eyes were the same hazel color, halfway between green and brown with flecks of yellow. Sometimes Abner's father would tease his mother and say, "You have seldom color eyes, a color you seldom see," or he would say she had cat eyes. When he would say that, he would laugh and give her a pat on her backside. Abner had not thought much about his father all day, but suddenly he missed him very much.

He looked at his mother. She was, without doubt, the most beautiful woman in the village. Nearly everyone said so, so it wasn't just because she was his mother that he thought so. When Papa was home, she smiled and sometimes she laughed, but not now. Abner couldn't even remember when she had laughed; it had been that long. It occurred to him that his mother missed Papa as much as he did. Now why hadn't he thought of that before?

"Jake," his mother asked; "Would you like to stay for supper? I don't have anything fancy, just noodles that I put to a beef bone, and cabbage slaw, but there's plenty and it's all ready."

"I'd be glad to stay for supper," he answered with a big smile. "It's been a long time since I've had any home cooking, especially Altland cooking. Nothing tastes as good as something made by family."

Rachel smiled when he said that, but turning to Abner, she said, with slight anger in her voice, "It wondered me where you've been. You usually aren't late for supper." Then changing to a softer tone, she asked, "What do you have here?"

"Grandma sent along some little cakes. There were more, but I gave some to Schotzy because..."

"You gave some to Schotzy! You gave some to Schotzy!" The anger was back in her voice. "Why did you do that?"

"Because he was hungry, that's why," he answered defensively. Suddenly he remembered his grandfather saying, "It's best to think before you talk." Changing the tone of his voice he said, "The little

12

cakes smelled so good, and I ran into Schotzy, and we were talking. It seemed like a good idea to eat some." He hoped he wasn't lying.

"Well, food isn't all that easy to come by, that we give it to just anybody," she said as she wiped her feet on the mat and went into the house. "Wipe your feet," she added. Abner and Cousin Jake dutifully wiped their feet and followed her into the house.

Abner washed his hands in the wooden basin and helped his mother set the table. "We need a spoon and a fork. Do we need a knife?" he asked.

"Yes, we'll have butterbread."* She looked in the breadbox. "It looks like the bread is just about all.* Son, will you run to the bakery and get a fresh loaf? And tell the baker I will bring him butter in the morning to pay for it."

Abner was out the door and running toward the bakery in a flash. He was hungry and besides he didn't want to miss anything Cousin Jake might have to say. He was halfway there when heard Schotzy hollering.

"Abner, wait up! WAIT UP! I WANT TO TELL YOU SOMETHING!"

"All right, all right! You don't have to make like the pigs are after you. Supper's on the table and I must fetch bread."

"Pappaw says that I can go along tomorrow to Widow Schneider's and he's going along, too, to help," panted Schotzy, out of breath from running.

"What?" Abner's mouth fell open and his eyebrows shot up in surprise. "Your pappaw never goes anywhere or does anything he doesn't want to. How come is he going?"

"I don't know," answered Schotzy, "I don't know what to make of it."

"I haven't had a chance yet to ask my mother about working with Grandpa because Herr Altland is at my house. We are having him

---

* butterbread: bread with butter on it; jellybread, bread with jelly on it; honeybread, bread with honey on it
* all: all gone

for supper. I hope I see you in the morning or maybe I'll see you later." Abner ran to the bakery, got the bread and ran home.

Everything else was ready when he got back. His mother sliced the bread and they all sat down, with Cousin Jake in Papa's place. It was the first time that anyone else had sat there since the soldiers had taken Papa away and Abner felt a lump in his throat just thinking about it.

"Abner, will you be the man of the family and ask the blessing on the food, please?" asked his mother.

They bowed their heads. Abner, who had never prayed aloud in front of a stranger, hesitated a bit, cleared his throat and said, "God is great. God is good. Let us thank Him for our food. By His hand we all are fed. Give us Lord, our daily bread, and God bless Papa and keep him safe wherever he is. In Jesus name, Amen."

Abner noticed that his mother had put butter, apple butter and smiercase* on the table as well as beef and noodle potpie, cole slaw, bread, and the little cakes. Nobody passed anything, they just reached into the middle and helped themselves to whatever they wanted. They ate their meal without talking.

As they ate, Abner thought about the differences between the Altlands and the Hartzells. The Hartzells talked and laughed during a meal, making jokes and sometimes even pretending they were somebody else. His papa was especially good at that. They passed their food from one to another, and Grandpa always saw to it that everyone was served before he ate. The Hartzells always said, "Guten Appetit,"* and they always seemed to enjoy their meals. Abner was glad he was a Hartzell.

After supper as Mama cleared the table, Cousin Jake said, "Will someone tell me what happened to Matthias? I keep hearing bits and pieces but no one has told me the whole story. I really want to know."

---

* smiercase: cottage cheese (sounds like smear case)
* Guten Appetit: enjoy your meal; literally, good appetite

Abner looked at his mother as she tried to tell about his father, but she choked up and couldn't talk. Tears came to her eyes and she said, "I'm sorry..."

"It's all right, Rachel," said Cousin Jake as he got up and put his arm around her. "Don't cry, I'm sure it will be all right."

"I wish I could say it'll be all right," she answered, and then looked at Abner. "You tell him." She wiped her eyes and continued to clear off the table. Then she poured water from a wooden bucket into a wooden basin and began to wash the dishes in the drysink.[*]

Abner didn't really know where to begin. He hesitated, and she motioned for him to go on. "Well," he said shyly, "last summer a man came and wanted to know who were the best stone masons in the village. The people in the village sent him straight to Grandpa and Papa. The man told them that the king was building a new palace for his son, the prince, because he's getting married next year to a princess from the country next to us. The man wanted to hire Grandpa and Papa to work for the king, but they didn't want to go. They shook their heads and said, 'No, it's too far, and besides, we don't want to leave our families and be gone the many months, or even years, that it would take to build the palace.' The man said that the king would pay them well, but they both said, 'No, thank you.' Then the man left and you could tell that he didn't like it a bit."

Abner took a deep breath, looked at his mother to see if she thought he was telling it right, and continued, "A cuppy weeks later soldiers came to take Papa and Grandpa to go to work on the palace whether they wanted to or not, but Grandpa was very sick that day. He wasn't sick the day before, and he wasn't sick the day after, and he hasn't been sick ever since. It was funny in a way. Grandpa looked so sick, that the soldiers wouldn't go near him. Grandma said that God's angels made him look sick because as soon as the soldiers left he was fine." He took another deep breath and looked at his mother again, rubbed his chin and went on.

"Papa said that he couldn't go because there would be no one here to look after his family, but the soldiers grabbed him, held onto

---

[*] drysink: a wooden work place in the kitchen without plumbing

him and told Mama to get his things ready. They said the king would be upset that Grandpa couldn't come and they weren't going to let Papa have a chance to get away."

"I'm glad to hear they didn't take your grandfather, but that's too bad about your papa," said Cousin Jake. "How long has he been gone?"

"Since last fall." Abner counted on his fingers. "Nine months."

Turning to Rachel he asked, "Have you heard from him?"

"No, not directly," she answered shaking her head sadly. "We heard some rumors that the king was going to send a number of stone cutters to Italy for marble. He really wants to impress the princess's father with this new palace. They say he is going to build a huge castle after this palace is done. When I think of what the taxes are now and what they will be, it just makes me sick. Everything just keeps getting worse all of the time. When there's war, the soldiers come and take everything, and when there's peace the king taxes us and takes everything."

Cousin Jake nodded sympathetically.

"It hasn't rained much this spring and it probably will be a dry summer and we won't have any crops," Rachel continued. "I don't know how I'm going to get along. The worst just keeps happening."

Ach, thought Abner, *I hate it when Mom runs at the mouth like that. She always expects the worst. She never says that something good will happen. When I talked about it to Grandpa, he said that it was just her way, or perhaps it was fear. Maybe she is afraid, but I've got the poops hearing it.* He started to say something, but inside his head he heard Grandpa say, "It's best to think before you talk," and he kept quiet. Instead, he changed the subject.

"Cousin Jake, will you tell me about your introducing my mama and papa."

His mother frowned, but Cousin Jake ignored her and began to tell the story, "Your papa and I were working down in the flat country building a rathaus* in the town near where your mother

---

* rathaus: town hall (sounds like rot house)

lived. I told your mother that this greistlich* fella that I worked with, had seen her and wanted to meet her. I told your father that my fat, funny-looking cousin had seen him and wanted to meet him. They both kept trying to avoid meeting each other, and at the same time they kept seeing each other and wanting to meet. It was a good trick, don't you think?" Cousin Jacob laughed and laughed.

Abner laughed, too. "My papa is the handsomest man in town and my mother is the most beautiful. That was a good trick. I guess I wouldn't be here if it hadn't been for you." Then he looked at his mother. She didn't like to be the butt of a joke any more than he did. He could tell that she must have been very embarrassed and still didn't think it was funny. He decided to change the subject.

"How long are you going to stay here, Cousin Jake"

"I plan to stay tomorrow which is Saturday; to worship with you on Sunday, and to leave early Monday morning."

"You can stay here if you like, Jake," said Mama. "We have plenty of room."

"Thanks anyway, Rachel, but I've already engaged a room at the gasthaus.* They serve breakfast and they are expecting me."

"I'd like to invite you for Sunday dinner, but we always go to Matthias' folks. How about tomorrow night?"

"Gut,"* Cousin Jake replied with a smile. "Thank you very much. I appreciate that, and I'll be here. But getting back to Matt. If you haven't heard from him, then he hasn't sent you any money. I am family, Rachel, and I care about you. How do you get along?"

Abner wondered what his mother would say. She wasn't much of a talker; in fact, she hardly ever said anything unless she was angry or complaining about something. He watched her a bit as she sat quietly and thought. When she began to talk Abner was really surprised because she said more than she ever did, and she told Cousin Jake all about how everything was.

---

* greistlich: ugly, disgusting (rhymes with spiced pig)
* gasthaus: inn (sounds like gast house)
* gut: good (rhymes with boot)

Rachel began slowly, "I have three cows and I sell milk. I make cheese and butter, and sell that, too." She stopped, caught her breath and then went on, "We have a sow and I give it the extra milk and buttermilk. She should have some little wutzies[*] before long. I"ll save one or two and sell the rest. I have a few chickens, so we have gockies[*] and a chicken to eat now and again. I always have a cluck[*] raise at least one setting of peeps.[*] Sometimes more. I try to have enough gockies or a chickens to sell or trade. Right now the hens aren't doing so good and we should be getting more gockies. I think so half that somebody besides Abner or me might be finding them." She sighed and thought a bit before continuing. "We've always had a big garden, but I doubt if Abner and I will be able to dig it around[*] like Matthias did. Still, if I keep working hard, and am careful not to waste anything, Abner and I might be all right until Matthias gets back."

Abner stared at her wondering what had come over her that she was talking so much. He realized he was staring at her, and looked away quickly, but not before he saw her set her jaw with that stubborn look he knew so well.

Just then Cousin Jake got up from the table, walked over to Abner, put his arm around his shoulders and asked, "Rachel, what kind of plans do you have for this young man?"

Abner listened, wondering what she would say. They had never talked about anything like that. He was surprised when she answered right away.

"Matthias and I always thought that he should learn one of the building trades. The Hartzells have always been builders," she said thoughtfully. "Most of the Altlands have been farmers and dairymen, content to stay on their own land and mind their own business, although I'll admit that you're an exception. But now

---

[*] wutzies: baby pigs (rhymes with footsies)
[*] gockies: eggs Hens cackle gock, gock, gock after they lay an egg.
[*] cluck: setting hen, (rhymes with look)
[*] peeps: baby chicks, from the fact that they go "Peep, peep, peep," all of the time
[*] dig it around: turn the ground over with a shovel and prepare it for planting

things are different. The king is pressing* builders into working for him. So I think it would be a good idea for Abner to be a dairyman. Then the king wouldn't take him away." Rachel paused, nodded her head and added, "Ya, I've thought about it a lot, and I want him to be a dairyman."

Rachel looked around the room, sighed and added, "I have three cows now. One is due to drop her hummy* in a week or two, and another in about three months. If they are heifers when they are born, I will save them to become cows. I'll keep on saving the heifers and that way I'll build a herd. By the time Abner is grown, there should be enough cows for both of us."

The idea took Abner completely by surprise. He thought about being a dairyman, and he knew he didn't want to be one. He knew dairymen had to milk the herd and shovel out the manure every morning and night, and he didn't want to do that for the rest of his life. And cows! He didn't like cows. Some cows kick, and some are mean, stubborn and contrary. They swish their tails when they are being milked and often hit the milker in the face!

Sometimes when cows are giving birth and the calf was having a hard time being born, the helper had to reach in up inside of the cow to his elbow or farther, and pull the calf out. Ooey-kuttz!* He hated that. Another job he hated was teaching a hummy to drink from a bucket. After it was a few days old it had to be taken away from its mother so that the milk could be sold. Besides, if it were allowed to drink all it wanted, it would get sick and die. Abner thought it was absolutely the worst job there ever was, worse even than shoveling manure. He hated having to put his hand into the hummy's mouth while trying to hold its head down in the bucket of milk. It naturally wanted to reach up and suckle from its mother, so it butted its head and sometimes knocked him down. He always tried to be sure there wasn't any manure around, because if there was any, sure as the

---

* pressing: involuntary servitude, forcing a person to work or join the army against his will
* hummy: calf
* ooey-kuttz: oh, puke

19

world, he'd land in it. After that happened, he had to get up, wipe himself off, and put his hand back in the calf's slobbery mouth until it learned to drink. The whole operation was greistlich, just plain greistlich. Abner shivered just thinking about it. It always took a few days until the hummy got the idea that milk could come from a bucket and not just from its mother. No, no indeed, he didn't want to be a dairyman and he wished his papa were here so he could talk to him and tell him so.

Cousin Jake looked at Abner and could tell that he didn't like the dairyman idea, but Rachel, wrapped in her own thoughts, hadn't even noticed.

"Hey, Abner, a pfennig* for your thoughts," he said.

Abner started to say something but Grandpa's words came to him again, "It's best to think before you speak." He shook his head, but he was thinking that he didn't want to stir up anything or hurt Mama's feelings. He wished he could talk to Grandpa because he knew he couldn't say what he wanted to say then, right out of the blue sky. He didn't know how Mama would take it, but he had a very good idea. Once she had made up her mind about something, it was just about impossible to get her to change it. He liked Cousin Jake, but it seemed as if he was stirring up trouble. All of this was coming at Abner just a little too quickly.

"The king never conscripts dairymen," Rachel continued, her jaw stubborn looking still. "My mind's made up. The king has been drafting many young men for his army, too. He wants a big army. He wants to be an important king. But, like I said, he never conscripts dairymen. He needs them to produce food for his army. We've even heard that he is going to draft men from this province into the army. Then he's going to hire them out to other countries so he can get money to pay for his new palaces. Abner will be ten years old next week. The years will go by fast, it won't be long until he is of an age to be conscripted."

Cousin Jake tried to soothe her by calmly saying, "It's hard to tell, Rachel, what will happen. You just have to put your faith in

---

* pfennig: penny

God. Don't be afraid of the future. Abner's future may be in America. And you, Rachel, do you have to stay here? Couldn't you go to America, too?"

Having brought up the subject of America, Cousin Jake let it drop. Turning to Abner, he asked, "Other than hoeing in the garden, what kind of plans do you have for tomorrow?"

"W-Well," he stammered, "I, I haven't asked Mama yet if I may, but Grandpa asked me if I would like to go along to Widow Schneider's first thing in the morning. He is going to work on her porch and replace her worn-down back steps. I'd like to go because I want to start learning the building trades." He turned to his mother, "Mama, I know that I need to know about cows, and how to farm, too. Grandpa says the more you know, the better off you are, because you never know when you're going to need to know something. You'd probably need to be able to build things when you live on a farm."

His mother didn't say anything. She just looked at him. He wished he knew what she was thinking. He was glad when Cousin Jake said, "I'm traveling all over this part of Europe to tell people about Pennsylvania. I'll find Matt and we'll talk. I'll tell him how you are. Then I'll come back and bring you the news. How does that sound?"

Abner felt as if a great load had been taken off his heart. He looked at his mother and saw her face light up, too. "Could you do that?" she asked. "I'd be so pleased if you did. It's awful, not knowing where he is, or how he is. I know he's concerned about us, too."

Cousin Jake took her hand as a worried look came over her face, and she continued, "You know, Jake, what you're doing could be dangerous. The king doesn't allow people to leave the country, especially skilled workers like Matthias. Besides, I can't imagine that he would put up with agents like you coming in and riling up the people. He's bound to look on you as a troublemaker. You will be careful, won't you?"

"I'm always careful, and I've got my tricks," he said. "Besides, I'm telling everyone that I came back here to find a wife," he laughed.

"In that case, I think he should go along to Widow Schneider's," said Abner, his eyes twinkling. "Mama, would you say that the widow's daughter is ugly or beautiful?"

Rachel nodded and smiled, "She's pretty."

"Mama, don't lie, she's greistlich," laughed Abner.

"Now I must see for myself," said Cousin Jake. "I've got tomorrow all figured out. If it's all right with you, Rachel, I'll go along with Abner to help repair the porch and rebuild the steps. It will feel good to get my hands back at building something. We'll stay until after dinner, say mid afternoon, and then we'll dig the ground around in your garden. How does that sound?" Abner was relieved when his mother agreed.

Cousin Jake got up to leave. He bowed to Rachel and said, "Thank you for a good meal and good company. Now have a good night's rest." To Abner he said, "I'll see you after the rooster crows."

Abner's mother waited until she was sure that Jake was gone, and then she scowled at him and said harshly, "Young man, I am not pleased with you. You were gone almost all afternoon and you didn't do your chores. You didn't empty the slop buckets, or feed the pig, or muck out the barn. Before you go to bed, you must empty the buckets and feed the pig. Bring in some wood and water, too. It'll be too dark to clean the barn, but you can get up early and do it before you leave."

"Yes, Mama, I didn't mean to be gone so long. Things kept happening."

"That's no excuse. Now get to it." Abner gathered up the table scraps and the peelings and put them in the bucket for the pig.

"Shall I give the pig this buttermilk, too?"

She nodded and went upstairs to her bedroom.

As he got the pig's slop ready, it occurred to him that the pig ate better than Schotzy did. It will be hard on him to work tomorrow since he had such a little bit for supper tonight, he thought. I'll get a cup and give him some buttermilk. I may as well give him a piece of bread and cheese and an apple, too. I'll take it to him and then come back for the slops.

Abner found Schotzy on the bridge watching the water and throwing stones in the stream as he often did in the evening. Abner motioned and Schotzy came over. "My mother said I could go tomorrow, but I have to muck out the barn first. By the way," he said as casually as he could, "We had this food left over, and I thought maybe you could use it."

Schotzy drank the buttermilk and began stuffing the bread and cheese into his mouth. "You would never guess what my pappaw is doing," he said between bites. "First he wanted me to cut his hairs.* You should have seen that!" Schotzy started to laugh and nearly choked on the bread. He coughed, cleared his throat and added, "The scissors were dull and wouldn't cut so good and I really didn't know how to go about it."

Abner laughed, slapped his knees and said, "I don't think I'd let you cut my hairs."

"Oh, that's not all," added Schotzy with a smile. "He's taking a bath!"

Abner's eyes popped open with surprise. "Is that the truth?"

"Every word of it," Schotzy said, scratching his head. "He's taking a bath!"

"My mom makes me take a bath every Saturday night," said Abner. "How about you?"

"I had one last summer before Grandma died. I figure I'll take another when it gets warmer. It's no use taking 'em too often."

Abner couldn't think of anything to say. He just shook his head and kept quiet.

"I must go now, but it wonders me just what that old man is up to," Schotzy added.

"Me, too, I'll see you in the morning." Abner went back into the house, picked up the slop buckets and started to carry them out.

---

* hairs: hair

"Abner! You come here, wunst!"[*] shouted his mother angrily from behind him. Abner jumped, he was that startled. "Where have you been?" she screamed, "I told you to do that a bit ago."

"I, uh, I," Abner didn't answer quickly enough for her. She grabbed his arm and shook him.

"Where have you been, and what did you do with the food you took outside? There is bread, cheese and an apple missing. What did you do with it? You didn't give it to the pig, did you? No, you haven't fed the pig yet. You had plenty for supper. I know you didn't eat it and it didn't get legs."[*]

Abner looked her in the eye and said, "I gave it to Schotzy. He was hungry."

"You gave it to Schotzy!" she continued in an angry, ugly voice that he had never heard before. And then louder and shriller, "You gave it to Schotzy! I told you before supper that food is too hard to come by to give away. If Walter Schotzenberger would get off his rear end and do a little work, Schotzy wouldn't be hungry."

"But Grandpa says he is sad."

This made her angrier still. "Grandpa says he's sad," she said in a mocking voice. "Well, I'm sad, too, but I keep on working. Did you ever think about that? My husband is gone and I don't know where he is. I keep on keep on working. My father died and my mother is not well. I can't just go off and leave the cows and see her. I must keep on working." She stopped, caught her breath and cried, "Oh, I miss your papa so much and I can't even write him a letter because women and girls are too dumb to read and write." She put her face down in her hands and began to sob. He had never seen her cry like this before either.

Abner looked at her and didn't have an idea about what to say. All he could think of was that when Papa was teaching him to read and write, he had wanted to teach her, too; but she didn't believe that she could learn and she wouldn't even try. All she ever said was, "I'm too dumb, and besides I have too much work to do."

---

[*] wunst: at once; as an idiom, sometime as in 'Come and see me wunst.'
[*] get legs: walk off by itself

Abner had never pitied his mother before. He looked at her and knew he had to say something. "I'm sorry I upset you, Mama. I'd write Papa a letter for you if I knew where to send it." He would have liked to have given her a hug like he had given his grandma, but his mother was a different sort of person. He picked up the buckets and walked out the door.

As he did his chores, he thought to himself, *I am sorry I upset her, but I'm not sorry I gave the food to Schotzy. She's afraid we won't have enough food, but we will. I know we will.* Looking up, he said aloud, "I swear to you, God, that I will never let anyone go hungry if I can feed him. I know that I must obey my mother, but how can I let Schotzy starve? I ask you to work this out, and I ask you to give me some understanding of my mother. She just keeps to herself and doesn't talk to anybody. It wonders me why she could talk to Cousin Jake and she never talked to anybody else like that, not even my papa." He stroked his chin and finished his chores.

When Abner came back into the kitchen, he saw that although the fire was banked and his mother was ready for bed, she was sitting in the candlelight mending one of his stockings. He sat down across from her and cleared his throat. He hesitated and cleared his throat again, feeling uneasy, "Mama," he said earnestly. "Will you tell me something? It wonders me, and I really need to know. What fer reason is it all right to feed Cousin Jake and not Schotzy? And how come you talk to Cousin Jake and nobody else?"

She looked at him like he must be stupid. "Because he's freundschaft.* We're Altlands. We're family and we understand each other. These people around here don't understand me and I don't understand them. The women go traipsing from house to house just to nose and gossip. Altlands don't do that. We stick to ourselves and take care of ourselves and we figure everybody else should do the same."

Abner started to say, "But Grandpa says..."

---

* freundschaft: family; any blood relative up to second or third cousins and even beyond (rhymes with find loft)

25

But her face hardened and she cut him off. "If we start feeding Schotzy, he will be like one of the barn cats. We'll never get rid of him. Now get ready and go to bed."

Abner washed his face and hands and went upstairs to bed. He rolled and tossed and couldn't sleep. "Dear Lord in heaven," he prayed, "Grandpa says one thing and Mama says the exact opposite. Show me the right way, and if Mama is wrong, show her the right way, too. Please send your angels along with Cousin Jake as he goes to find Papa, and keep Papa safe. If you will bring our family together where we can live safely, I will worship you forever. In Jesus name, Amen." He rutched and rolled and wondered where his papa was. Finally he slept.

CHAPTER THREE

"It can't be time to get up," Abner groaned when his mother knocked on his door.

"Ya, and it is, and breakfast is ready," she replied. "There's panhas* and apple snitz* down there for you. Get right up. I mean it. I'm going to milk the cows now."

Abner stretched in his feather bed and though he knew that no bed had ever felt better, he got up. It was a cold morning, so he quickly closed the window and dressed even quicker. Downstairs in the kitchen, he washed his face and hands and combed his hair with the family's ivory comb. He began eating the food his mother had prepared for him. The panhaus was warm and crisp, just the way he liked it; and the apple snitz, which she had soaked over night and warmed for him, were sweet and tart at the same time. Last fall his mother and grandmother had worked together preparing the apples, and he had helped to cut and dry them. It was a lot of work then, but definitely worth it. "Ummm," he sighed. "That was good eating." He was glad there were still some apple snitz in the cellar because he liked eating them either dry as a snack or soaked as part of a meal.

Abner started for the barn but he did not have to go outside because it was not a separate structure. Instead, the house and the barn were directly attached, all under one roof, with a gable on each end. The front gable, where the living quarters were, faced the street. Abner's bedroom and his parents' bedroom were on the second floor and each had a window with a window box for flowers. There were two more rooms upstairs. One was a spare bedroom, and the other was used for storage.

As his mother never threw anything away, the storage room contained all sorts of things, from Abner's baby clothes and toys,

---

* panhas: scrapple, finely chopped pork and broth, thickened with meal, cooled, sliced and fried crisp

* apple snitz: dried apple slices

seasonal decorations, baskets, sewing materials, large and small spinning wheels, out-of-season clothing and bed coverings. Everything was in chests, bureaus, and boxes, or neatly covered with old quilts and blankets to keep off the dust, and his mother knew the exact location of every article.

The stairway was beyond the storage room, and there was also a door that led from the second story of the house to the loft of the barn. The back of the barn, called a bank barn, was dug into the side of the hill in order that wagons could be driven up into it and emptied of the hay that would feed the animals all winter. This floor was the ground level on the north side and the second story on the south side as the structure was set on a slope. There was also storage place on the upper level for a wagon, plow and large tools that were used on the outside. Downstairs under this area was a mudroom for changing boots and dirty clothes, and a washroom with a fireplace for laundry. Next there was a workroom with a workbench with all of his papa's hand tools.

Beyond the workroom was the barn, with a section for horses, which was empty now because they had no horses. Abner never went through it without thinking, *I wish I had a horse, and when I grow up, I'm gonna get me a horse.* Sometimes when he was cleaning out the barn he'd think of names for his horse, like *Thunder, or Zeus, or Siegfreid.*

Beyond the section for the horses was the section for the cows. This part faced south so that the warmth of the sun heated the barn and made it possible for the cows to go outside in the wintertime, protected from the cold wind. The pigpen was farthest from the living quarters. In the cellar below was a spring where milk was kept cool. A stone conduit carried the water out of the barn and down to the stream.

Abner heard his mother talking to the cows when he walked into the barn. "Ach, Beppy,[*] I know how you feel." She scratched the cow's forehead. "You sweet girl. Your baby will be here soon and then you will forget all about it. And Gretel, I'll milk you only a few

---

[*] Beppy: baby

more days and then you need dried up so your strength goes into your baby." She patted Gretel on the back, pulled up a three-legged stool and sat down to milk her. The third cow started to bawl. "Yes, Dolly, I know you are there. I'll turn you out soon."

What got to Abner was how sweetly his mother talked to the cows. *I could never talk to cows like that*, he thought. *And she wants me to be a dairyman! I can't be a dairyman. Kootchy, kootchy coo, sweet cows.* He shivered, made a face and said, "Greistlig."

"Guten morgen,"[*] he greeted his mother when he caught her eye. She nodded and kept on milking. He picked up a broad wooden shovel and began shoveling up the manure that the cows had dropped. Dolly kicked at him. "I don't like you either," he hissed at her, "and if my mother weren't here I'd give you a good slap." The cow kicked at him again, but he adroitly dodged her hoof.

Just then Cousin Jake came in the barn door smiling and said, "I came here because I don't know where Widow Schneider lives, and I have never met your grandfather. Do you mind if I help you muck out the barn?"

The idea that anyone would object to having help to shovel manure out of a barn tickled Abner. "Cousin Jake, you're funny," he laughed, and it felt good.

Rachel finished milking, unlatched the stanchions and let the cows out. Cousin Jake helped her carry the milk down to the spring, and then picked up another shovel and got to work. In no time at all, the barn was clean. Abner smiled at Cousin Jake gratefully.

"We'll see you then, Rachel," said Cousin Jake as he and Abner headed down the street towards the Widow Schneider's.

It was a beautiful morning. The sun from the east touched just the tops of the evergreens on the western slopes and the frost on them glistened like nothing Abner had ever noticed before. They were absolutely gorgeous. He was glad he was up, even though it was early and pretty nippy, too. He was glad, too, for the warm jacket that his grandparents had given him.

---

[*] guten morgen: good morning

When they got to the work site, they saw that Grandpa and the Schotzenbergers were already there. In what he hoped was his most polite manner Abner introduced Cousin Jake to Grandpa first, then to Herr Schotzenberger and last of all, to Schotzy. "We had Cousin Jake for supper last night and he said he would like to tag along," explained Abner.

"I've wanted to meet you for a long time, Herr Hartzell," said Cousin Jake. "Your son Matthias is a friend of mine." Turning to Abner he said, "You certainly do favor your grandfather. You can just look at him and know what you will look like in forty or fifty years."

The idea tickled Abner and he thought, *Will my hair turn gray and get thin? Will I have such big ears with hairs growing out of them? Will I have a big nose and bushy eyebrows? Will my beard be long and curly? Will I really look like Grandpa? I suppose I will. Lots of people say so. One thing's for sure, I'd rather look like my grandpa than Schotzy's.* He smiled at the idea.

Coming back to what the men were saying, he heard Cousin Jake tell Grandpa, "Your son Matt often talked about you. He said that you have an interesting and unusual story, but he never told me what it was. I've waited close to a dozen years to hear it. I hope you'll tell me." Abner hoped Grandpa would tell it again, too, because he loved hearing the story about when Grandpa was a boy.

While the men talked, Abner looked at Schotzy's Pappaw. He certainly didn't look like he had the day before. His straight gray hair, as stiff as a hair brush, was hacked up to be sure, but it was clean. His hands and face were clean, too, not kruttzy[*] as they usually were. His clothes were clean and good quality, although they smelled musty and didn't fit him very well. On the other hand, Schotzy was just as dirty as ever, and his clothes sure couldn't keep him warm. Abner could tell he was cold and he wished he could run home and get his sweater for Schotzy, but he didn't dare for fear of what his mother would say.

---

[*] kruttzy: dirt encrusted, filthy, scabby (rhymes with muttsy)

Widow Schneider came out to greet them. "Thank you, Herr Hartzell, for coming over to repair this for me," she said, "You know I can't pay you, but if I can ever do anything for you, just ask."

"Í just might do that, and sooner than you think," replied Grandpa with a smile.

The Widow Schneider looked around the group and spying Herr Schotzenberger said in surprise, "Why, Walter, I haven't seen you for a long, long time. What are you doing here?"

"I came along to help. I heard you needed some help, and I came along to help," he repeated himself, somewhat flustered.

"I'm really glad you came." Her eyes sparkled with pleasure and she smiled all over her soft round face.

Herr Schotzenberger smiled back showing a few yellow teeth. He looked pleased with himself.

Abner, continuing his introductions said, "This is my mother's cousin, Herr Altland, who has been to America, and this is Schotzy, my best and only friend."

Widow Schneider greeted Cousin Jake, and she smiled another big smile at Herr Schotzenberger. She looked at Schotzy and then back at his grandfather. "Does that mean that this handsome young man is your grandson?" she asked. When he nodded, she said, "I used to call your grandfather 'Schotzy' when we were both young. When we were about your age we used to go down by the creek to the briar patch and pick berries, and into the woods to find nuts. Do you two boys do that?"

The two boys were so surprised; they just nodded their heads.

"So your nickname is Schotzy," she continued, "What is your right name?"

"Ephraim." He hung his head. He did not like his name.

"Ephraim Schotzenberger, how do you do?" She reached out and shook his hand. "That is an impressive name and I predict that you will be rich and famous some day. Ach, your hands are cold. I believe so half that there's an old coat upstairs that used to belong to my son, Klaus. He's all growed up and a soldier now. He's never going to need it. I can just see his big body in it." She laughed gaily

31

at the very idea. "I'll go in the attic and root it out." Turning to the men, she asked, "Can I get you coffee or something to eat?"

When they said, "No, thank you," she motioned to Schotzy and smiled again, "Come on into the house and warm up while I find the coat. I may have a cap, too, that will fit. Besides, Trudy is making fastnachts* and she needs someone to test them to see if they are all right." He followed her into the house.

Abner and the men began the project. Grandpa got out a cold chisel and a hammer and asked, "Who would like to chip out the mortar between the stones on the worn down steps?" Abner was surprised when Herr Schotzenberger said that he would give it a try. Abner followed Grandpa and Cousin Jake onto the porch, then turned around and waited to see what Herr Schotzenberger would do. Abner saw him carefully climb up to the third step and pick up the cold chisel and hammer. He had pounded on it just a few times when he let out a tremendous yelp.

The Widow Schneider shot out the door and asked, "Oh, Schotzy, what have you done?"

"Ach, I hit my thumb and I believe I'm going to have a blood blister. I may even lose my thumbnail," Herr Schotzenberger moaned.

"Oh you dear man, come into the house and let me see what I can do for it," she said in a concerned voice.

"I'm coming, I'm coming," he said, shaking his hand as if to shake the pain away. He put the hammer down, got up, and walking as if he were really suffering, went into the house.

"I guess that job is mine now," said Cousin Jake. He stepped down to where Herr Schotzenberger had been working, picked up the cold chisel and began pounding away at the old mortar between the stones on the top step.

Grandpa and Abner began by checking out the boards on the porch. Grandpa marked the boards that were rotted, and then

---

* fastnachts: heavy fried cakes or doughnuts made with yeast dough and traditionally eaten on the day before Lent (rhymes with frost nokts)

showed Abner how to use the wrecking bar to pull them up from the floor joists.

"This is fun," shouted Abner over the sounds of the pounding and ripping.

"Careful now," said Grandpa. "You don't want to get carried away. That's when accidents happen. Watch out for splinters."

Abner just began to feel as if he were getting good at ripping out the boards when Schotzy came out wearing a dark brown knee-length coat and an old fur cap. They both had seen better days, but they were warm. Abner saw that he had crumbs at the corners of his mouth and was glad that he had been given something to eat. Abner ripped up a few more of the marked boards, then handing the wrecking bar to Schotzy, asked, "Would you like to give it a try?"

Schotzy placed the bar as Abner showed him and ripped out three or four boards. He then reached down and cleared away the rotted wood. "Oops," he said, "I've got a splinter."

"You'd best go into the house and get that tended to that right away," said Abner, looking at his dirty hand. Schotzy knocked on the door and was let in by Trudy. Abner finished ripping out the boards.

"What shall I do next, Grandpa?" he asked.

"You can carry this rotted wood down to the wood pile, and then bring up an armful of the new boards." directed Grandpa. Abner, handling the wood carefully to avoid splinters, had finished carrying all of it away by the time Schotzy came out. Abner saw that there was a neat, clean bandage on his recently washed hand. In fact, both hands were clean.

"Do you want to help me carry up the new boards?" asked Abner. Then as they walked over to get them, he said, "I know I'm nosy, but you've just got to tell me. Where did your pappaw get those clothes? I've got to know. He looks almost like a fine gentleman."

They both laughed at the idea of Schotzy's pappaw looking like a fine gentleman.

"They were Uncle Pete's that died," Schotzy said. "Remember last year, about now, my father and I borrowed your wheelbarrow? We went down beyond Partenbuhl where Uncle Pete lived, and we brought a lot of stuff back. We made three trips."

Abner nodded.

"Well, Pappaw didn't want anything to do with it, and Mammaw was too sick to take care of it. So it was just piled in a corner and there it set until yesterday. Then Pappaw started muttering to himself saying, 'I'll bet Pete had some clothes,' and he started rooting. Ach, what all he found!" Schotzy laughed. "Uncle Pete had some nice things. You come over some time and I'll show you."

"Ya, I'll be glad to," answered Abner.

The boys loaded up their arms with the boards and carried them up to the porch.

"Hey, Herr Altland," said Schotzy, "You're a fast worker. You almost have all of the mortar removed. I don't think my pappaw would have worked that fast."

Cousin Jake laughed. "I don't know about that," he said. "He may be a faster worker than you think." At that remark, Grandpa laughed, too.

Abner shook his head and Schotzy scratched his; and they both asked, "What's he talking about?"

Then Grandpa said, "We'll just see which way the wind blows," and the boys looked more confused than ever.

Just then the Widow Schneider came out and said, "Kumm essa."* It was time for the midmorning break.

The men put down their tools, brushed themselves off and headed for the door. "Wipe your feet," said Grandpa, and each one dutifully did so.

It was warm in the house and it smelled good.

"I don't believe we've met," said Cousin Jake to his hostess's daughter.

---

* kumm essa: come eat, (kumm rhymes with doom;) When a human eats, the word used is 'ess;' but when an animal eats, the word used is 'fress' unless it implies that the human is eating like a pig.

"I'm sorry," said Abner, embarrassed. "Let me introduce you. This is Fraulein Trudy Schneider, Widow Schneider's daughter; and this is my mother's cousin, Jacob Altland. He's been to America and he's just come back. He said he'd like to come along and help today."

"I'm pleased to meet you," said Trudy. "Much pleased I am, too, that you would give us a hand. Now do sit down and help yourselves." Trudy nodded her head and smiled.

"We'll be glad to, thank you. It looks very good."

Abner saw a nice spread of cold meat, bread and butter, fresh warm fastnachts, and coffee. He also saw Herr Schotzenberger sitting at the far side of the table near the window. He had a huge bandage on his thumb and looked as if he owned the place. Everyone took off his coat, sat down and started to eat, except Grandpa. He was praying silently, asking God's blessing on the food.

Oops, thought Abner. *Next time,* and dived in.

"This is wonderful good food. I could fress this all day," said Cousin Jake, smiling at Trudy. "And such good strong coffee! It's worth souffing!* I believe it would put hair on your chest."

"Not mine," said Trudy, laughing, and it was Cousin Jake's turn to be embarrassed.

Abner looked at Trudy. She was average height and slender, with wavy blond hair and big, round, blue eyes. She wasn't beautiful like his mother, but she was pretty and had a sweet smile. She had nice ways about her too, and she could cook. She would make Cousin Jake a fine wife. It occurred to Abner that being nice might be more important in a wife than being beautiful, especially if you were old like Cousin Jake.

After a bit Trudy asked, "Herr Altland, we've heard about America and I'd like to hear more about it, but first, tell us why you came back."

---

* souffing: drinking, often hard liquor; a souffer is a drunk (ou in souf sounds like ou in south)

35

"I can tell you why he came back," said Abner, smiling mischievously. "He came back to get a wife."

"Abner!" said Cousin Jake, looking at him as if he would like to wring his neck. Trudy turned bright red and left the room.

"Well, that's what you said you were going to tell people," said Abner.

"That was my cover story in case I got picked up by the authorities," said Cousin Jake. "But maybe it is a good idea. Maybe I should look for a wife."

"I think you should," answered Abner. "You are getting pretty old."

"I'm thirty-five," laughed Cousin Jake, "and that is not as old as you think."

"Abner," said Grandpa sternly. "What did I tell you yesterday about thinking before you speak?"

"I'll try to do better, Grandpa." Abner said, hanging his head. "Sorry, Cousin Jake." Abner continued to eat, but he was not enjoying it much because something smelled bad. The house had smelled good when he came in, but now… It had to be Schotzy. *I better wouldn't* say anything, he thought.

Widow Schneider spoke up, "I really do want to hear about America, Herr Altland. Will you tell us about it?"

"I will at dinner time," he said. "It's really time for us to get back to work. By the way, do you have a brush we could use to sweep away the old mortar?"

"Certainly, I do," she said. "I'll bring it out to you."

The boys and the men, including Herr Schotzenberger, got up, thanked the widow for the food, put on their coats, and went out. Cousin Jake resumed removing stones from the steps with the cold chisel and hammer. Herr Schotzenberger stood around with his bandaged thumb sticking out, not acting as if he really wanted to work.

"Who would like to hammer one of these pegs in?" asked Grandpa.

"Me," said Schotzy, before Abner could get his mouth open, so Grandpa gave Schotzy the mallet and the peg and showed him how to hold it. Schotzy began pounding it in. Just then Widow Schneider came out with the brush. Schotzy looked up, and not watching what he was doing, pounded his thumb.

"Ach, Ephraim, you poor boy," she said, putting her arm around him, and handing the brush to Abner. "Come right into the house with me. I'll take care of it. Ach, it looks bad. We'll soak it in some salts." Herr Schotzenberger followed them in without saying a word to the other men.

Grandpa, Cousin Jake and Abner watched them go into the house, and Abner wondered whether Herr Schotzenberger was going to work or not. What had Mama said about him last night? Turning to his grandpa, he asked, "What would you like me to do?"

"You can sweep away the old mortar and dust while Jake stands up and takes a little break,' said Grandpa, "I'm sure his knees are tired. How about it Jake? Would you like to change jobs awhile?"

"Ya, and I sure would," he said. "It's good to get my hand back into it, but it is hard on the knees. Why don't I help you finish the porch and then we can work together finishing the steps?"

"Good idea," answered Grandpa and the men began reinforcing weakened floor joists and replacing the ripped up boards on the porch.

Abner swept the old foundation of the steps quickly, but his grandpa was not satisfied with the job. "You don't just sweep where the king walks.* You sweep all over. You must do it again, Abner," he said sternly as he inspected the job. "It must be very clean or the fresh mortar won't hold. Sweep until you can't raise any more dust. Remember this, you don't have to seek honors in this life because if you do good work, your work will honor you. Good work always honors the man."

"I thought it was clean enough," grumbled Abner, but not loud enough for Grandpa to hear. He swept and swept until he was sure it would do, and then he went to the men and did fetch-me's* until Grandpa asked him if he would like to try pounding in a few pegs.

---

* where the king walks: down the middle
* fetch-me's: fetching whatever is needed

"Now be careful and pay attention to what you are doing," warned Grandpa. "It's when you don't pay attention that accidents happen."

Abner pounded in several pegs and was just beginning to feel like an expert, when one of the neighbors came out onto his back steps and called, "You're doing a job that's needed to be done awhile. Do you want to do mine next?"

On hearing the man speak, Abner looked up, lost his concentration, and pounded his thumb. He said a couple of words he would rather his grandpa wouldn't have heard and began to cry.

Grandpa didn't scold for the bad words he'd heard, and neither did he sympathize. He merely said, "Let me look at it." Then he added, "It'll be all right before you're married. You might lose the nail, but if you do, it'll grow back. Mine always have." He showed Abner his rough, callused hands, his gnarled fingers and his broken nails. "You'll get tougher as the days go by. Now stop your brutzich* and get back to work. I must speak to this neighbor man to see if he really means business." Abner picked up the mallet and continued to pound in pegs, muttering to himself once in awhile about Schotzy going into the house while he had to keep on working.

"What are you growling* about?" asked Jake. When Abner didn't answer, he continued, "Here's something to cheer you up. There's only one more board and then we'll be done with this job. You take a break and I'll finish it."

Abner smiled at Cousin Jake, stood up and stretched, just as Grandpa came back.

"What do you want me to do next Grandpa?" he asked.

"There is more to do, of course, but first, there is something I want to say to you. You can call it your first big lesson as a builder."

Abner's face lit up as he thought, *Wow! My first big lesson as a builder! I can't wait to hear it,* and he said eagerly, "Ya, I'm listening."

---

* brutzich: whining, crying; brutz is the verb (rhymes with put stick)
* growling: grumbling, complaining

"If you want to be a builder," said Grandpa seriously, "there is something you must know. You will pound your thumb with a hammer; you will get blisters, and you will ache in spots you never knew you had. If you are not careful, you can really hurt yourself, but you are not to brutz and grex.* You set your jaw. You bite your lip. You face it like a man, and you keep on working. Do you understand?"

Abner's face fell and he thought, *Boy, some lesson,* but he nodded his head respectfully and said, "Ya."

Grandpa smiled at him kindly, "All right then, we agree. You are not a mama-baby, and you are on your way towards becoming a builder and a man. Now, see that pile of dressed stones over there," he said, pointing to the back of the yard. "They have been chipped to the right size and are ready to use. They need to be loaded into the wheelbarrow and brought up to the steps." He added, "When you load the wheelbarrow, don't fill it too full. It is better to take several trips than to pull a muscle trying to handle too big a load."

The stones weren't all that heavy, but Abner's back knew he was lifting something it wasn't used to. He put six stones into the wheelbarrow for the first trip and soon realized that that was too many. He could barely push it. He had to take one of them out and then another. He had made several trips, his arms ached, and he had the start of a blister when Schotzy came out.

Abner noticed that there were crumbs around his mouth again and signs of milk, too. "I'm glad to have you back," he said. "Do you want to help me with these stones?"

Schotzy began lifting stones, but the job was too much for him. He was panting in no time. He dropped a stone, just barely missing his foot, but breaking off a fingernail back to the quick. Pushing the wheelbarrow was too hard for him, too. Abner forgot that Schotzy was half starved. He grabbed the wheelbarrow handles and pushed it as hard as he could, blistering the palm of his hand in the process.

"Come, you two, and I'll show you how to mix mortar," called Grandpa. "We can be glad that the foundation and the sides of the

---

* grex: fuss and moan

39

steps are still good, otherwise this would have taken all day." Then smiling at Jake, he added, "We're sure glad you showed up."

Abner nodded, "Ya, we sure are glad you came along, Cousin Jake. We needed your help since we haven't got much from other people." Schotzy didn't say anything, but if Abner had noticed, he would have seen a hurt look on his friend's face.

Grandpa frowned, letting Abner's remark pass without comment. "Now, boys," he said, "when you want to mix mortar, you take one shovelful of lime to three shovelfuls of sand. That is always the ratio, one to three. Now I know that one of lime and three of sand is not going to be enough, so I am going to put in three shovelfuls of lime. How much sand will it take?"

Abner had started to count on his fingers when Schotzy said, "Nine."

"Good for you, Schotzy," said both Grandpa and Cousin Jake.

Abner scowled and thought, *It's only yesterday he told me to learn them. When would I have had time? Good for you, Schotzy, my eye!*

"Now this is the way you mix the sand and lime together," said Grandpa, not seeing Abner's face. "You push and then pull the hoe back and forth until it is mixed. You don't add the water until the sand and lime are well mixed, and I mean well mixed. Speaking of water, would you boys go and fetch a bucketful?"

"I must go to the outhouse first, sir," said Schotzy.

Abner stalked to the spring, frowning and muttering all of the way, "Good for you, Schotzy, good for you."

After he had filled the bucket and had carried it nearly all of the way to where Grandpa was mixing, Schotzy came running and said, "I'll help."

"I'm doing it," growled Abner, and jerking the bucket away from his would-be helper, he spilled part of the water on himself and the rest on the ground. "Now look what you made me do," he said. "I've a mind to rub your nose in it." Abner didn't know what he would have done if Widow Schneider hadn't come to the door just then and called, "Kumm essa."

CHAPTER FOUR

The lime and sand were mixed together, but as Grandpa had not yet begun adding the water, they could leave it and go eat. Abner refilled the bucket, and, pushing Schotzy aside, carried it up to the work site so it would be ready when they came out after dinner. It really hurt his blistered hand to carry it, but he did not let on. He was too proud. He followed the rest as they clambered up the foundation of the steps and went in for dinner.

"Wipe your feet," said Grandpa. Abner wiped his feet thinking, *Grandpa always says wipe your feet and so do my mother and papa. I would think by now that they would know that I would wipe my feet. But no, they will probably always tell me to wipe my feet until I'm an old man. I get tired of being told to wipe my feet.*

Widow Schneider held the door open and as Schotzy went past her, she gave him a hug and said, "Here is my little hero, my brave little hero! Wounded he was, so many times and each time as I tended to his wounds, all he could say was, 'I must get back out. I must work. They need me out there.' Come my brave little soldier, I will seat you at the place of honor." She put him at the head of the table next to his pappaw who was already seated back by the window, and obviously all ready to eat.

Abner's anger bubbled up inside and he thought, *What about me? I really worked hard this morning.* He held his tongue, however, and looked at the food. The table was full and it smelled good. There was roast pork and sauerkraut, fresh baked lake trout, buttered noodles, red beets and red beet eggs,[*] beans with speck,[*] cole slaw, smiercase and apple butter, chow-chow, fresh bread and butter. On the sideboard, there was apple cake and a custard tart. The widow asked Grandpa to ask the blessing.

---

[*] red beet eggs: boiled eggs pickled in beet juice and vinegar and sometime spices
[*] speck: the fatty part of ham or bacon; any animal fat

"Would you like to have some pork, Ephraim?" Widow Schneider asked Schotzy, as soon as the blessing was finished. "Here is the tastiest part; the part I like the best. I give it to you. You deserve it," she gushed. "And here is some of the speck from the beans. You will find it very delicious." She noticed his broken fingernail. "Ach, I knew you were a brave soldier. Shall I bandage it for you, the fingernail? No, we'll wait until after dinner. I'll tend to it then. Ya, you can be sure I'll tend to my brave little man. Here, let me get you some fish. Trudy baked it in butter, with crumbs and herbs." Schotzy sat there eating everything she gave him, as happy as a pig wallowing in a mudhole, licking his fingers and smacking his lips. Abner shook his head. This was too much.

The men ate and talked. Trudy served. Widow Schneider made over Schotzy. No one paid any attention to Abner. Suddenly he realized that the room no longer smelled very good, and of course, it was Schotzy.

"Schotzy," Abner said loud and clear. "You stink. You should go outside and air out your stinks, or better still, I'll throw you in the horse trough as soon as we get outside." Schotzy turned a bright red, but didn't answer.

"Abner!" said Grandpa sternly. "That was uncalled-for and I will talk to you later." The rest looked at him the way people look at bad boys, then looked away, ignoring him completely.

"Herr Altland, you said that you would tell us about America," said Trudy, "What do you think is the most interesting thing about it?"

"Not many people ask me what I think about America," answered Cousin Jake thoughtfully. "They usually ask what it looks like, or how to make a living there. Let me see, uh, the most interesting thing about America is that everyone doesn't do things the same. Here in this country most people do things the same way, and when they go to America, they keep on doing them the same. When I got to America, I found that Englishers do things different from us and the Swedes do things different still. The Indians plant in different ways and hunt in different ways from the way Europeans do. In America, everybody learns from everybody else, and sometimes someone comes up with an altogether new idea.

"Take homes for instance. The Swedes build houses out of logs, notching them out at the corners so they fit together, then filling places between the logs with mud or mortar. They call them log cabins if they are small one story affairs and log houses if they are larger and have two stories. They can be built quickly because there is no fine finish work that takes time. The English like a grander house with fine wood and a center hall from the front door all the way to the back door. If there's an air going,* it comes right through and keeps the house cool. Our countrymen like to build solid houses of stone or brick if they can afford it. It is interesting to walk around a city or town and see all of the different kinds of houses."

"What do you think is the best thing about Pennsylvania?" asked Schotzy, leaning forward and looking interested. "I'm going to go there when I get big."

"Are you, Schotzy?" Cousin Jake smiled at him and said, "That's good to hear. I'll try to tell you what's best, but that's hard to say, too. It depends on what you want or what you are interested in. If you're a farmer there's wonderful rich farmland, lots of it. There are more trees than you can imagine if you want to build houses and barns. There are stones for building, too, right on the surface of the ground, and out in the forest, too. All you have to do is pick them up.

"As for food, there's plenty of game to be had, rabbits, partridge, grouse, deer and bear. Even the squirrels are good to eat. And there are no laws against hunting like there are here. Everyone can hunt, not just the members of the royal family. There are rivers and streams full of many kinds of fish and eels. In the hills, pigeons nest by the millions, and they aren't afraid of people. You can walk right up to them and gather up the young squabs. They taste wonderful good in pie. Everybody's interested in food, not?"

---

* air going: breeze blowing

"What about worshipping God?" asked Grandpa thoughtfully. "What church must Pennsylvanians attend?"

"Haven't you heard?" Cousin Jake's eyebrows shot up in surprise. "William Penn gave the people of Pennsylvania what is called The Charter of Privileges, a guarantee of religious freedom. No one who lives in Pennsylvania can be forced to attend any particular church or pay taxes to any church."

"Wunderbar!" gasped Grandpa in amazement. "I never heard of such a thing." A look of pure joy came over his face and he added, "Well, you tell William Penn when you see him that it's a wonderful thing he did."

"I wish I could tell him, but God rest his soul, he passed away in 1718, by near fifteen years ago. His son, Springetts, is in charge now. He is a good man, too. It's a sad thing that William Penn passed away. He was a good and godly man. I believe God chose him to do a mighty work. Penn called it his Holy Experiment. His idea was to help poor, godly people of Europe to move to Pennsylvania and settle there, establishing a land based on godly principles. Being allowed to worship in the way that he wanted was most important to him. I heard that he went to jail sixteen times because he didn't want to worship in the king's church. But even though he is gone, the experiment is working and the charter can never be revoked. No king, no government can ever take it away."

"How come?" asked Trudy. "In this country, it seems like the king can do anything he pleases. Why would it be different in Pennsylvania?"

Cousin Jake looked at Trudy and smiled. "That's a good question, Fraulein. It has to do with English law. About five hundred years ago, there was an English king named John. He was a bad king and he did whatever he pleased. After years of this kind of behavior, the noblemen of the country got together and decided that they had had enough. They wrote a paper which guaranteed the noblemen certain rights, and gradually over the years, those rights have been extended to the common people.

"One day when the king was out for a ride in his royal carriage these noblemen captured him and took him to a high wall overlooking the sea. They said, 'Sign this paper that will guarantee us certain rights, or we will heave you over this wall and you will land in the sea.' He knew that it would be the end of him, so he signed it. They called it the Magna Charta, or great charter, and Englishers have had more rights than the rest of the world ever since. I believe it's God's doing that much of North America is governed by the English, because I believe that God wants it to be settled by His people, not just English or Dutch or French, but His people. That's why I am here, to persuade God-fearing people to move to Pennsylvania."

Abner had been listening very intently. "What does 'rights' mean, Cousin Jake? I don't understand."

"Your father is a good case in point." continued Cousin Jake. "No English king could, by law, take him away, and make him work without his consent. That is involuntary servitude. It is against the law in England, and in the English colonies in America, too, except for the African slaves. A person has the right not to work for someone he doesn't want to work for. That is just one right. There are several others. A trial by a jury of one's peers is another. If you are arrested for a crime, you have a right to a trial by a jury of your own kind of people. You cannot be thrown into jail for no good reason."

"So that's what 'rights' means," said Abner. "I never heard of such a thing. That's a good idea. I wish we had them in this country."

"There are even more rights that I haven't even told you about," Cousin Jake added. "You know how soldiers come sometimes and stay at people's homes without paying? They just move in and stay and you can't get rid of them. That's called billeting. They can't do that in England or in her colonies, either. They say a man's home is his castle, and no one has the right to invade it. That would mean a lot to people around here, not?" Cousin Jake thought a bit, then added, "I believe there are more rights, but I can't think of them now."

"What about Indians?" asked Herr Schotzenberger. "I don't think I'd want to go there no matter what you say. I've heard that they are filthy, thieving, savage beasts and that they eat little children."

"That's not true, sir." Abner was pleased that Cousin Jake answered firmly and politely. "William Penn made a rule that everyone is to treat the Indians fairly. Penn made a treaty with the Indians and promised that white people would not take land without paying for it. I have met some Indians, and I am not afraid of them. If you treat them decently, they will treat you decently."

Abner could tell by his face that Herr Schotzenberger did not like to be contradicted. "I don't care what you say," he grunted, "I wouldn't ever want anything to do with those dirty heathen."

Widow Schneider shivered a little and smiled at Herr Schotzenberger. "Ach, I give you right* about that."

Ignoring Herr Schotzenberger and Widow Schneider, Cousin Jake smiled at Trudy and said, "We are not going to get those steps finished if we sit here and run at the mouth all day. I have not had any of that delicious looking cake. Are you going to let me have any of it?"

Trudy blushed and offered everyone either apple cake, sour cream custard tart, or both. They both looked so good that Abner had a hard time deciding, but he chose cake, and so did his grandpa. Schotzy took both, as did his pappaw and Cousin Jake.

Herr Schotzenberger ate them up quickly, and asked for more, saying, "That is the best dessert I have ever eaten. You two should start a dessert bakery. They are wonderful, just wonderful." With a broad smile he said to Widow Schneider, "Gretchen, I had no idea you were such a marvelous cook and baker! How lucky your husband was. How fortunate your family! It is too bad you have no man to cook for now. He would be the most fortunate of men."

After listening to Herr Schotzenberger talk, Abner thought, *That it doesn't sound the way that old man usually talks. I wonder if he means all that.* Abner found himself scratching his head like

---

* give you right: admit that you're right

46

Schotzy did all of the time. Then he had another horrible thought, *What is Grandpa going to say to me? What is he going to do to me? He told me to think before I speak. What is he going to do to me? Schotzy does stink, but I'm in trouble because I said so.*

Schotzy stood up and stretched at the table, sighed and said, "I'm so full I could bust."

"Happy it makes me to hear that you enjoyed it, my dinner," Widow Schneider said, reaching for his hand, "Let me tend to it now, your fingernail."

Pulling his hand away, Schotzy said, "It's all right. I must get out and do my part."

"What a wonderful boy you are. You are so much like your grandfather," she answered, patting him on the back. "You go out with the other men, but come back in if it bothers you."

The men thanked their hostess, arose from the table and went outside and the boys followed. Cousin Jake began placing the stones on the bottom step, fitting them together like a puzzle. Grandpa picked up the hoe and said, "Abner, fetch another bucketful of water. Schotzy, you can take the hoe and start mixing the mortar like I showed you before dinner. Here, take the hoe. Good, you are doing it right. Back and forth, gradually mix the water in. Here, we will pour in some more water… What the…?"

Without any warning, Schotzy threw up, into the mortar and all over himself. He was still heaving when his pappaw took hold of his shoulder and shook him. "You stupid, ignorant, ugly, dumkopf!" Herr Schotzenberger said and then he slapped him upside his head. "You wutz!* Now what are you going to do? You have no clothes but these and you kuttzed* all over them. I told you the other day I had half a mind to bind you out to some farmer, and that is exactly what I am going to do. I don't need no puking brat in my house and the farmer will give me a dollar a year for you to work for him. I can use it. My mind's made up. I'm going to bind you out as soon as I can!" He took hold of Schotzy's arm and began to shake him.

---

* wutz: hog (rhymes with puts)
* kuttzed: vomited, puked (kuttz rhymes with mutts)

47

Grandpa reacted immediately. "Take your hand off that child. How can you punish a sick child? What kind of a person are you anyhow? Do you mean to say that you wish to bind out this boy on account of his throwing up?" His eyes blazed with anger. "Then I will take him! You want a dollar? I will give it to you. You meet us on Monday afternoon at the magistrate's and we'll sign the papers. Schotzy can stay with me from now on. So Herr Schotzenberger, I bid you good day! Schotzy, say 'Goodbye' to your grandfather." He glared at Herr Schotzenberger as if to say, "YOU HAD BETTER LEAVE NOW!" Herr Schotzenberger left without looking back.

Grandpa composed himself and said in his usual kind voice, "Here's my handkerchief, Schotzy, wipe your mouth. Don't worry, we'll take care of you. Abner, take Schotzy to my house and help your grandmother heat some water. This mortar will have to be thrown out. It would never set up. It needs to be mixed with lots of water and washed down the creek. Jake, will you take care of it? I must speak to Widow Schneider. I'm glad she didn't see what happened. I'm going to tell her that something came up that we can't finish this afternoon. We'll do it Monday morning."

"When I get the board cleaned up I'll leave it on the porch, so it will be here for you on Monday," said Cousin Jake. "You just do what you have to do. I promised Rachel I would dig her garden around this afternoon, so I'll go there when I'm finished. If you need me for anything, just let me know."

Abner went over and put his arm around his friend. "I'm sorry I was ugly to you. I promise you that from now on I'll be a better friend."

"I didn't mean to leave you with all of the work," answered Schotzy. "I'll work harder next time."

As the boys walked to Grandpa's house they spied someone riding a horse up the road toward their village. "Who do you think it is, Abner?" asked Schotzy. "Can you make him out?"

"Oh, no, I believe it is a soldier," gasped Abner. "What do you suppose he wants? You don't suppose he's come for Grandpa? Let's get behind this bush so he won't see us. I don't want him to see us. There haven't been any soldiers here since they took Papa away."

"I don't want to hide in a bush," said Schotzy. "I don't feel so good."

"It's not going to hurt you to hide in the bush a couple of minutes 'til he goes by," insisted Abner.

As the soldier came along side the bush Abner peeped out from his hiding place. "Oh," he whispered, "it's Klaus Schneider. You remember Klaus Schneider, don't you? What's he going to say when I tell him you puked on his coat?"

Schotzy didn't answer. He just began to shake. "I feel sick. I told you I feel sick. Oh, oh, oh," he groaned, and bent over still shaking.

"What's the matter?" asked Abner. "Why are you shaking? Now stop it."

"I can't. I...ooh, ooh," moaned Schotzy. He clutched his stomach, fainted and slumped to the ground.

"Schotzy, what is the matter with you?" shouted Abner, taking hold of his arm. "Come on, open your eyes. Ach, what am I to do? Schotzy wake up!" But Schotzy just lay on the ground in a heap and didn't open his eyes.

Klaus, hearing the commotion, got off his horse, tied it to the bush, and came over to investigate. He picked Schotzy up in his arms and said, "Where do you want me to take him?"

"To my Grandpa Hartzell's. He's going to stay there awhile. Be careful, he's my best friend in the whole world."

"I will carry him like a baby, you can depend on that," said Klaus. "You're the Hartzell boy, aren't you? I saw your papa awhile back. He's over at Lebensbuhl. He's all right. He's a good mason, but he complains a lot. The king doesn't like that. Isn't this your grandpa's place?"

"Yes, and we had better go in the back door." Abner knocked and Grandma answered. She didn't recognize Klaus immediately and was bewildered upon seeing Abner and a soldier with Schotzy in his arms.

"Grandma, I can't explain this," said Abner, "but Schotzy is sick, and he is going to stay here awhile. Grandpa said. He also said to heat water so Schotzy can have a bath."

"Ach, I'm all ferhuddled,"* she said, as she shook her head in confusion. "What is the soldier doing here? Yesterday, I dropped a knife. Remember?"

"Frau Hartzell, you remember me, don't you?" asked Klaus kindly. "I'm Klaus Schneider, Karl and Gretchen Schneider's son. I've been a soldier for a long time and I'm going to come home to stay soon. It can't be too soon for me. This little boy fainted and your grandson asked me to bring him here. Where shall I put him?"

Grandma indicated a cot in a small room off the kitchen. Klaus put him down gently and took off his shoes. "Poor little fella has no stockings, and his feet are icy cold." Klaus covered him with a quilt, and added, "I want to tell you I saw Matt not long ago. He was all right, but unhappy about being away from home. I didn't know I was coming here or I'd have brought you a message from him."

"Thank you, for bringing that much news," answered Grandma. "We were worried about him."

"Thanks for helping me, too, Herr Schneider," said Abner. "I don't think I could have carried him."

"That's all right, lad, I was glad to do it, and don't call me Herr Schneider. Call me Corporal Schneider. I'll see you at Sabbath meeting tomorrow." Klaus waved goodbye and said as he left, "I hope your little buddy will be all right."

"I'm glad he went out the back door where he came in," Grandma said after he had gone. "Soldiers going out a different door would be very, very bad luck."

"Grandma, where did you learn all this stuff? Next you'll say that Schotzy is liver-growed."

"Well, he could be liver-growed. That no doubt is what's the matter with him," she said. "Let's see how he's doing."

---

* ferhuddled: confused, bewildered, (hud rhymes with stood)

Abner and Grandma gently pulled the quilt from Schotzy. He moved, stretched, opened his eyes and said, "Some big angel picked me up and brought me here. I thought I'd died."

Abner couldn't help but laugh. "That was the soldier we saw. He's Corporal Klaus Schneider, Widow Schneider's son. Imagine that, Grandma, he thought an angel carried him. How are you feeling, little buddy?"

"I'm all right. Let me get up and take off this coat. I'm hot."

Grandma touched his forehead and said, "Ach, you are hot." She reached into her pocket and pulled out some yarn. "I'm going to measure you quick for the takeoff."* Going down to his feet, she measured one of them with the yarn, then folded the yarn seven lengths of his foot. Then she measured him from head to foot to see whether Schotzy's height was seven times as great as the length of his foot, and it was. "That's good," she said. "Now we tie it around his waist. He'll be better in the morning." She mumbled a few words that Abner could not quite hear. He didn't know whether it was a prayer or what it was.

"Grandma, listen to me. Grandpa said to heat water for a bath for Schotzy. He'll be here soon."

"I know, that's why I had to hurry and measure him. Your grandpa wouldn't let me do it if he were here. You know that much."

Ya, I do know that much, thought Abner, *but I'm not going to say anything.* "I'll stir up the fire and get some water," he said. "You just stay right where you are, Schotzy. We'll take care of you."

"It won't do me any good to take a bath," objected Schotzy. "I won't have any other clothes to put on."

"Of course you will," said Grandpa, wiping his feet as he came in the door. "Abner, go to your house and get a set of your clothes that you've outgrown. They'll do just fine."

---

* the takeoff: one of the healing rituals in powwowing, a mixture of superstition and Christian doctrine

CHAPTER FIVE

Abner stood inside the back door of his grandparents' house, totally perplexed. "Ach, du lieber!* what now?" he said, scratching his head. He just stood there thinking, *I know my mother will not give me clothes to give to Schotzy. I know that as sure as I was born. Now what am I supposed to do?*

Grandpa motioned for him to go, and out the door he went, down the step, and slowly uphill toward home. When he came to the neighbor's house just before his, he could see Cousin Jake spading the garden, and his mother coming out of her little greenhouse. *Now I'm in for it,* he thought. *There is no way I could sneak in and smuggle clothes out. She'd know. She always knows. Dear God, what am I going to do?*

Just then his mother spied him, and smiled. Abner was so surprised by the smile he smiled back and waited to see what she would say.

"Jake told me how hard you worked this morning and how you never complained. He said that I should be proud of you and that you probably have blisters." She reached her hand out and took his and examined it. "I'm glad to see that the blisters aren't broken. They'll heal up faster that way." She gave him a pat on the shoulder.

Abner stood still wondering what to do when she walked over toward her little greenhouse and said, "More cabbage and parsley plants grew than I'll be able to use, so will you take them back down to your grandma? I'm sure she'll be glad for them. I may as well give her some celery plants, too. I'm glad Jake is here so you and I don't have to do all that digging. I sure hope your papa will be home next year to do it."

Abner started to ask her about the clothes, but then remembered Klaus. "Mama, Klaus Schneider, the soldier, is home, and he said he

---

* ach du lieber: good heavens

saw Papa over at Lebensbuhl. He said he's all right." He looked at her and could see she was fighting back the tears.

"Good," she said, "Now Jake will know where to go to find him." She wiped her eyes, picked up the plants and handed them to him, saying, "Here, take these to your grandma. I took notice yesterday that her lettuce was nice and her peas and onions were just peeking out of the ground."

There was nothing for him to do but take the plants and carry them back downhill to his grandparents' home. When he got there, he set the plants down next to the back door, petted Princess and thought about what he would say. He knocked and when Grandpa came to the door, he motioned for him to come outside.

"Grandpa," he whispered when his grandpa got close. "My mother always saves my clothes to send to her sister's children, and she sends them whenever she gets a chance. She might lend you some clothes until you could get some made. I know there are some because she hasn't sent any for awhile, but it wouldn't do any good for me to ask her. Maybe if you asked her..."

"Hmm," said Grandpa stroking his chin, "I see what you mean. You go in and talk to Grandma and tell her I'll be right back."

When Abner entered the house his grandmother asked in an exasperated voice, "Now where did that grandpa of yours go? Schotzy is too big a boy. He doesn't want to be bathed by a strange woman. Why did your grandpa go and let* Schotzy here like this? Abner, you will just have to help him wash his hairs. Here is the soap. It's ready, the water. Schotzy, hold them over the tub, your hairs, and Abner can pour the water over them. Abner, rinse them good, then soap and rinse them again. Then scrub all over. Here is a washrag and a towel." Grandma turned to Abner and asked, "Where are the clothes that you were supposed to bring?" Abner could tell she was fussed up.

"I didn't get a chance to ask my mom about them. As soon as I got there, she gave me some cabbage plants, some parsley plants,

---

* let: leave

and some celery plants from her little greenhouse for you to plant out in your garden."

Grandma gave a squeal and a holler. "Ach du Lieber, ach, ach! Doesn't she know that transplanting parsley is about the worst bad luck there is? Where are they? Take them out from under my roof!"

Abner had never seen Grandma in such a state. "Mama didn't know. I'll take them away, but what about Schotzy?"

"Just take them away from the house, then come back and take care of Schotzy.

"Gott in Himmel!* Terrible bad luck this means! I need to talk to Herr Kessler, the pow-wow* doctor. No doubt he'll know what to do." Grandma looked frantic as she fanned herself with her apron.

"I'll be right back," said Abner as he rushed out the door. "Watch out, cat, I don't want to step on you, and I don't have time to play." He picked up the plants and looked for a place to put them. *Any old place will do, I guess. I never heard that transplanting parsley could be bad luck, and I'm sure Mama never did either. How can Grandma believe such nonsense? What am I going to say to Mama when she asks me if Grandma was pleased with the plants? She won't like it one little bit if I tell her, and she'll notice if they are not planted.* Abner put them down at the edge of the garden and hurried back into the house.

Grandma had left the room, and Schotzy had his shirt off, ready to get his head washed when Abner came in followed by Grandpa with his arms full of clothes. "All right, young man, take that string off from around your waist. Frau Hartzell knows I don't believe in that powwow business. It's just plain superstition, no more, no less, and I won't have it."

Schotzy removed the string and then dipped his head into the tub. Abner began to rub his hair with the cake of soap. It took a lot of soap and a lot of rubbing to form a lather. He poured more water from the tub down over Schotzy's hair and began rubbing it with the

---

* Gott in Himmel: God in heaven
* powwow: Rituals that have had their roots in both Christianity and superstition. The word itself may have been borrowed from the Indians, but such rituals were practiced in the old world.

soap again. He kept at it until it was good and soapy, and then he poured clean water over it. "My, look at the color of the water!" he said in astonishment.

Schotzy opened his eyes to look and howled, "Soap in my eyes. I got soap in my eyes!" He tried to get away.

"Just stay where you are, young man," said Grandpa. "We don't have all of the crust off of you yet. Take the washrag and wash your front. We'll scrub your back and then we'll get clean water."

Schotzy had nearly finished washing himself when he began to shake again, so Grandpa told him to sit down and put his feet in the tub. "Your face, hands, feet and most of your body will be clean anyway. Go over what's left of your body with the rag, and the rest of the crust will have to wait 'til next week."

"Next week?" protested Schotzy. "I never have a bath that often!"

"You will if you live around here," Grandpa assured him.

Grandpa helped him dry off and dress. "How do you feel now?"

"I feel a lot better, Herr Hartzell. I just never ate that much before. I'll know better next time."

"Just so you learn from it, son." said Grandpa kindly. "Incidentally, I never asked you how you felt about living here and working for me for the next seven years. That's what it means to be bound out. You must decide if you want to or not. You don't have to. However, if you don't, I won't teach you and your grandfather may bind you out to someone else. I don't believe in teaching a person for nothing. People appreciate what they work for. You don't have to decide right now. You'll have until Monday."

When Grandpa finished talking to Schotzy, Abner stroked his chin and said, "I'd better tell you, Grandpa, Grandma's pretty fussed up."

"Ach du lieber, what happened now?"

"Mama sent over some parsley that she had grown in her little greenhouse for Grandma to plant in her garden, but Grandma says that it's the worst bad luck there is to transplant parsley. Mama didn't know."

"Ya," said Grandpa nodding his head. "To her, that is about the worst; that, and dropping a dishrag. I'd better go find her."

After Grandpa left, both boys sat quietly for awhile, without saying anything. After awhile Abner said thoughtfully, "All of this came about quick, didn't it? No one would have guessed yesterday when we heard Cousin Jake at the square, that all this would happen. What do you think, anyways?"

"I don't know. I want to learn, but what if my pappaw needs me? He's getting old and I help cook and get in the wood and build the fire and do a lot of work around there. What if he'd get sick? If he decides to cut down a tree, he needs someone to go along with him to the forest. It is not safe for a woodcutter to go to the forest all by himself. I tell you, he needs me."

"But he said he was going to bind you out to some farmer."

"Nah, he doesn't mean it. He says dumb stuff like that all the time."

"You must know," said Abner, shaking his head. "If you're all right, I'll go on home. My mother may want me to plant or something. Are you going to stay here tonight?"

"I don't know yet," answered Schotzy. "I feel a lot better now. I think I'll walk on over to my house and talk to Pappaw. I'll find out what he wants."

"Your hairs aren't dry yet. Rub them with the towel and stand by the fire a while," said Abner. "When they are dry, I'll walk along, just in case you don't feel as good as you think you do. We'd better tell Grandpa. I'll find him and tell him you're going home and I'm going with you."

However, Grandpa and Grandma returned to the kitchen without Abner having to hunt them and they were still arguing about the parsley. "Well, I'm planting it and that's that," he said. "All this silly superstition is just too much."

"Well, I suppose you'll do it no matter what I say," said Grandma with a look of resignation on her face. "But we'll all pay for it in the end," she added, squinting her eyes. "You just wait and see!"

Abner hated to hear them argue in front of Schotzy, but then he thought, *well, Schotzy might as well get used to it if he was going to stay. But what if he weren't? Who knew what was going to happen?* So he said to them, "Schotzy wants to talk to his pappaw. I'm going to walk along with him."

"You aren't feeling all that well, Schotzy," said Grandpa. "Are you sure you want to go? You don't have to, you know."

"I 'preciate the chance you have offered me, Herr Hartzell, but what if my pappaw needs me? He talks mean sometimes, but that's just his way. If Abner's mother ever talked mean to him, I know she wouldn't, but if she did, he wouldn't leave her. I know he wouldn't. A person doesn't just leave because somebody talks mean to him once in awhile. I do need someone to teach me, but . . ."

In the meantime Grandma was walking around picking up Schotzy's dirty clothes. When she found the string on the floor that she had put around his waist, she shook her head and carried everything out to the washtubs, growling under her breath.

When she returned, Grandma said, "It's getting pretty black over to the west and I believe it's going to make down* before long. As black as it is, it could be pretty hard. If you are going to go, you best hurry. We don't want either of you to get wet. We'll see you tomorrow at Sabbath meeting and after meeting for dinner. And Abner, would you please tell your Cousin Jake that we would be pleased if he comes for dinner, too." She gave him a hug and a kiss, and to Schotzy she said, "You come back if you want. Herr Hartzell needs a boy around here to help him. We will make you welcome, and you won't be sorry if you decide to come." She gave him a hug, too.

Abner looked at his friend fondly, but suddenly it occurred to him that if Schotzy became Grandpa's bond servant, he would be at Grandpa's all of the time, and when he came to see Grandpa and Grandma, he wouldn't find them alone as he was accustomed. Schotzy would be there. From now on it would be different, and he

---

* make down: rain

57

wasn't sure he would like that. He frowned and thought, *I prayed for help for Schotzy, but this isn't what I had in mind.*

As the boys walked over the bridge and up the path to see Schotzy's pappaw, Abner, looking down at the lake, shouted excitedly, "Look, the wild geese are here! I knew we should have put out snares long already* but maybe it's not too late. I'd sure like to get a goose. It's been a long time since we had a goose to eat. Mama would be pleased to get feathers for pillows or the feather bed. She's run out of goose grease to rub on my chest if I get a snootful*, and we need quills for writing when Grandpa teaches us. That is, if you really are going to be bound out to Grandpa."

"I just don't know yet," said Schotzy. "There's my pappaw sitting in the sun. I guess I'll soon find out."

"He won't be sitting in the sun long," said Abner. "Those clouds are getting darker all of the time, and feel that wind!" Abner saw that Herr Schotzenberger had changed his clothes and had put his dirty old ones back on. He wondered how on earth a person could possibly stand it to put on such dirty clothes, especially since he'd had a bath the night before.

Herr Schotzenberger looked up, and seeing the boys, drew himself up as tall as a short man could, and said in a slurred, sarcastic voice, "Well, look at Herr Fine Feathers, all dressed up in Hartzell's castoffs! Don't you look like a big shot! And why would you want to come here, since you've been taken in by those big-feeling* Hartzells?"

Anger hit Abner like lightning. "Don't you call the Hartzells big-feeling, you...you...you...." He was so angry he couldn't even think of a thing else to say.

"But, Pappaw," protested Schotzy, "I just wanted to talk to you about..."

"Nothing to talk about!" Herr Schotzenberger interrupted. "Just get off my property, you ingrate, and take that Hartzell brat with

---

* long already: awhile back, a long time ago

* get a snootful: to catch a cold

* big-feeling: pompous: arrogant, acting as if one is more important than he is

you. If I don't never see you again, it won't bother me none. It's not long 'til you'll be just as big-feeling as the Hartzells and that brat's uppity mother. Now raus mit du!"[*]

Abner was fuming, ready to tear into him, but Schotzy grabbed his arm and held on tight. "Nein,[*] nein, nein!" he scolded, "Just keep out of it. It won't do no good; it's just the beer talking. You can't talk to him when he's like this. Let's go. Let's go!" Schotzy pulled Abner down the slope and across the road, but as soon as they were out of Herr Schotzenberger's sight, he sat down, exhausted. When he tried to get up, he couldn't.

"Schotzy! Schotzy! SCHOTZY!" screamed Abner . "Don't do this again. Come on. Come on!" He tried to lift him to carry him, but he could not. The only person anywhere near was Schotzy's pappaw, but asking him to help was out of the question. He could hardly stand up, much less help anyone. Oh, no, it started to rain just as Grandma had predicted. It was just a gentle spritz[*] at first and then it really began to make down hard. Abner tried to drag Schotzy, but it was hard, hard on Abner and hard on Schotzy.

Abner looked around frantically. He didn't know what to do. There was no one to call on, no one to help. Then he seemed to hear a voice inside his head saying, "Why don't you pray?" He closed his eyes and said, "Father in Heaven, please help us. Send your angels to help us. I thank you." A sense of peace came over him; he looked up, and there was Klaus walking toward them. Abner could have fallen over in surprise.

"Well, what's with our little friend again?" asked Klaus, as he gently picked him up and started to carry him toward the Schotzenberger's house.

"He passed out again, but don't take him to his house, carry him back to my grandpa's."

"That's good, I sure don't want to see old man Schotzenberger right now," replied Klaus. "I was out for a walk and then planning

---

[*] raus mit du: get out (raus rhymes with mouse)
[*] nein: no (same as nine)
[*] spritz: sprinkle, noun or verb: gentle rain or mist

on going to your place. I want to meet your cousin Jacob Altland. Trudy went on about him and I want to see what kind of a man he is. My papa always ran off any man or boy who was interested in Trudy. I always thought that was unfair, but that was his way. Anyhow, I want to meet Herr Altland. As man of the family, I must protect my women folks."

Klaus walked rapidly in the downpour and Abner had to run to keep up, so he couldn't take up for Cousin Jake like he wanted to. Klaus carried Schotzy to Grandpa's back door again and Abner knocked. Grandma came to the door just as she had before, only this time she wasn't surprised to see them. Abner and Klaus wiped their wet feet and apologized for tracking up the kitchen.

Just before Klaus put him down, Schotzy opened his eyes, threw his arms around Klaus' neck and said, "Thank you again, Big Angel, I know my papa sent you to help me this day."

Klaus sat down, and holding Schotzy on his lap, took off his wet clothes and dressed him in Grandpa's nightshirt. He gently massaged his feet until they were warm, laid him on the cot, covered him and gave him a friendly pat, saying. "You rest now, little soldier."

"I'm all right," said Schotzy. "I'll see you tomorrow in at Sabbath meeting." He looked up at Klaus, smiled at him in gratitude, closed his eyes and promptly went to sleep. Grandma came over, tucked him in and walked Klaus to the door.

Abner watched Klaus leave and realized that he did not hate him. In fact, he suddenly knew that he liked him. Since the soldiers had taken his papa away, Abner had allowed hatred to grow in his heart. He had loathed soldiers fiercely, and yet here was Klaus, who was obviously a kind man. It was something new to think about. He would like to talk to Grandpa about it, but he was nowhere to be seen. He told Grandma he'd be back later to see how Schotzy was doing. He ran out the door and shouted, "Corporal Schneider, wait up, I'll go along with you since it's not making down so hard right now."

When they got to his house, Abner knocked on the front door nervously, and wiped his feet. He wiped them again, just to make sure. He rarely used the front door because his mother always kept the parlor scrupulously clean. In a village where every woman kept her house spotless, Rachel was known as being crazy clean. She came to the door and stood there perfectly still.

Abner saw that she was startled to see the soldier. "Mama," he said, "you remember Corporal Klaus Schneider, don't you? He's Widow Schneider's son. He can come in, can't he? He wants to meet Cousin Jake."

Abner could tell that she was not pleased to invite him in, but it had begun to pour again, and as the wind was blowing rain into the house, the door had to be closed. "Come in," she said with a look of distaste on her face. She did not ask Klaus to sit, nor did she offer him anything to eat or drink, as was the custom.

Abner knew he had to explain why Klaus was with him. "Schotzy wanted to see his pappaw, so I thought that I should go with him since he wasn't so good."* Abner stopped, took off his wet coat, hung it up, and considered what he was going to say next. It didn't seem right to blurt out everything that Herr Schotzenberger had said, but he had to say something. He looked at his mother. She had her hands on her hips, looking back at him as if her patience was near its end.

"After we saw his pappaw we headed back to Grandpa's," Abner continued. "But Schotzy fainted again and Corporal Schneider found us in the rain. Was I ever glad to see him! He carried Schotzy to Grandpa's house and Schotzy thought that Corporal Schneider was an angel. And you know what? He acted like an angel. He took Schotzy's wet clothes off, dried him, put him to bed and Schotzy went right to sleep. If he is well enough tomorrow Grandpa will take him to church. Grandma is drying his clothes by the fire; and it's a good thing that he is sleeping, since he has no other clothes to put on." Turning to Cousin Jake he said, "Corporal Schneider wanted to meet you and hear about Pennsylvania, too."

Klaus spoke right up. "Trudy says that you were in America, that you are going back, and that you want other people to go with

---

* wasn't so good: wasn't feeling well

you. Why would you do that? Your family is here and your roots are here. It is a beautiful place, our country. If you want to go, that's all right, but why do you want to uproot a lot of other people?"

"Yes, our country is beautiful and most people who leave it don't do so willingly," said Cousin Jake, "but once they get to Pennsylvania they discover that it is beautiful, too. Those who would never have a chance to get ahead here, or own their property, can do so there. Land sold in Lancaster County not long ago for 16 and 18 pfennig an acre. You could buy five acres for less than a dollar."

"That's cheap enough," said Klaus skeptically, "but is it any good?"

"It's good land all right," said Jake, "and now land is becoming available further west beyond the Susquehanna River. The Penn family wants to get it settled as soon as possible to protect its rights to that section, and the right of the people to worship there as they please. The Calverts, the family that owns Maryland, want only Catholics to live on any land that belongs to them. If Marylanders move onto the Penn family's land, and claim it for Maryland, there will be less freedom of religion because only Catholics will be allowed to live and worship there. Do you understand?"

"Ya, I see your point."

"As for the land," Cousin Jake continued, "the Penn family will keep some land west of the Susquehanna for themselves, and they will sell the rest but the Calverts do not sell land outright to the people. They plan on keeping title to the land forever so they don't sell it, just the right to build on it. That way the Calverts will always be paid ground rent for the use of the land in Maryland."

An understanding look came onto Rachel's face. "That's just as bad as here," she said.

"Exactly," nodded Cousin Jake and continued. "I'm not quite sure what the Penns will be charging for land in the newly opened section, but I do believe it will be less than what they've been charging east of the Susquehanna River. They want it settled quickly and it's further from civilization."

Abner began to worry that Cousin Jake would forget that Klaus was a soldier and would say something that would get him into trouble. Cousin Jake probably didn't know that Klaus was one of the king's own guards. Abner began to pray silently, "Father in Heaven, help Cousin Jake think before he speaks and keep him out of trouble."

When he stopped praying he heard Klaus say, "In other words, the Englishers want our people to go and fight their battles for them."

Cousin Jake thought a bit before answering. "You have a good point and I honestly never thought of it that way," he said. "I guess some people might look at it like that, but I don't believe that's the truth. William Penn was a good and godly man. He believed that God wanted him to give poor people an opportunity to go to America so they would have a chance to live better lives, but most important of all to him, was for people in Pennsylvania to be able to worship God as they wished."

Cousin Jake smiled and put out his hand to shake hands with Klaus. "I am pleased to meet you. I met your mother and sister this morning and enjoyed a wonderful dinner at their house. I don't usually get off on the subject of Pennsylvania quite so quickly."

"Actually, I was on my way over here when I came upon the two boys," answered Klaus. "Trudy asked me to seek you out, Herr Altland."

Abner could see that Cousin Jake looked very pleased when he heard that, but he didn't say anything.

Klaus looked at Rachel and said politely, "May I please sit down? What I have to say is very personal, and may take a little while."

Rachel nodded stiffly and Klaus sat down on the hardest chair, cleared his throat and spoke with difficulty. "My papa was a very hard and bitter man. I ran away when I was very young to join the army. The first time I ran away I was too young and the army wouldn't have me. I had to come home or starve, so I came home. Papa was meaner yet after that, and he beat me and made me work terrible hard. I counted the days until I was old enough to run away again. When I was gone, he took his meanness out on Trudy. He ran off any man or boy that ever came near her. Now that he's gone, my mother has convinced Trudy that she is too old and not pretty enough ever to get a husband. That's why she is nearly thirty years old and still unmarried. She was quite pretty when she was young, but now she's given up and figures she doesn't have a chance."

Abner glanced at his mother and noticed that a softer look came over her face. Cousin Jake sat forward in his chair and paid close attention. Abner wasn't surprised that Cousin Jake was interested and he thought, *Everything is happening so fast. These last couple of days have been unbelievable. Weeks can go by and nothing happens and then Cousin Jake shows up and suddenly everything is upside down.* He listened to hear what Klaus would say. He looked over at his mother and was surprised and pleased to see how interested she looked. This was exciting! *What could Klaus possibly say next?*

"Trudy asked me to come over here and inquire if you knew of anyone who needs a bond servant in Pennsylvania. Something very strange happened at our house today. I found a piece of the puzzle that helps explain my father and his ways. It doesn't excuse him, but it does help explain. When I got home, my mother was so happy, she was like a silly young girl. 'My true love has come back to me,' she said. She threw her arms around me and said, 'I'm going to marry him after all these years!' and she gave me a big kiss!'"

Abner's mouth fell open and his eyes popped out in surprise. *Klaus is talking about Herr Schotzenberger, Schotzy's pappaw, the person who had just told Schotzy to make like horse manure and hit the road, the person who had called me a brat, the Hartzell's big-feeling and his mama uppity! Widow Schneider liked Schotzy's pappaw and wanted to marry him!* Abner shook his head in surprise and kept his eyes riveted on Klaus.

Klaus continued, "My mother told me that she and Walter Schotzenberger grew up together and always wanted to marry, but her father had other ideas. She was very beautiful, I know. In fact, she still is. My father wanted her, too, and he had money and property. Herr Schotzenberger had none and no trade that would make a good living. Her father forced her to marry my father against her will.

"My father thought that once they were married, she would grow to love him. She says she never did, and my father knew it. He took it out on me and Trudy, but he always tried to please my mother. In all these years, she never let on to us children how she felt. But on the other hand, she never took up for us either. Maybe she felt guilty. Trudy never suspected such a thing, and neither did I."

Abner remembered Widow Schneider's pleased look when she saw Schotzy's pappaw this morning and how strange he thought it was.

"Anyways, she told us that she's made up her mind that she is going to marry him; and nothing we can say will stop her. She says that he hasn't asked her yet, but he will. Trudy does not care for Herr Schotzenberger at all. Just looking at him gives her the shivers, and she says she will not live in the same house with him. So now you know why I wanted to see you, Herr Altland. When are you going back to America, and can you find a position for Trudy? She is determined to go."

Abner sat on the edge of his chair and listened. He wondered what Cousin Jake would say. He had never sat in on such an adult conversation before and he didn't want to miss a word, and he especially didn't want to be sent out of the room. He needn't have worried; no one was paying a bit of attention to him.

"I take it as a great compliment that you would trust me enough to ask such a thing of me," said Cousin Jake seriously. "But before I agree, I must get to know Trudy better so that I can make a good choice for her." Then he laughed a loud joyous laugh. "Who am I trying to fool? I want to get to know Trudy better, just because I want to know Trudy better! Klaus, may I call you Klaus?"

"Yes sir, you may, and what shall I call you?"

"Well, Jake, of course. In Pennsylvania they have a saying, 'It's jake with me.' which means, 'It's all right with me.'"

Both men stood and shook hands again. "Now I have a favor to ask of you," continued Cousin Jake, smiling. "May I call on your sister so that I can get to know her better?" Cousin Jake laughed again like a silly young boy.

"It's jake with me," said Klaus, and they all laughed, pleased with themselves. Even Rachel had loosened up.

CHAPTER SIX

"I must not take up any more of your time, ma'am," said Klaus as he stood up.

"You don't have to go," answered Rachel. "I'm about to make all of us some tea." Abner just about fell off his chair in surprise. The offer of tea meant that Rachel liked Klaus, too.

"Well, thank you," Klaus answered with a smile. "I'd be pleased to have something hot to drink. I got chilled in the rain and it is still raining." Rachel went to the kitchen to make the tea, leaving Abner with the men. He had expected to have to build up the fire in the kitchen or help his mother in some way, but not! He could stay with the men.

"Tell me, Jake," said Klaus, "when you went to America, did you have any trouble be-ins you didn't talk the same as the people there?"

"There are lots of places in Pennsylvania where only our language is spoken, but I tried to learn English as quickly as I could. If you want to deal with the English, you have to speak their language. They aren't about to learn yours."

"Was it hard, Cousin Jake?" asked Abner.

"I made a lot of mistakes, and people made fun of me, until I met a man who was willing to teach me. I did him favors and we became good friends, but sometimes we would play tricks on each other." Cousin Jake laughed at the thought of it.

"What kind of tricks?" asked Abner. "Not mean ones, I hope."

"No, not mean ones. Just a little something to lighten the load. Like the time I needed a cap because I had lost mine. I asked him the word for cap. Nearly everybody who ever stays at an inn gets a louse or two, and also fleas. So to have a little fun with me, he told me that the word for hat was louse cage. I went to a hat store and asked for a louse cage. The storekeeper nearly died laughing and the other customers downed[*] me and said said I was a dumb Dutcher. I didn't know why they were laughing until somebody told me what I had said. But I have my tricks and I got him back."

"That sounds like tricks soldiers would play on each other," said Klaus. "How did you get even? It must be good."

"Well, it was good," answered Cousin Jake. "He got married and I organized a rattle band. Not many people over there had ever heard of a rattle band."

"They never heard of a rattle band!" exclaimed Abner. "They sure miss out on a lot of fun."

"The bride and groom didn't know what to make of it," continued Cousin Jake. "Everybody in the town heard the hullabaloo and came out of their homes. We told them to get pots and pans and broom handles, horns and drums or whatever else that would make noise, and come on over. Everybody made as much racket as they could. We told them not to stop until the bride and groom came to the window. When they stuck their heads out, we told them we wouldn't go away until they invited us in and gave everybody something to eat and drink. We had a party that lasted way into the night. Even the sheriff came."

"That must have been fun," said Abner. "Let's have one when Widow Schneider marries Herr Schotzenberger."

"God forbid that she does marry him," said Klaus. "But if she does, by all means have one. I doubt that I'll be there."

"Me neither," said Cousin Jake, shrugging his shoulders.

Rachel came back in with the tea, and some bread, butter and honey. Abner helped to serve, while Cousin Jake kept on talking. "English is hard because they put their sentences together different from the way we do. If I want you to feed the cow, in English they say, 'Throw some hay over the fence to the cow.' But we say 'Throw the cow over the fence some hay.' They think that sounds funny and would ask me questions so that I would answer, 'Throw the horse over the fence some hay.' One time they got me to say,

---

[*] downed me: put me down

68

'Throw the baby down the steps a cookie.' That time they laughed until their pants split."

"I don't see why," said Abner with a frown. "I don't think it's funny."

Cousin Jake smiled and said, "I guess you had to be there. Maybe you'll think this was funny. I played a trick I played on my friend's father. He was a joker and he would set me up to say something that would sound stupid to the others. He did this all of the time, and he got such a kick out of it, that I decided to fix him. When my friend's wife had a baby, I sneaked over after dark and put up a lamp and a sign in front of his house that said, 'NEW BABY, NEW GRANDPARENTS! WE ARE CELEBRATING! COME ONE, COME ALL! COME IN FOR A PARTY!' Then I stood back and watched the people knock on the house and go in. He never did know who did it. He blamed everybody but me. He didn't think I knew enough English to make a sign like that." Jake laughed hard and slapped his knee at the memory of it.

Abner was thinking, what a good time they were all having and wishing his papa were there, when Klaus stood up and said, "Thank you for your hospitality, Frau Hartzell. It looks like that was the clearing-off shower and I really must go now. I appreciate your letting me come in. I know you can't help distrusting soldiers after what happened to your husband. If I see him, I'll tell him I saw you. I want you to know that if I can ever help him or you, I will."

"Thank you, Klaus," said Rachel, wiping her eyes. "Tell Trudy that if I can do anything for her, I will and she should not hesitate to ask."

"I think I'll walk along with you," said Cousin Jake. "Since it's clearing off, I'll ready some more stones so the steps can be laid more quickly on Monday."

"And you just might see Trudy, ain't?" teased Abner. He knew there were too many chores to be done even to ask if he could go along, especially since he wanted to go back down to Grandpa's to see how Schotzy was doing. Still he wished he were a little fly on the wall so he could hear what was said. He didn't think he was nosy; he just liked to know what was going on.

"I'll be back for supper," said Cousin Jake, "and I might get back in time to help with the chores, unless Abner is so eager to do them himself that he wouldn't want me to help." He winked at Abner, smiled at Rachel and left with Klaus.

Rachel immediately got up and started to get ready to go to the barn. "Aren't you coming with me?" she asked Abner.

"Yes, Mama, I will do my share, but first, may I go over to Grandpa's and see how Schotzy is?"

"What is this about Schotzy being at your grandparents?" she asked. "Why did Klaus take him there?"

Abner was glad that she had asked and proceeded to tell her just about everything that had happened. "This morning Herr Schotzenberger and Schotzy were at Schneiders' when we got there. Widow Schneider was really glad to see Schotzy's pappaw. It really surprised me. Schotzy wanted to help but it was easy to see that he was cold, so Widow Schneider asked him to come in and get a coat that used to belong to Klaus. When he was in the house he had a fastnacht to eat, but that was all right because he probably didn't have any breakfast. After Schotzy went into the house, Herr Schotzenberger started to remove some old mortar with a cold chisel, but he pounded his thumb. At least he acted like he had pounded his thumb, so he went into the house, too. After a bit Schotzy came out and began to work, but he got a splinter in his hand. You know that it needed to be tended right away, his hand was that dirty, so back in he went. After that was tended to, he came out, but his pappaw didn't. He stayed in the house until Widow Schneider called us in to eat our mid-morning meal."

"Was it a nice meal?" asked Rachel.

"Ya," said Abner, nodding his head and went on with his story, not realizing that his mother was more than a little interested in what they had to eat. "When we went in is when Cousin Jake met Trudy. You could tell right away that he liked her. After we had eaten, all of us men went out again. Herr Schotzenberger just stood around, but Schotzy wanted to work. He was doing all right until he

70

pounded his thumb and back in again he went. His pappaw followed him in and that's all the work Herr Schotzenberger did this day. Schotzy came out again and this time he broke a fingernail, but he didn't go back in until it was time to eat again." Abner did not mention pounding his own thumb, Grandpa's lesson about acting like a man, or his own anger.

"At dinnertime the widow kept giving Schotzy so much food! And he ate every bit of it. He got so full he couldn't hold it all, and when we got outside he got sick all over himself. Herr Schotzenberger was outside too, and you know what? He hit Schotzy and called him names for throwing up. As if Schotzy did it on purpose!" Abner added indignantly. "And then his pappaw said that he was going to bind Schotzy out! Can you imagine that? Ya, and to the first farmer who would take him!"

Rachel nodded her head and answered, "There are a lot of mean people in this world."

"Really? I think that the rest of the people around here are pretty nice."

Rachel rolled her eyes and said, "Go on with your story."

"When Grandpa saw Schotzy's pappaw hit him, it made Grandpa mad. I never saw Grandpa get mad like that before. Instant mad, like I do sometimes! He really got hot under the collar, especially when Herr Schotzenberger called Schotzy names and told him that he was going to bind him out. It was then that Grandpa said that he would take Schotzy in. I think Grandpa really had him scared."

Rachel leaned forward and listened intently, while Abner continued, "Schotzy needed a bath. Ach, did he ever need a bath, so Grandpa told me to take him to his house and help Grandma make the water hot. On the way, Schotzy passed out just when Klaus came by, so Klaus carried him to Grandpa's. After Schotzy had his bath and had rested awhile, Grandpa asked him if he really wanted to stay there."

"The poor little lad! I had no idea," said his mother kindly. "Bound out children don't really have any say in the matter, and they all come from poor families; families with too many children to feed." Bitterness crept into her voice as she continued, "The pet of the family doesn't get bound out and neither does the one who works the hardest at home. The dollar a year sometimes makes a difference, too. It doesn't go to the child who earns it, no indeed. It goes to his or her father, or in Schotzy's case, the grandfather." She took a deep breath and added, "I didn't mean to interrupt, go ahead with your story."

Abner looked at his mother strangely and wondered, *What brought that on?* He rubbed his chin and continued, "Schotzy said that he wanted to go talk to his pappaw, so I went along with him after his hairs were dry. Schotzy insisted on going, even though Grandma said it looked like it might make down before long. He said that his pappaw needed him and would have no one to take care of him if he got sick or had to go into the forest to cut wood. I went along because I could tell that Schotzy wasn't so good yet. When we got there, that old man talked to him worse than he had before. He said that Schotzy should go hang with those big–feeling Hartzells."

Abner's voice rose in anger as he continued. "He called us big-feeling! Can you imagine that? That old man said he never wanted to see Schotzy again and Schotzy took it all in without even getting mad. He just said that it was beer talking and wouldn't even let me say a word to him. He pushed me away; and when we were out of his pappaw's sight, he passed out again. It started to rain and I didn't know what to do. Just then Klaus happened by and carried him back to Grandpa's."

"That's some story," said Rachel. "Do you think Schotzy has been mistreated since his father died? You never know, do you? I'm sorry I was ugly to you last night for giving him food."

Abner was surprised by the apology, but he didn't let on. "That's all right, Mama," he said.

"I know how it feels to be young and hungry and have no one to watch after you. I don't think you know about it, but I was bound out when I was younger than you are now. I don't even think your papa knows. The subject has never come up."

"Oh, Mama, I'm sorry. Was it awful?"

"Ya, it was. I had to milk cows early and late, tend to bawling babies, change and wash dirty diapers all day long. I also had to cook and clean, hoe the garden, and do any other work that Frau Slaybaugh could think of," Rachel said angrily. "If I thought I'd get a chance to sit down and rest a minute she was after me, calling me lazy. Her good-for-nothing miserable overbearing* oldest daughter was the one who was lazy."

My goodness, thought Abner. *She's still angry after all these years.* He knew he couldn't comment on her anger, so he asked,"How long were you bound out?"

"Five years, from the time I was eight until I was thirteen. Then Herr Slaybaugh started to pay too much attention to me. I ran away, and went back home. My papa went to talk to Herr Slaybaugh and he let me out of the contract. Then Frau Slaybaugh spread stories about me that I didn't want to work, but the neighbors knew better. Papa went back to Herr Slaybaugh and told him to shut his wife up or he would tell everyone how he acted towards me. After that I worked in people's homes by the day, but I never stayed overnight."

"Poor Mama," said Abner. He walked over and gave her a hug without even thinking about it. "Five years is a long time."

Rachel, surprised by the hug, was stiff at first, then loosened up, smiled and gave him a little hug back. "Ya," she said, "five years is a very long time when you are eight or nine or ten years old and away from home. I was just a little girl! Anyone ought to be ashamed to do anything like that to a little girl, or to any child for that matter."

Abner looked at her in surprise that she had talked so much, but more surprising still, she kept on talking. It was like she'd turned on the spigot.

"What always got to me was that Johannes, my brother who came just before me, never was bound out. He was Mama's favorite, and she spoiled him rotten. Our brother next older than Johannes died when he was real young, so I guess Mama was afraid she'd lose Johannes. She made up for the one she lost by turning

---

* overbearing: bossy, arrogant, acting like a bully

73

him into a mama-baby. Now he's a good-for-nothing, big-feeling somebody if you ever met one."

"How do you know, Mama, since you haven't seen him for ten years or more?"

"I know," she insisted. "That kind never changes. I made up my mind I'd never spoil any of my children," said Rachel, setting her jaw stubbornly.

Abner wanted to say something, but he couldn't think of anything to say, but he was thinking, *She sure has done a good job of not spoiling me.* Their special time was over and his mother was back to every day things.

"What shall we have for supper, be-ins Jake will be here?" she asked.

"I think apple dumplings would be good," said Abner eagerly. "We have a few apples in the cold cellar* yet." Apple dumplings were one of his favorite foods and he was even willing to peel the apples if his mother would make them.

"All right," she said, "You go and get the apples and I'll start the crust. If you help, we can get them in the oven before we milk the cows. We'll have a good, easy supper. I know Jake likes apple dumplings with cream. You can go see Schotzy as soon as the chores are done."

It sure is nice to have Mama in a good mood, thought Abner as he made his way to the cold cellar. *I hope it lasts.* He picked over the apples as he had been taught, choosing the ones that were pelthy* and any with bad spots. He knew that apples keep over the winter if they are kept cold and the bad ones are picked out. *What if she wants only the good ones for Cousin Jake's dumpling? Ach du lieber, there's always something to think about. Dear God, don't let me do anything to upset her.* He chose some spotted ones, some pelthy ones, and several perfect ones, just in case, and carried them up. She didn't make any comment about them, but just made the

---

* cold cellar: a deep cellar with a ground floor where vegetables and fruits are kept
* pelthy: withered or spongy

dumplings, put them in to bake; and then they both went to do their chores.

Rachel milked the cows, strained the milk and tended to it, while Abner fed the pig, cleaned the barn, fed the chickens and gathered the eggs. He counted the eggs and noticed that there were quite a few more than there had been for awhile. *Those hens really outdid themselves today,* he thought. *Mama will be pleased and everything has gone well so far.* Cousin Jake had not come back and supper wasn't quite ready, so he told his mother about the eggs and asked if he could go to see how Schotzy was doing.

"Make yourself back soon," said Rachel. "I'm not going to hold it up, the supper, on account of you." Abner knew that warning voice.

It was a perfect evening. There was a nice air going and the smell of spring was everywhere. The birds were back and the robins and larks, or whatever they were, were singing as if the whole world depended on it. Ahead of him on the street was a stranger, a short little man, darker in complexion than the people who lived in his village. He had a pack on his back, and he was dressed in a heavy coat, wool cap and leather boots. Not unusual for this part of the world, but still he looked different from anyone Abner had ever seen before. In his hands he carried a small box. It wasn't often that strangers came to their village, and he couldn't help but wonder who he was and why he was there. It was hard to believe, but he must have come over the mountain pass. It was a very difficult and dangerous undertaking at this time of the year, and no one would even consider using it unless he had an urgent reason to do so. At least that's what Grandpa always said. Later in the season when the avalanche season was past and the snow had melted, many people used the pass, including armies invading the country, but not this early.

When Abner got to his grandparents' he forgot about the little man. He noticed that the peas and onions were up and the parsley, celery, and cabbages were planted. He couldn't help but wonder if Grandma's superstitions could be true. If something bad were going to happen, what would it be? No, no, he didn't believe in superstition. If Grandpa didn't believe in it, he wouldn't believe in it either. He shook his head, rubbed his chin, wiped his feet, petted the cat, opened the back door, and went in.

Schotzy was still in bed. He looked very pale, but he was sitting up eating a piece of toast. "I feel better now," he said. "The powwow doctor came and powwowed over me, but it wasn't the powwow doctor that made me feel better."

"Is that right! What did he do?" asked Abner. He had never been powwowed-for, and he was eager to know what it was all about. He was also wondering where Grandpa was when all this happened. "Tell me all about it."

"The powwow doctor had a string, just like your grandma did, but he used it differently," continued Schotzy. "He took it from the top of my head down to my feet. I had to step over it, and then he brought it back up to my head. Then he took that string and wrapped it around an egg and put it in the fire. The string burned off without breaking the egg and he said that was good. He wanted to know if I wanted to eat the egg, but I didn't, so he ate it himself." Schotzy started to laugh.

"What's funny?" asked Abner, and he started to laugh, too, because Schotzy was so tickled.

Schotzy tried to go on, but he still had the giggles. Finally he got hold of himself and said, "He made me crawl around the table leg three times and then he said some words that I didn't understand. I felt silly but I didn't laugh. He said that if I was liver-growed it was all cured. He said I was as good as new, except for the wart on my hand." Schotzy put out his hand and showed Abner a large wart on his palm."

"Ooh, that's greistlich. You never showed me that before. What did he say about it?"

"He said to get a rotten potato, put part of it on the wart, and bury the rest of it at the full moon."

"Rotten potatoes stink so bad, I think I'd just as soon keep the wart," said Abner.

"Well, your grandma said we'll do it, come full moon. I'm tired of this wart."

"It is big and ugly," said Abner with a grimace. "I can see why you want to get rid of it, but what I want to know is: does Grandpa know that the powwow doctor was here?"

"Ach, ya, and he does. You should have been here. Your grandma left* the powwow doctor in the front door. Your grandpa was out back. When he came in he didn't say anything ugly to the powwow doctor, but after he was gone, your grandpa said, 'Stand back woman! I'm going to pray.' You should have heard him. He sounded like thunder. She stood back all right, and didn't give him any lip. He laid his hand on my chest and called on Jesus' name to rebuke, I think that's what he said, to rebuke any sickness I might have. Then he asked God to send down his healing hand. He rubbed some oil on me and thanked God for my healing. It was awesome. I felt better right away."

"How about that!" said Abner. "You felt better right away! How did you feel after the powwow doctor worked on you?"

"Not any better really, and I felt so silly crawling around that table leg. If you would've seen me you would've laughed your head off," said Schotzy, starting to laugh again. "I wouldn't have done it for anyone but your grandma 'cause I knew it wasn't gonna do any good."

"What did Grandpa say about the wart?"

"He said there may be a substance in a rotten potato that kills a wart, and if that was so, you wouldn't need to bury it during the full moon to get rid of it. Your grandma says, 'We'll see.' They're funny. You are so lucky to have grandparents like yours."

"I am more than lucky, I am blessed," answered Abner.

"And I'm blessed that they will take me in," agreed Schotzy with a smile.

"So you are going to stay?"

---

* left: let, allowed

"Well, I guess so. I guess I better would*. I don't know what else to do. Your grandparents are good people and Pappaw could bind me out to anyone, the first one that came along with a dollar. I'm not very old to be deciding this stuff for myself, but ever since Klaus came along I've felt as if God was watching over me."

"That's good," said Abner, remembering how he had prayed for Schotzy.

"I can't help worrying about Pappaw and what will become of him. It wonders me, too, where he got money to buy the beer that he was souffing. Nobody would trust him to pay later, and nobody that I know of likes him enough to buy him any. It's a puzzle."

Abner didn't care a bit about Herr Schotzenberger, but he wasn't going to say so and hurt his friend's feelings, so he decided to talk about something else. "I forgot to tell you," he said, "there's a stranger in town, a very different looking person. He had a pack on his back and a box in his hands. He must have come over the pass, and I believe that he was headed for the inn. I'm going to tell Cousin Jake to look for him."

Grandma came in carrying little cakes on an old plate. "I promised you more little cakes today," she said, giving Abner a hug. "You need to remember to return the basket if you want more."

"I'll return it after supper if you want me to, or else tomorrow. Where's Grandpa?"

"He's studying his Bible. It must be wonderful to be able to read. It's too bad that girls are too dumb to learn how to read. I believe I'd enjoy reading a Bible if I could do it. The preacher told him that part of what he was preaching tomorrow was from Psalm 139. Your grandpa read one verse to me that said that no matter where you go in this whole wide world, God will be with you there, so going to America might not be so bad after all."

"Grandma, you surprise me!" said Abner. "Why did you say that? Would you really go to America?"

"If I thought that the king would take you away like he did Matthias... Yes, I'd go to America just to keep you from being

---

forced to go into the army. I've been thinking about this for awhile. Your grandpa doesn't have many jobs and when he does have one, the people have a hard time paying. What stirs him up the most is not being able to get nails. Going to America would be hard for old people like us, but still we probably could do it. Would you like to go, Abner?"

"Yes, Grandma," Abner answered, "Schotzy and I are planning to go when we're big enough."

"That's interesting," said Grandma, raising her eyebrows and nodding her head as she looked toward Grandpa who came into the room carrying his Bible.

"I thought I heard you out here," he said. "I want you to think about this in preparation for church tomorrow. It's the beginning of Psalm 139. **"Oh Lord, thou hast searched me, and known me. Thou knowest my downsitting and mine uprising; thou knowest my thoughts afar off. Thou compasseth my path and my lying down, and art acquainted with all my ways.'** Verses nine and ten say, **'If I take the wings of the morning, and dwell in the uttermost parts of the sea, even there shall thy hand lead me, and thy right hand shall hold.'**[*] Wunderbar! We wouldn't have to be afraid to go to America. God would be right there with us."

"Frederick," said Grandma, "what are you saying?"

"I've been thinking on it, Bertl," he answered, "ever since they took Matthias away. That was a close call for me, too. I know you are going to argue about it, but I'm going to ask Jake for more particulars about Pennsylvania when he comes for dinner tomorrow. We must think about it and pray about it, too."

Grandma laughed. "So you think I'm going to argue about it. What if I tell you I was thinking about going to Pennsylvania, too? I kind of want to go, but then I think how old we are, how schuslich[*] I've been lately, how far it is all the way across the ocean, and how much it would cost..."

"Like I said, I'll talk to Jake..."

---

[*] *Authorized King James Version (KJV)*
[*] schuslich: shaky, unsteady

79

"Oops," interrupted Abner, "I forgot to ask him. So much happened, I just forgot. I hope it's not too late."

"What do you mean, you hope it's not too late?" asked Grandma.

"He went with Klaus to see Trudy. She may ask him for dinner, too. I'm sorry." He decided not to say anything about what he had heard Klaus say about Trudy.

"You ask him anyway," said Grandpa. "There will be enough one way or the other. We can always eat leftovers, can't we, Schotzy?"

Schotzy nodded and said, "Leftovers are lots better than nothing." It wasn't until later that Abner thought about Schotzy at all, or wondered how he would fit into the picture as far as going to Pennsylvania was concerned.

"I've been here a lot longer than I meant to be," said Abner. "I'd better get home quick." He waved to Schotzy and Grandpa, received his usual hug and a kiss from Grandma, grabbed the little cakes and out the door he went, almost falling over Princess. "Watch out, cat. It's good you've got nine lives."

Cousin Jake was there and dinner was ready when he dashed in the door. He forgot to wipe his feet and was glad that his mother had not noticed. That was one thing that could really get her going. Abner could tell that they had been talking seriously and didn't seem to mind that he was late. He couldn't help but wonder what had come over his mother. Whatever it was he was certainly glad for it. He forgot that he had prayed for that very thing the night before. Earlier in the day Rachel had made a big pot of vegetable soup with a bit of beef, and Abner thought that it was extra good. A supper of soup, fresh butterbread, and apple dumplings with cream, what could have been better?

Rachel was pleased when he said, "Good supper, Mama. We got a great do on those apple dumplings, didn't we?"

"Ya, and you did," put in Jake with a delighted look on his face. "A lucky girl it is that gets you for a husband. You can do all the cooking! Ya, that was a very special supper. Thank you." He nodded, smiled and patted his stomach. "I am eating good up here in the hills, what with your supper last night; Widow Schneider's dinner today; your supper tonight; and Widow Schneider's dinner tomorrow. I'll be busting out of my pants if I keep this up."

It was then that Abner thought of his grandparents' invitation. "I forgot to tell you that Grandpa and Grandma asked me to invite you for dinner tomorrow, too. I'm sorry."

Rachel's eyes flashed with anger. "I've told you often and often," she said. "Sorry isn't enough. You can't make up for this, can you?"

"It's all right, Rachel," said Jake soothingly. "I really did want to get to know Trudy better. Perhaps we can both come over to Hartzell's after dinner. I do believe that it will all work out. Don't you worry about it."

All Abner could think was, thank you, Cousin Jake, thank you.

"It's been a long day for you, son," said Rachel, stiffly. "I suggest you take your bath right away. Jake and I will go into the front room. You are big enough to take care of yourself." Abner guessed he was forgiven.

Rachel quickly cleared the table while Abner went upstairs to get his nightshirt and slippers. When he came down the tub was in place. The water, which had been heating in a kettle over the fire while they ate, was ready, and the grownups had left the kitchen. He figured that Cousin Jake must have helped.

This was the first time he had ever had to bathe completely by himself. He was glad. He knew that he had grown up a lot since his papa had left, and lately he had been feeling self conscious about having his mother help. He soaped his head, and began to pour clean water over it when he thought about Schotzy. *What would happen to Schotzy if they went to Pennsylvania? Could he go along? Would his pappaw feel the same about binding him out when he was sober? How much would it cost for all of them to go? Would they have enough money for the trip and to buy land, too? Nobody in his family ever talked about such things in his hearing. It would be good to know a little about the family's money. After all, he was almost ten years old, and how could he think if he didn't have any facts to think with?*

It was funny, scrubbing himself in the middle of the kitchen thinking all these deep thoughts. He had never had a chance to do that before. His mother always said not to fool around, get washed, and get it over with.

He looked at his body. He had no hair on his chest or under his arms either. *Maybe if I drank coffee I would get some like Jake said. Ya, I'll start drinking coffee tomorrow if my mother will let me.* With a shiver and a shake, he grabbed the towel and dried himself off. *It would be nice,* he thought, *if there were a little room in the house just for bathing.* He put on his nightshirt and slippers, combed his hair, and stood near the fireplace to dry it. Then he emptied the tub into the slop buckets, put fresh water on to heat for his mother and went into the parlor.

Cousin Jake and his mother were sitting comfortably near the fireplace. Rachel looked at Abner and said, "If Schotzy is going to be living with your grandparents, he needs some decent clothes to wear to church. Bound out children don't need to look like poor souls.[*] I remember what that felt like." She smiled and added, "I have an idea. Let's lend him the lederhosen[*] that you just outgrew. You can take it over before church in the morning." Abner was so surprised he couldn't think right away of anything to say. He just stood there like a dumkopf with his mouth open. Finally he smiled and said, "Thank you, Mama. That's real nice."

Rachel nodded her head as if embarrassed to be thanked and asked roughly, "Are your hairs dry?" He nodded and she added, "Say good night to Cousin Jake then."

"Must I go to bed so early?" He knew before he asked, but it didn't hurt to try, and one of these days, she would say, "Why not? You are nearly grown. Stay up awhile."

Before he went to bed, Abner got down on his knees and said, "Thank you, Father, for this day! Thank you for answering my prayer about Schotzy, and that my mother was happier today. I wanted to understand her better and you made it happen. I ask you

---

[*] poor souls: persons who are slow and can't help themselves
[*] lederhosen: short leather dress pants (rhymes with raider chosen)

to keep my papa safe, and I thank you for it. In Jesus' name, Amen." He was asleep as soon as he hit the pillow.

CHAPTER SEVEN

"Clang! Clang! Clang! Clang! Clang!" Church bells rang early and loud in the village where Abner lived. *They must awaken the whole village and the next village as well*, he thought as he rolled over in bed. It seemed as if they'd never quit. "Clang! Clang! Clang!" He wouldn't be surprised if they even awakened the dead. He got out of bed and put his window down, but the ringing still resounded in his head.

Why don't they stop, he thought, *they aren't even from our church. The men who ring the bells want everyone to go to their church, but Grandpa says that just because they broke away from the Catholic Church doesn't mean that they're right about everything. They told Grandpa that I'll go to hell because I haven't been baptized, but Grandpa told them that I would get baptized down in the water like Jesus was, when I am old enough to know what it is all about. It wonders me. What if they are right and Grandpa is wrong? No, I'm not going to get worked up*[*] *about it. Grandpa's never wrong.* Abner dressed quickly and surprised his mother by opening the door just as she knocked to tell him to get up.

It was another beautiful day. Now that the bells had stopped ringing he could hear the birds singing. It sounded like the wrens were back. It was always good to have the wrens back. It meant that spring was really here. Abner didn't mind being awakened by the wrens or robins or any other birds, except cuckoos. He and his Papa had built some new wren houses and put them up last fall just before he went away. Abner hoped the wrens would like them and move in. The robins had tried, but they were too big. It was funny to see them with their heads stuck in the hole, unable to get out without a struggle.

Abner and his mother did the chores quickly, ate their breakfast, and then she gave him the lederhosen to take to Schotzy. Actually it

---

[*] worked up: stirred up, worried, in a nervous state

84

was the whole outfit: short leather pants, suspenders, knee-high stockings, a dress shirt, a jacket and a felt hat with a feather in it. She carefully packed it all, including some underwear, in a pillowcase and handed it to him.

"Now don't go over there and visit," she said. "Come right back. We don't want to be late for church."

"Thank you, Mama, for letting Schotzy wear this." She smiled and nodded. *Evidently having him bound out made him an entirely different case,* thought Abner. *He was the same person, wasn't he?* Abner stroked his chin. *Adults are hard to figure out sometimes.*

He hurried to his grandparents' wondering what this day would bring. Schotzy was dressed in the same clothes he had worn yesterday, but he looked different and he obviously felt better. His hair was combed, which made Abner wonder who had combed it. It would have been a job. He was sure that Schotzy would get a haircut before the week was out. Grandma would see to that. Grandpa and Grandma must have been upstairs dressing for church. "I have something for you," he said as he offered Schotzy the pillowcase.

Schotzy looked confused. "No, not the pillowcase, what's inside it," Abner laughed. He watched Schotzy open the pillowcase. He didn't want to miss the surprised look on his face when he opened it and saw the lederhosen.

"Lederhosen!" exclaimed Schotzy in a pleased tone of voice. "I never thought I'd ever have lederhosen and I always wanted some. Imagine that! Thank you very much." He smiled a big smile and said again, "Thank you very much."

"My mother sent them over to you. She thought you'd enjoy them," said Abner, and suddenly he had a bright idea. He grinned and added, "I'll tell you what! Go in the room and put these on. Then come out as if nothing is different. That will be a good trick. I wish I could see their faces when they see you, but I must go." Abner was so tickled he laughed all the way home. Cousin Jake was there already but he didn't have time to tell him about the trick. He didn't want to be late for church. That would be a sure way to make

Mama mad. He dashed upstairs, changed his clothes, and was down in record time.

"You forgot to wash your face and comb your hairs," she said as soon as she saw him. "You always forget something." Abner didn't think he did, and started to talk back, but decided it would be better not to. He looked over at Cousin Jake and saw him make a sign of approval. That made keeping his mouth shut worth the effort.

Abner did as he was told and they all left for the Sabbath meeting place. It wasn't very far and the walk was good. Services were held in a small building that was as plain inside as it was outside, not fancy like Protestant and Catholic Churches. Everyone sat on benches: the men and boys on one side, and the women and girls on the other. Grandpa always sat close to the back because he liked to be where he could keep an eye on everything. Cousin Jake and Abner sat with him and Schotzy. Rachel sat with Grandma nearer the front. Widow Schneider and Trudy sat in front of them. They were all seated when Herr Schotzenberger came in with a flourish, decked out almost like a nobleman, not in plain dark clothes like the rest. He had on a coat of royal blue wool with buttons of gold, and he carried a hat of the same color with a large white feather plume. Abner knew that it was the first time that he had ever attended their services. He bowed to Widow Schneider and took a seat just opposite her. She smiled a sweet smile and turned beet red, knowing that everyone was watching and wondering. Abner could hear the people say, "Oooooh." It was hard to keep from laughing, but he knew he better wouldn't,[*] especially as he was seated next to Grandpa. A rap on the knuckles or the back of the head could come swift and hard.

The service was simple but not short. It consisted of a hymn, a prayer, another hymn, a long sermon, more prayer and a closing hymn. Abner tried to pay attention and remember everything. Elder Wentz prayed that everyone would be courageous and know that God was always with them. The Old Testament lesson was from Joshua and it told the people to be strong and courageous, to think

---

[*] better wouldn't: had better not

about God's word and they would be prosperous and successful. They were not to be terrified because God would be with them wherever they would go. The lesson from the New Testament said that Jesus would be with them always, no matter what happened. Abner wanted to remember this because it was good stuff to think about if you were scared or didn't know what to do like yesterday when Schotzy fainted.

After a while, Abner's mind began to wonder and when it came back to the sermon, he had no idea what Elder Wentz was talking about. Who was going where? Abner wanted to go to Pennsylvania, but that would be a long time from now. Of course, Cousin Jake had been telling people about going, but a sermon about it? It seemed strange. The elder was saying about the Hebrews leaving Egypt and some of them didn't want to go and some wanted to go back as soon as they got to the Red Sea. God said they were stiff-necked people. Then he said that God never met people more stiff-necked and stubborn than those sitting right here in this congregation. He said that God had promised a land where his people would be safe, but the Hebrews refused to enter it once they got there. Because they refused to trust God, and believe that he would take care of them, all of the older ones died after forty years, except Moses, Joshua and Caleb.

Elder Wentz went on to say that again God had prepared a place for his people, a place called Pennsylvania, a land of milk and honey, but people would have to bestir themselves. They couldn't just sit comfortably in their homes and expect to be safe.

Abner sat up and started to pay attention when he heard Pennsylvania. He was surprised to hear that William Penn had spent time in prison because he wanted to worship God in the way he felt God wanted him to; and the government said that he could not. This was part of God's preparation. Another thing that was interesting was that William Penn did not feel that anyone was any better than anyone else. He refused to bow down to the English king and even wore his hat in the king's presence. *I wouldn't trust to do that in this country,* thought Abner. *Our king would probably cut my hat off right down by my shoulders.*

Abner sort of lost the thought of what the Elder Wentz was saying for a bit, and when he got back to it, he was saying that William Penn said that it wasn't right for the government to tell the people how to worship. He said he believed it was none of the government's business how anybody worshipped. He said that the king was a man just like anyone else, and that, for political power, he should not be able to force anyone to worship any particular way.

"The church and the government want us to go back to the old ways when most people were ignorant and no one could read," said Elder Wentz. "They want people to follow them blindly, but those days are gone forever. More and more people can read now, but those in authority want everyone to stay ignorant and are clamping down on those who don't believe as they do.

"Martin Luther found fault with the Catholic Church and the Protestant movement was begun," Elder Wentz continued. "Now that Protestants have had some control for a long time, they are just as fiercely protective of their power as the Catholics ever were of theirs. Each group of Protestants wants everyone to worship their way and won't settle for anything else. Another thing, even though the Bible does not mention infant baptism, they say that it is wrong for anyone to wait until adulthood to be baptized, but the Bible says to repent and be baptized. How can a baby repent?"

I don't really know what repent means, thought Abner, *but whatever it is, I'd better do it. I'll ask Grandpa.*

"They are willing to persecute us for the differences in our beliefs," continued Elder Wentz. "We can either leave here, or stay and be persecuted. We can cross the Jordan as the Hebrews did under Joshua, except in our case it is the Atlantic Ocean. They call us Dunkards* and mock our baptism. They call us Anabaptists, saying we are against baptism. We are not against baptism; we are

---

* Dunkards: members of the Brethren Church because they baptize by full immersion; from dunk, to dip, thus mocking their baptism

88

against infant baptism. We will have a baptism next week in the river. Anyone who wants to be baptized then should let me know."

Elder Wentz pounded the pulpit and raised his voice. "Right in our midst today is a man who knows all about persecution. He came over the mountains from a country to the south. His entire family was burned at the stake for worshipping and believing as we worship and believe. He alone escaped. God is giving us an opportunity to leave here before the persecution gets worse."

Abner craned his neck around to look to see if it were the man he had seen the night before, only to be rapped by Grandpa. Persecution. He had never heard the word before, but whatever it meant, it wasn't good if people were burned at the stake for it.

Elder Wentz was winding down now. It seemed to Abner that he had talked a long time. "Herr Jacob Altland is here to tell us about going to America because I believe that it is God's plan for us. We are few in this country and they are going to hound us out. It seems, too, that it would be wise for us to go as soon as possible. Herr Altland, will you come forward and talk to the people?"

Even though Cousin Jake was a talker, he was totally surprised by the request. He stood, cleared his throat, thought for a moment and said, "I'm pleased and surprised to be asked to address you, but I don't think this is exactly the time for it. You people pray about it and talk among yourselves. I will be back in two or three weeks. At that time I should have all of the particulars, the cost of land, the cost of ship fare, the cost of shipping household goods, and the cost of shipping cattle. I should also have a list of people who are willing to pay the fare of anyone who has no money, but is willing to work for seven years to earn the way across. Generally there are more requests for bondservants than there are persons to fill them. The Americans know that our people are honest and hard working, and there is always a demand for that kind of person. Think about what has been said here today and I will see you when I get back. Like Elder Wentz, I feel that God's hand is in this. William Penn called his project 'A Holy Experiment.' He wanted to offer land to the persecuted Christians, so that they could have a safe place where they could live and worship." He looked around, nodded his head, smiled, and sat down.

Abner reached over, patted him on the knee and whispered very softly, "Good job."

Everyone stood for the last hymn and final prayer. Cousin Jake put his arm around Abner's shoulders and gave him a squeeze. It was a good feeling.

Elder Wentz finished by saying, "Second Timothy 1:7 says, **'For God hath not given us a spirit of fear; but of power, and of love and of sound mind.'** First John 4:4 says, **'Ye are of God, little children, and have overcome them:'** that is the evil ones, **'because greater is He that is in you, than he who is in the world.'** The evil ones are those in the world; and you have the power to overcome them, but you are too comfortable. I sense that there will have to be martyrs here before you truly believe that there is a danger. Go in peace."

The congregation left in a very subdued mood, all except Widow Schneider. Abner could see that she was excited by Herr Schotzenberger's presence. He looked around and wondered where Cousin Jake had gone and then he spotted him near the doorway. He had made his way quickly to the strange little man who had sat clear in the back. Abner saw Cousin Jake mouth the word, "America," and saw the little man nod his head. He watched Cousin Jake put his hands together with his fingers out straight and push away from himself like a boat going through water, then point to himself and to the man and say, "America." The man understood! Abner couldn't take his eyes off them.

All of a sudden out of nowhere there was a strong squeeze on his arm and his mother whispered, "It is very impolite to stare at people. You know better."

"But, Mama, they are talking without words," he whispered back.

"You can't talk without words."

"Yes, you can, watch Cousin Jake." She turned and looked and saw him point to the sun and then hold up his fingers indicating fifteen or twenty. He pointed to himself and then put his hand out as if to show that he was going away and then coming back, then

90

showed the fingers again. Rachel looked away, embarrassed to have been staring.

"See, Mama, I told you."

"It's still impolite."

Elder Wentz walked over to the men, greeted them, and spoke to the man in what must have been his language. He introduced him to Cousin Jake and the man said something to him. Abner tried to get near enough to hear what was being said, but his mother took a firm hold of his arm, and he could not move.

"You are pretty nosy, aren't you?" she whispered, and unexpectedly she laughed. "I'll admit that it is interesting," she added, "but still impolite." She took his arm as if he were a man and they walked around greeting people. When they saw Schotzy, she said, "You look nice, very nice. I hope you wear those clothes in good health. We'll see you at dinner in a little while." She had no intention of letting go of Abner's arm. She steered him toward Widow Schneider in order to speak to her, but when Herr Schotzenberger spotted them, he took the widow's arm and pulled her away, pretending that he did not see them. It was an insulting gesture.

"Well," snorted Rachel, her eyes flashing, "I guess he meant what he said last night."

"Don't let him bother you, Mama," Abner whispered back. "He's nothing and nobody."

"Nevertheless," she replied, "it's never good to have an enemy, no matter who he is."

On the way to his grandparents', Abner was warned by his mother that he and Schotzy were not to talk to each other loudly or carry on in any way. "It is the Sabbath, the Lord's day," she said. "One of the Ten Commandments is to remember the Sabbath and keep it holy. You have been told this many times, but today, with Schotzy there, you may be tempted. Do not give in to temptation, or someone may have to remember the proverb about sparing the rod and spoiling the child. You know what is expected of you. You are to sit quietly all afternoon. Perhaps your grandfather will allow you to look at his Bible."

It took about an hour from the time they arrived from church until the women had dinner ready and on the table. Everything had been cooked or baked or roasted the day before. All that had to be done was to warm it. Grandpa was not there yet as he usually stayed and talked with the men about affairs of the brethren. The boys were told that they could sit in the corner of the kitchen and talk quietly. Abner asked Schotzy how he liked the lederhosen and Schotzy said he liked it fine. Abner told him he looked good in it and Schotzy thanked him. Other than that, Abner couldn't think of anything to say, and neither could Schotzy. Abner would have liked to talk about going to America, but he didn't know if Grandpa was going to take Schotzy along. He hadn't said he wouldn't, but then again, he hadn't said he would either. This was strange. He and Schotzy had always been able to talk and talk and talk, but now that they were told to sit and talk, they couldn't. Abner giggled at the thought of it and his mother shot a warning glance in his direction. Abner was afraid that this was going to be a long day.

Abner looked again at Schotzy's lederhosen and thought of something. "What did my grandparents say when they saw you all decked out in that outfit?"

Schotzy smiled and said, "You should have seen their faces. They were so surprised! They both asked, 'Where did you get that?' I told them, and your grandma had to cry. She said this outfit belonged to your Papa as well as to you. I didn't know that. They were pleased that you were willing to let me wear it."

"Boys, you are getting a little loud."

"Schotzy was telling me that he surprised you this morning, Grandma," said Abner.

"Yes," she responded loudly, trying to look cross and shaking her finger at them. "He did, you little nix-nooks,* playing tricks on your Grandpa and me. I know you put him up to it!"

---

* nix-nooks: a young mischievous trickster, a bad boy (nooks rhymes with books)

"Who is this noisy person, talking loudly on the Sabbath?" asked Grandpa, as he walked in the door. Grandma covered her face with her apron and tried to smother a laugh. After a bit she put the apron down and, seeing that he was no longer in the room, she said, "He caught me in the act, didn't he?" She laughed so hard she had to sit down. Abner thought that maybe today wasn't going to be so bad after all.

As they sat there, Abner took notice[*] of his Grandma's kitchen as he never had before. There were hearts almost everywhere. Grandpa had carved hearts in the cornices above the windows, on a whatnot shelf, on the slaw cutter, and even on the woodbox. Grandma had appliqued hearts on her curtains, on her tablecloth and on her apron. She also had cross-stitched hearts on dish towels and stenciled hearts around the doorways. *Looks like she likes hearts,* he thought. It struck him as funny and he giggled, but not much. Grandma could get away with it, but maybe he better wouldn't find out if he could. He looked over at Schotzy. He had his hands clasped together and he was twirling his thumbs – forward for awhile and then backward. He noticed a pfennig on the windowsill. Widow Schneider had one on her windowsill, too. He wondered why. There had to be some reason. He started to say something about it when Grandma asked, "Would you boys like to help carry the food into the dining room? You better would wash your hands first." They were more than happy to get up and move around. He forgot to ask about the pfennig. He had forgotten to bring back the basket, too.

For dinner there was baked chicken with filling[*] and gravy that smelled wonderful good,[*] sliced buttered carrots, baked caramelized onions, buttered cabbage, dandelion slaw with hot bacon dressing, pickled red beets and red beet eggs. The dandelion slaw was special because it could be had only in the early spring before the plants

---

[*] took notice: noticed, paid close attention, studied
[*] filling: dressing or stuffing
[*] wonderful good: especially good

93

blossomed. After that, the greens became bitter and they weren't fit to eat.

Abner wondered who had gathered the dandelion greens. That was usually his job because he liked dandelion slaw so much. In the early spring, nothing tasted better to him than dandelion slaw. Grandma had made rolls, as light as an angel wing, according to Grandpa, and there were cherry preserves to go on them. For dessert, there was currant cake and a mixture of dried fruit that Grandma called compote.

As they sat down to eat, Abner couldn't help but whisper to Schotzy, "I don't hope you eat as much today as you did yesterday."

Showing Abner a doubled up fist under the table, Schotzy whispered back, "If it wasn't the Sabbath and we weren't here at the table, I'd get you for that."

"Boys," said Grandpa sternly. He bowed his head and asked the blessing, thanking God for each kind of food. He also asked God to bless the hands that prepared it, and praised Grandma for how beautiful the food looked and smelled. He then indicated that they could begin eating by saying, "Guten appetit."

CHAPTER EIGHT

After they had been eating for a short while Grandpa looked at Abner and asked, "What did you think of the sermon?" Abner looked up in astonishment and thought, *I don't want to talk. I want to eat. What did I think of the sermon? I didn't even know I was supposed to think about the sermon. Listening to it should have been enough.*

"Abner," said Grandpa sternly, "too fast you're eating, and anyways, I asked you a question. What did you think about the sermon?"

"He said something about persa... persa... some word I never heard before," he mumbled, with food in his mouth.

"That was what it was about, not what you thought of it, and please don't speak to me with food in your mouth." Abner stared at his Grandpa in disbelief. He had come to this house for dinner every Sunday for ten years, and this was the first time Grandpa had ever asked him such a thing. It was embarrassing to be asked in front of Schotzy.

"I took you by surprise, didn't I, Grandson? Do you remember asking me two days ago if I would teach you? Yesterday I taught you a lesson about being a builder. Today's lesson is about being a Christian. The lesson is: Listen to the sermon, think about it, and if you ever hear the pastor or anyone say anything that you don't think is the truth, look it up in the Bible and read it yourself. The main reason for learning to read is to be able to read the Bible and know what it says. Next week I will ask you about the sermon, and what you think of it. I suggest that you be prepared to answer. I plan to ask you every week. You, too, Schotzy. I'm not asking you today, because you are a guest." He smiled and asked, "Do you understand?"

The boys nodded their heads and Grandpa added, "Good, go ahead and eat; we'll talk more about the sermon after dinner."

Grandpa turned to the ladies. "What was Jake going to do today, Rachel?"

"He was invited to Schneider's for dinner, but he planned to come over here this afternoon," she answered. "He wants to visit with you."

When everyone had finished eating, the women and boys redd up* the kitchen and then all of them went to the front room. Abner sat in his customary chair by the window and Schotzy sat in a hard chair in the corner. As the adults talked, Abner looked out. It was an absolutely beautiful day and he longed to be outside, but he knew that he and Schotzy would have to stay in and be quiet all day long. It didn't seem right to him that God would make such a perfect day and not want anyone to be out enjoying it. He'd been staying in on the Sabbath for all of his life and he still didn't think it was right. He began to feel that if he didn't stand up and move around he'd fall off the chair with his rutching. Then he had an idea. "May I go to the outhouse?" His mother nodded and out he went. He relieved himself, and then, out of sight of the adults, he ran back and forth as hard as he could for as long as he dared stay out.

Just as he was about to go back in he noticed three boys pointing toward the Protestant Church steeple and bell tower, making motions and laughing. He walked in their direction until he could identify them hoping that no one in the house was looking out and seeing him. He knew who the boys were all right: Max Bosserman, Otto Schwartz and Willy Gruver, rowdy boys whose parents belonged to the same group of believers that Abner belonged to. Their parents were sort of strict in Sabbath meetings, but they seemed to have no idea how much mischief the boys got into during the week when they were out of sight. These boys were older than Abner; and as he didn't want them to see him, he ducked his head and hurried back, but not quickly enough.

"Hey Abner, Abner Hartzell!" yelled Max, the largest, and the ring leader, "Come here boy, we like you and we want to be your

---

* redd up: clean and straighten

friends. Come on," he coaxed in a pleasant voice as they came nearer. "We want to talk to you."

Abner knew that he should walk away, maybe even run. Everyone in the village, except their parents knew that these boys were troublemakers.

Max smiled and continued to speak nicely, "Come on, Abner. We don't want everybody in the world to hear us. We need you. Don't run away. Come closer so we can tell you all about it."

Abner relented and walked closer, but when he drew near them; Max lunged at him, grabbed his wrist and twisted it. "We are doing something historic in this village, and you will be proud to be part of it, but don't you say anything or we'll fix you good," he threatened.

"I don't know, I think I. . ."

"We have a job for you one night this week," said Max, twisting his arm again, only harder. "See if you can get some rags and bring them to us. We have a project and we need somebody your size to help. It's going to be fun and exciting. Are you with us or not?"

"I'd rather not. I'm going to be very busy every night this week." Abner gave a quick jerk, broke away, and ran as fast as he could back to Grandpa's, rubbing his wrist and thinking, *Those overbearing rotten eggs, I'm going to hang away from them as far as I can from now on.*

"Mama-baby, mama-baby, that's what Abner Hartzell is, can't do nothing without asking his mama," they yelled, but they didn't chase him. He was glad for that, because he knew that Willy could run very fast.

He was almost back to Grandpa's when he saw Cousin Jake, Trudy, and Klaus coming up the street. Pretending not to see them, he ran to the back of the house. He petted Princess until he got his breath, and then walked in, trying to look as if nothing had happened. He looked down at his wrist and saw that it was red and sore. He pulled his shirtsleeve down so no one would notice.

The knock on the front door told him that the guests were there. Abner, who was closest, answered it. Cousin Jake greeted him with twinkling eyes and a whisper, "I hope you had a good run. Has

Schotzy been out?" Abner shook his head. "Well then," he continued, "we'll have to see about that." After they were in, had greeted everyone and got settled, Cousin Jake said to Schotzy, "Abner was out and I imagine you need to go out, too. Am I right?" Schotzy, who had been quiet all afternoon, nodded his head gratefully and looked at Grandpa. He nodded his permission and Schotzy left the room.

"While he's out, sir," said Cousin Jake, "I want to warn you about Herr Schotzenberger. I don't know what he's up to, but..."

"Don't worry about it, Jake," interrupted Grandpa. "That's just the way he is. I'm not going to worry about it, and I don't want you to worry about it either." Turning to Abner, Cousin Jake said, "Please don't mention this to your friend. It would upset him, and we wouldn't want that, would we?"

"No, sir, but if you would have heard that old man last night..."

"Abner!" scolded his mother. "We never speak disrespectfully of anyone, no matter who he is."

"But that's what Schotzy calls him."

"It doesn't matter to me what Schotzy calls him. It's what you call him that matters to me. In this family, we don't talk that way. Do you understand?"

Abner was so embarrassed at being called down in front of everyone that he hung his head and couldn't say anything. He was glad when Schotzy got back.

Cousin Jake saved the day by saying, "Herr Hartzell, I've wanted to hear your story long already. Do you mind telling me how come you can read, have a Bible, and are so well educated? How did that come about? It is most unusual for this time and place."

Abner was grateful that everyone's attention shifted from him to Cousin Jake and then to Grandpa.

"I haven't told this story for quite awhile and I'll be glad to," he said with a smile. "It brings back memories, both good and bad. Have you ever heard my story, Schotzy?"

"No, sir, I haven't, and I'd be pleased to hear it," he answered, sitting up straight and looking interested.

"It is time for me to tell the story again, because it is important for these boys to take advantage of every opportunity that comes along. That is what happened when I was eight years old, younger than Abner and Schotzy are now. The king began looking for a companion for his son, the prince, who was eight years old also. He did not want a companion of noble birth because he needed a whipping boy, as well. You see," he said turning to Abner and Schotzy, "a member of royal family could not be spanked, but sometimes a young prince needed to be punished. What do you think of that?"

A look of horror spread over Abner's face as he asked, "Do you mean to say that if the prince was bad, you got the spanking?"

"That's right, absolutely right," answered Grandpa nodding his head. "If the prince was bad, and he was bad pretty often, I got the spanking, but I sure tried to keep him from doing anything bad or getting in trouble. At the beginning, I got spanked and sometimes whipped a lot, sometimes two or three times a day."

"Oh, Grandpa," said Abner, his voice showing anger, outrage and pity. "If I'd have been there, I would have protected you. I wouldn't have let them do that to you."

"You poor soul," said Cousin Jake sympathetically. "Does this still go on?"

"It may, and probably does, but I don't know for sure," answered Grandpa.

"I've heard of such a thing," said Cousin Jake, "but I've never known of anyone involved in the practice. How did the king choose you?"

"He sent emissaries throughout the country to search for a boy who would be a good companion for his son. He wanted someone who would fit into court life, who was healthy and strong, who wasn't a mama-baby, and who would benefit from the education that came along with it. One day they came here to this village and chose me.

"My papa decided to let me go but my mama was against it. He said that it would be good for someone in the family to be able to

99

read the Bible. He hoped that if I learned, I would teach others. By this time some ordinary people were able to read, but before Martin Luther's time only members of the nobility and those who studied to be priests were taught how. My father figured that they were hiding something from the people. He had heard of Luther, Calvin, Zwingli, Hus, and other reformers, and he wanted to know more. My papa was a wise man and he hungered for the truth. He was to be paid five dollars a year for my services, and I was to stay for five years. If the king found my behavior to be satisfactory, I would be given a five dollar bonus when the time was up. So I went."

"Didn't you get homesick?" asked Rachel

Grandpa took a deep breath, as if remembering, and smiling at Rachel fondly said, "Ya, Rachel, and you know I did, because you get homesick still, don't you?"

Rachel nodded and wiped her eyes but did not answer. Abner, who had never been away from home, wondered what homesick meant considering that it made his mother almost cry. He had never heard the term before and wondered if it would ever happen to him. He shrugged his shoulders and listened to his grandfather.

"It was especially bad when the prince would pull the maids' pigtails or trip them when they were carrying food to the table, and then take delight in seeing me punished. At times I got so angry I thought I couldn't stand it. All I thought of was running away from the palace and going home, or busting him a good one, right in the mouth, but I knew that I daresn't do anything that would bring disgrace to my family. I also knew that if I did anything out of line, someone would beat me unmercifully. They beat me hard enough as it was. I figured that worse yet, they might put me in the dungeon forever, or maybe even kill me. Even so, I was beginning to think it would be worth it. I was really tempted."

Abner had heard parts of the story before, but never this. "What did you do, Grandpa?" he asked. "Did you get him back? Did you hit him?"

"No, Grandson, I didn't hit him. I wouldn't be here today if I had. The only reason I was able to control myself was God's great grace and mercy. He sent a heavenly visitor to me one night when I was at the end of myself." Everyone in the room was quiet, wrapped up in the story. Even Grandma, who had heard it many times, never failed to be thrilled to hear this part.

"Ya," Grandpa continued nodding his head, and even after all these years his voice was full of wonder. "A heavenly visitor came to see me. He told me that I had been chosen by God to read so that I could help lead His people out of darkness, and when the time came I should be ready. He said that my parents were praying for me every day, and that those prayers would give me the strength to take whatever came my way. He said that learning to read was important, but learning self-control was more important; and that I was well on my way. The next thing he wanted me to do was to help the prince learn self-control. The way to do that was to pray for him and to be a good example. Next, he told me that I should pray to find favor in the prince's eyes. Then he would like me and would feel bad if I were punished. The result would be that he would behave better, and control himself when he had an impulse to do something naughty. If he liked me and thought of me as his friend, he wouldn't want to see me punished."

Schotzy had sat very still, taking it all in, until suddenly he interrupted, "Do you mean to tell me that all of this is true? That everything they say in church is true? That people can pray and there is a God who listens and answers?" He scratched his head.

Grandpa looked kindly at Schotzy. "Yes, my boy, it is all true, and the more you hear the more you'll believe, because faith comes from hearing and reading the Bible and hearing stories like mine and others who have learned to know God. That's why God wants his people to learn to read."

Schotzy smiled and said, "I'm glad to hear that."

"Go on with your story, Grandpa," said Abner impatiently. "Did the prince like you after that?"

"It was gradual, but, ya, he did, and he began to behave better. One day I realized that I hadn't been whipped for awhile. That was partly the queen's doing. She always treated me kindly and did not approve of me being punished for the mean and thoughtless actions of her son."

"Did the heavenly visitor have anything else to say?" asked Cousin Jake.

"Yes, he told me to study the life of David when he lived with and ministered to King Saul because David acted wisely in the palace and in his dealings with King Saul. He said that the king was the anointed one of God put in that position for God's purposes, and I should remember that. He also told me to study St. Paul's letter to Titus. In it, he talks about self-control and how important it is in a person's life. Before he left, he told me he would come again with further instructions. In the meantime, I was to be strong and courageous because God was always with me; and his angels were always watching over me to keep me safe."

Grandpa thought a bit and then continued. "The next time he came was three years later. This time he told me that the Lord was pleased with me, and so was the king. I had studied hard, behaved myself, and helped the prince to learn the wisdom of self-control. The prince and I studied the Proverbs in the Bible and we learned about self-control from them, too. The queen could read and often sat in on our lessons.

"I was allowed to go home for one week each year. One time when I was home, a tramp came to our house asking if he could work for food. He carried his belongings on his back and among his possessions was a Bible. At night after work he read the Bible to my parents and anyone in the neighborhood who wanted to hear. He had been a priest but was defrocked[*] and excommunicated[*] because his beliefs changed and the Catholic Church would not put up with them."

From the looks on Abner's and Schotzy's faces, Grandpa could tell that they were confused. He smiled and added, "Defrocked means that the Catholic Church took away his priestly garments and did not allow him to wear them any more. That meant that he could

---

[*] defrocked: not allowed to be a priest any more
[*] excommunicated: thrown out of the Catholic Church

no longer be a priest. Excommunicated means that he was no longer be a member of the Catholic Church and according to them, he would surely go to hell."

Abner gasped, "Do you believe that he'll go to that place, Grandpa?"

"No, of course not. He read the Bible and believed that it was the word of God. Besides that he was a godly man who believed that one should lead a plain and simple life, never go to war, never fight back and never get even. He said that every true follower of Christ always turns the other cheek just as Jesus did. He also taught that one should get baptized down in the water only after he or she has been taught and believes. This is called believer's baptism. He said that infant baptism was wrong. He taught us right out of the Bible, something neither my parents, nor I, had ever heard before. The lesson that made a big impression on me was from St. Paul's letter to the Ephesians."

Grandpa began to quote, "This is from the second chapter, the eighth and ninth verses, **'For by grace are ye saved through faith; and that not of yourselves; it is the gift of God, not of works, lest any man should boast.'** This was an eye-opening message. As you know, the king rules the entire country but each principality or province is governed by a prince. As part of the treaty following the Thirty Years War the king and the leaders of the Reformed Movement, that is the leaders of those who followed the teachings of Luther and Zwingli; together with the Roman Catholic Church, agreed to the idea that everyone who lived in a given principality would follow the its prince's beliefs and worship in whatever church its the prince worshipped in. As a result of this law, parts of the country were sometimes Lutheran, sometimes Reformed, and sometimes Catholic depending on the beliefs of the current prince. Can you imagine how confusing it was to the ordinary people when a prince died and his successor believed and worshipped differently from the previous one? This seemed to happen all of the time. Some people tried to go along with it, some people resisted, some people were just plain confused, and some didn't care at all.

"Under the Catholic Church they had been taught that they had to earn their way to heaven by good works, and if they had not done enough good works, or prayed enough, they could give money to the church and the priests could pray them into heaven. Often a family would give everything they had to ensure that someone who had died would go to heaven. Old beliefs die hard. At the end of the Thirty Years War, there weren't enough Protestant pastors to teach the people properly. Much of the old superstition and wrong teaching remained, and even now, most people aren't willing to put their faith in the simple truth, that only by the grace of God are we saved.

"About ten years ago I learned that a group of men who believed as the itinerant preacher taught, had met at Schwartzenau in 1708 and formed a group that they called 'The Brethren.' We joined them soon after I learned of them, and that is the group to which we belong."

"When I went back to the palace after being at home, I asked the queen if we could study Ephesians. When we came to the eleventh and twelfth verses of the third chapter the queen read them aloud and read them again. They say, **'According to the eternal purpose which he purposed in Christ Jesus our Lord: In whom we have boldness and access with confidence by the faith in him.'** This means that through faith in Jesus, we may approach God with freedom and confidence. We had never been taught that. We thought that only preachers or priests knew how or were allowed to pray to God. The queen and I discussed this. We read all of Ephesians time and again. We could understand what it said and it became a great pleasure for her and me, and to some extent, the prince. One day the queen asked me if I thought that she should tell the king what we had learned. The Bible says that a person needs to repent of his sins, to be baptized, to love others, and to lead holy lives. But none of this is possible without the grace of God. Each and every person is saved by the grace of God. No one is ever good enough all by himself." Grandpa looked at the boys and asked, "Do you understand what I'm saying?"

"Yes, Grandpa, I think I do," said Abner, and Schotzy nodded his head.

"What I want you to understand is that God loves us so much, that he forgives us immediately if we are truly sorry and are willing to try to do better. All that God asks is that we believe in His son, repent of our sins, love him and obey him. Repent means to be truly sorry that you have sinned and vow that you will try to do better."

So that's what repent means, thought Abner. *Now I don't have to ask.*

"Jesus told us that he would send the Holy Spirit to help us. Martin Luther had discovered the same thing nearly two hundred years before, but we didn't know that. You see, it is impossible to know the truth without the word of God, because the word of God is the truth.

"The queen agonized over whether she should tell the king, and she finally decided that she must. She didn't know what to expect. She asked me to pray that he would look favorably on what she had to say. We felt that she should have no fear because God was with her; nevertheless, it is not easy to be brave under such circumstances. The king was pleased to hear what she had to say, but not for the reason she had hoped. It was because he was glad for an excuse to get out of paying so much money to the church.

"However, the king was not pleased to hear of my part in it. He said to me. 'You know, Frederick, this whole thing was settled long ago at the end of the Thirty Years War, and I want no part of stirring up the people. If this is what you are teaching my son and my wife, perhaps bringing you here was a mistake. However, if you are willing to give up this foolishness, I will forget about it and send you to the university as I would like to do."

Abner was sitting on the edge of his chair, imagining what it would be like to be a friend of the queen. He brought himself back to Grandpa's story. "Before this the king had wanted me to study and possibly become one of his trusted advisors; but when the five years were complete, I chose to go home. I learned the building trade just as our Lord had done. I was glad to come back here to my own village and I resolved to be ready at all times to do whatever the Lord called me to do.

"The last thing the queen did before I left was to give me a Bible of my own. I could never have got one any other way because they were rare and expensive. That dear lady, she thought of me, and saw to it that I was given the desire of my heart, a Bible of my own. I still think of her and of her kindness. The prince kept his feelings to himself. He really had no convictions and no backbone either. He just wanted to have an easy life with no trouble, but he found that life doesn't work that way. His father died shortly after I left, and he became ruler. He was too young and his advisors gave him poor advice. He did not want to antagonize anyone, but he managed to antagonize just about everyone. He had learned some self-control, but not enough to be a real leader, not enough to be a good king. Thank goodness he didn't have a lot of ambition. His son, the present king, is ambitious and the less we say about that, the better. All we can do is hope for the best.

"So I left the palace and all of the people there with no regrets. In fact, it felt very good to get away. I began learning the building trades as soon as I got home. My father had saved the twenty-five dollars that the prince gave him for my years of bondage but he didn't give my father the bonus. I believed I deserved it, but as I said, the ruler does as he pleases. My father gave the money to me when I finished my apprenticeship and wanted to get married. I will always be grateful to him for saving it for me because it was his to keep. It gave me a helpful start in life." Grandpa smiled and added, "And that's my story."

Everyone in the room was so touched that they sat quietly for a while. Cousin Jake was the first to speak, "So did you ever miss court life and the excitement that went along with it?"

"Ach, no," replied Grandpa. "I wouldn't wish court life on anyone, but I am very glad for the education and the Bible that was given to me. I know that I have been greatly blessed, and I often wonder if God has something in store for me yet. His ways are mysterious."

"Sir," persisted Cousin Jake, "do you mean to say that you were never sorry that you gave up a university education and all of the power and wealth that would have gone with a position at court?"

"No, indeed," answered Grandpa shaking his head. "Advising the ruler of a country, that is a precarious job. A wrong recommendation, and there goes your head! I've been blessed with a quiet life. I wouldn't have wanted it any other way." He smiled fondly at Grandma and she smiled back.

"Did the king really cut off people's heads?" Abner asked, his eyes round with surprise.

"He was a good king in many ways," said Grandpa, "but he did have heads cut off, more than one while I was there, and he had people hanged, too. That puts fear into everyone. But I must say that he was more likely to have them whipped. A king has power to do just about anything he wants."

"Not in Pennsylvania," interrupted Abner. "Remember what Cousin Jake said yesterday? People have rights in Pennsylvania." Grandpa nodded in his direction.

"Thank you very much, Herr Hartzell," said Cousin Jake. "I appreciate your taking the time to tell us your story. Matthias was right when he said that it was worth listening to. I may call on you for advice before I return to America, and I hope that you will consider going along with us."

Grandpa looked serious and said, "Thank you. We'll see. You just never can tell what will happen."

Cousin Jake looked around the room and said very formally, "I have something to tell you. I know it is a short time that I have known her, but I have asked Trudy to marry me. She says she will go to America as a bondservant because she isn't sure about marrying me, but I say that seven years would be too long for me to wait. I do need a wife; and if Trudy waits seven years, she may be too old to have children. I know that it is very soon to make a decision, but some situations require it. Will some of you put a good word in for me while I'm gone?"

Abner jumped up off his chair, grabbed Cousin Jake's hand and shook it. "I told you Trudy would be a good wife for you," he said, grinning all over his face. "She'll do it, I'm sure. You just leave it to us; we'll convince her, won't we, Schotzy? Won't we, Mama? Ya, we'll do better than that, even. We'll pray about it."

Rachel was smiling, too. She liked Trudy more than she liked anyone else in the village. Trudy looked shy and didn't say anything, but Klaus looked pleased and shook Cousin Jake's hand.

Abner looked over at Schotzy and realized that he had been very quiet all afternoon. "What's the matter, Schotzy?" he said, "Has the cat got your tongue?"

"Abner, that wasn't polite, and it's time for us to go home," said his mother. "Apologize and we'll go. We have chores to do."

"Ya, Mama, sorry Schotzy." He stood up and went to get his coat, hanging his head in disgust with himself and thinking, *Why do I always say something that I shouldn't? If I had been in Grandpa's shoes, I probably would have had my head cut off. Grandpa said that words have consequences and he was right.*

As Trudy, Klaus, and Cousin Jake prepared to leave, Rachel invited them to come for supper. That was a surprise to Abner even though they did refuse. However, Cousin Jake promised to stop by to see her and Abner later that evening.

As they were about to go out the door, Klaus spoke up. "I'm thinking about the friendship that we have formed here this weekend. I treasure it and yet it worries me. I am afraid that the prince is planning to enforce the law in this principality so that it is a completely Protestant state. That means that everyone who worships as we do will be forced to leave or change back and worship as the prince does. I don't hold with his faith but the king doesn't know that. I couldn't keep my position if he did. Sometimes he rotates his guards to outposts where we are supposed to listen to what's going on and report back. My turn is coming up to be rotated." He looked at Abner and Schotzy and continued, "What I want you to know is that if I should be sent here, it may be safer for you, and for me, if you don't know me and I don't know you." He smiled at them fondly and asked, "Don't speak to me first. If I speak to you, then everything's all right. Do you understand?"

Schotzy went over to him, saluted, and said very seriously, "Ya, we do, Big Angel. We'll do whatever you say. Ain't so, Abner?"

Klaus lifted Schotzy right off the floor with a big hug and said, "No matter what happens, I'll always try to be there for you, little buddy. I'll be back as soon as I can." With a courtly bow, Klaus, along with Jake and Trudy, left for the Schneider's.

As Abner was putting on his coat, he heard Grandpa say, "I think I'll wander over to see Herr Schotzenberger. There are a few points we need to clear up before we sign any papers, and I need to know if he wants to go through with binding Schotzy out to me. Do you want to go along, Schotzy?" Abner wished he could go, but he knew he couldn't. Well, Schotzy would tell him about it the next time he saw him. He hugged his grandma and thanked her for dinner. "I forgot to bring your basket back," he said, "but I'll try to remember it tomorrow."

"You better would remember it, or you just might never get any more little cakes," teased Schotzy. "I'm here now to eat them."

"I'm really worried about it," laughed Abner, as he and his mother went out the door. They walked home quietly, changed their clothes, and did their chores. Rachel warmed up leftover vegetable soup for supper, and just as they had finished eating, Cousin Jake and Trudy came.

"Klaus and I are both leaving early in the morning, but we think it best that we not be seen together, so I will be leaving first," said Cousin Jake. "Like I said, I will find Matthias and tell him I saw you, and I will try to be back in two or three weeks." He turned to Trudy and said with a smile, "If this woman will agree to marry me, she should be ready for a ceremony when I get back. How about that?"

"Fraulein Trudy, look how handsome he is," said Abner earnestly, "He really likes you. Can't you tell? He wouldn't lie to you and say he wants to marry you if he didn't want to, would he, Mama?"

Rachel smiled. Trudy turned red and said, "We'll see. This all has happened too fast." Then she added thoughtfully, "Someone must watch after my mother. Klaus will get out of the army in two years if there is no war. He plans to come home and he will be here for her then. Of course, there is the case of Herr Schotzenberger. Will she really marry him? Ach, I hope not, and yet if she does, it will free me up to go to Pennsylvania and maybe marry Jake. I must really think on it hard before I decide."

Rachel spoke up. "Trudy, your mother is well and she could take care of herself until Klaus comes home. If anything would happen to her, 'The Brethren' would look after her. Look how my father-in-law is fixing her porch. That is an example of how our people look after each other. Do not be afraid of the future. God is watching after all of us. Pray about it."

Abner looked at his mother in total surprise and thought, *Was this the same woman who was crying two nights ago?*

Rachel continued, "If you marry Jake you will be part of my family, so if there is anything I can do for you, all you have to do is ask. I will help you in any way possible. That's the way Altlands are. They help family. Since Jake has no mother, I will play mother of the groom."

Trudy giggled and said, "Rachel, you are the same age as I am. You must have given birth to Jake before you were born." With that, everyone laughed and hugged and said, "Goodbye, may God go with you," and Jake and Trudy were gone.

For his prayers that night, Abner thanked the Father for the wonderful day and for his mother's change of attitude. He asked that God would help him to mind his tongue and to remember that words and actions have consequences. He asked also that He would keep Jake safe and help him find his papa and bring him home. He prayed that Trudy would decide to marry Cousin Jake and become a member of the family, and that everything would work out for the best for Schotzy. While he was trying to think about something else to pray about he remembered the strange little man that had come to their church. He had forgotten to ask Cousin Jake about him. He asked God to bless him and keep him safe too, thinking that it must be awful to lose all of your family. Having Papa gone was bad enough, but losing your whole family, how could anybody stand it? It wasn't easy to doze off after thinking such thoughts, but after awhile Abner went to sleep.

CHAPTER NINE

The next morning was cold and foggy; the perfect morning to stay in bed and sleep, not that Abner ever got such a chance. He could feel the cold creeping in the window and hated, hated, hated, to get up. "Raus mit du!" said his mother.

"Ya, ya, I know," he answered grumpily.

"If you think it's nasty for you, think of poor Jake and Klaus, on the road long already. But then again, it's probably better for Jake to travel away from here and not be seen by a lot of people. Get up, you must not be late getting to your Grandpa's. I fixed your breakfast. I made a dippy egg* and toastbread. I'm going to the barn now."

Abner crawled out, ran quickly to the window, closed it, and got into his clothes as fast as possible. The fog had drawn into them, and they felt cold and clammy. Brrr, he shivered. *I thought that winter was over and here it gives cold again.* It was warmer downstairs and he stood in front of the fire for a bit, rubbing his hands together, and then rotated front and back until his clothes had warmed and dried. He had forgotten to ask his mother for coffee. He looked at the coffeepot and thought about wanting hair on his chest. No, he better wouldn't souff her coffee without permission! He knew better than that, so he ate his breakfast, dipping the warm toast into the soft egg yolk. It hit the spot. His mother had also set out some softened apple snitz, and a cup of milk. Good breakfast! That would hold him for awhile. He went into the mudroom, pulled on his barn boots and coat, ran through the barn and did his chores as quickly as possible.

"Ach, young man, I hope you are doing a good job, as fast as you are going at it," his mother called to him from where she sat milking a cow. "Take your time and do a good job or you'll have to do it over." Abner slowed down and finished without spilling anything,

---

* dippy egg: toast dipped in a soft boiled or a sunny-side-up egg

upsetting anything, or making a mess as he usually did when he hurried. *It's a wonder,* he thought, *but on the other hand, I'm pretty grown up now and I can do a decent job when I really try.*

"It looks like pretty good to me, Mama. I'm going to go now." He tore back to the mudroom, put on his other coat and boots, washed his hands, grabbed his slate, and was off. Oops, he forgot to wash his face and comb his hair. Too late now!

The fog made the whole world strange. It looked different; it smelled different; it felt different, and even the sound of the creek was muffled. The fog was creeping through his coat and he was beginning to get cold. He had forgotten his gloves and he shoved his hands deep into his pockets. Abner hoped that he and Schotzy would have lessons first and not have to go outside to work until the sun came out and burned off the fog. Here it is the first day of a new beginning and it is foggy. What would Grandma have to say about that? He was sure that she would see it as not a good sign. Everything that happened had some kind of a strange meaning for her. Grandpa was right: superstition added a lot of worry to a person.

The fog was thicker by the stream and he could scarcely see his hand before his face, but he could swear that there was someone across the street. That person was pulling his coat up tightly around himself and covering his face. Was he doing that to keep warm or was it so that no one could tell who it was? It couldn't be Cousin Jake or Klaus. They both had horses and probably had left long already. Abner turned to Grandpa's and the man, if it was a man, hurried away, keeping his head down and his face averted.

Grandma was, as always, very glad to see him. "Ach!" she said, "Were you so much in a hurry that you couldn't take the time to comb your hairs and wash your face?" She went to the dry sink and got the comb and a washrag. She dipped the rag into some warm water and washed his face, got the sleeps out of the corners of his eyes, and began to comb his hair.

Schotzy walked in without Grandma seeing him, and behind her back, smiled and wagged his head and pointed. Silently he mouthed and mocked, "Grandma gotta wash your face, Grandma gotta wash your face!" He put his thumbs in his ears and stuck out his tongue and made fun, enjoying himself tremendously. Abner could do nothing about it except to vow that he would he never again leave the house without washing his face and combing his hair. He also decided to get Schotzy later.

Grandpa began the day with prayer and Bible reading. "I shall read from the first Psalm, the first three verses. It will tell you what kind of men I want you to grow up to be. That is what we are aiming for. First I will read it and then you shall copy it." Grandpa began to read and Grandma came in to listen. **"Blessed is the man that walketh not in the counsel of the ungodly, nor standeth in the way of sinners, nor sitteth in the seat of scornful. But his delight is in the law of the Lord, and in his law doth he meditate day and night. And he shall be like a tree planted by the rivers of water, which bringeth forth its fruit in its season; his leaf also shall not wither; and whatsoever he doeth shall prosper."**

Grandpa had a slate for Schotzy and the boys began to copy the verses. Schotzy clutched the chalk, stuck his tongue between his teeth and worked very hard at his task. For Abner, it was easier, because his father had been teaching him for several years. Grandpa showed Schotzy how to form letters that he was unsure of and then he asked, "Do you both know how to write your names?" Abner did and Schotzy didn't, so Grandpa wrote "Ephraim Schotzenberger" on the back of his slate.

"Do I have to write Ephraim? Can't I just write Schotzy?"

"I'm afraid not. Ephraim is your legal name and you may have to write it soon, perhaps this afternoon." Then, giving in a little, he said, "You must learn to spell Ephraim. Schotzy is easy if you know Schotzenberger. Besides, the name Ephraim itself is a wonderful blessing. It means 'Fruitful in a land of suffering.' In other words you will do well no matter what happens."

Schotzy smiled a big smile and said, "Well in that case, I'll try very hard to learn it quick and write it nice."

After a bit it was time for numbers. Grandpa showed the boys how to write the numerals correctly and asked them a few questions to see how much they knew. He instructed them to write on their slates the addition combinations that they did not know and to say them out loud. Two hours went by quickly. Abner looked out the window and saw that the sun was peeking through the fog. It was time to get to the outside work.

As they walked along the path to Schneider's, Abner said, "You didn't tell me what happened last night when you went over to see your pappaw."

"He wasn't home," said Schotzy, "so I went in and got some of my father's clothes. Your grandma said that Widow Schneider sews for people sometimes and maybe she would cut them down and make clothes for me. I need some to work in. I hope she will. I think she will, don't you?" Abner and Grandpa agreed that they were sure she would.

When they got to Schneider's, Abner immediately noticed that Widow Schneider was by no means as friendly as she had been on Saturday. He could not help but feel that it was strange. She offered them something to eat, but seemed relieved when they refused, and then went back into the house immediately. The boys got to work mixing the mortar as they had been taught. Then Grandpa showed them how to smear the mortar on the backs and sides of the stones, put them in place, fill in the cracks between, make sure they were level, and clean the mortar off the stones. Grandpa and the boys were able to finish the steps quickly because Jake had chipped, fit, and placed the stones properly on Saturday. "That Jake is a good man," said Grandpa. "Trudy would do well to marry him."

When they were finished and cleaned up, Widow Schneider asked them in for dinner. Abner noticed that today's spread was not nearly as sumptuous as Saturday's had been. There was enough, but nothing like before. There was pork and sauerkraut, noodles, butterbread, and cake left from Saturday; not the kind of a meal generally fed to workers. Abner noticed, too, that Widow Schneider kept an eye on him all of the time. She never smiled, nor did she say much to Schotzy. Abner was glad when the meal was over. He wondered if Grandpa had noticed anything, but he didn't ask. What would Widow Schneider say if he mentioned how weird everything seemed? The idea tickled him and he smiled. She didn't like that either. Was he the only one who noticed the tension, and where was Trudy?

Before Abner had a chance to ask about her, Grandpa smiled and said, "Frau Schneider, the other day you said that if there was ever anything that you could do for me, all I had to do was ask. Now I'm asking. Would you make some clothes for Ephraim? He needs them badly."

"Well, I don't know," she answered, not at all politely, "Trudy is over talking to Rachel. She's talking about needing a wedding dress and I was wanting a new dress for myself. But, beings I promised..." She looked toward Abner and continued, "Send Ephraim over late this afternoon, before it gets dark; and I'll measure him, but send him by himself. I'll get to making his clothes as soon as I can."

Abner cocked his head and looked at her in wonder. What could this be all about?

As soon as they got outside Abner whispered to Grandpa, "It wonders me..."

Before he could finish, Grandpa nodded his head and whispered, "Me, too."

Schotzy spoke up; "Widow Schneider wasn't very friendly, was she?"

"No she wasn't," answered Abner. "She really worked on my nerves.* How about you?"

Schotzy scratched his head, thought a bit, and said, "I wonder what my pappaw told her. It musta been something strange or she wouldn't have been acting like that. I can't think of any other reason, can you?" Abner and Grandpa both shook their heads. It was a puzzle.

As they walked toward Grandpa's house, Abner couldn't help but think of what was going to happen this afternoon at the magistrate's office. He knew it was none of his business, but he

---

* work on nerves: make nervous

wanted to go along. He held his tongue as long as he could, and then he blurted out, "Grandpa, please, can I go along this afternoon with you and Schotzy?"

"Ya," Grandpa answered without hesitation. "I was just going to ask if you would like to go along. I think you should because it's part of everyone's education to see and learn about the workings of the law. First, you must go home, clean up, and put better clothes on. It is always best to show respect for the law. You don't have to wear your very best, but you show respect by not wearing your dirty work clothes. The Bible says that laws and governments were set up by God for the good of the people. That is why we respect them."

Abner hurried home, told his mother what was going on, greeted Trudy, changed, and was back at his grandparents' home in record time. Grandpa inspected him. "Not clean enough, your face and hands." Oh, no! Not this again! Grandma got the washrag, but this time Abner took it from her and wiped his own face and hands. He looked over at Schotzy. His hair was combed; his face was clean and most of the imbedded grime was off his hands and neck. He looked a lot better than he had last week.

"How are you doing, Ephraim?" asked Abner.

"Fine, thank you very much," he answered.

Abner smiled and thought, *He's not going to let anything stir him up.*

Schotzy continued, "It just wonders me if my pappaw will be there. Do you want to bet? I'll bet he's not there, and you bet he is."

Grandpa frowned. "We don't bet around here."

"I'm sorry, sir, I didn't know that," said Schotzy. "But I think he won't be there still. How about you?"

"Time will tell," answered Grandpa. Abner thought he would be there because he wanted the money, but like Grandpa said, time would tell.

When they got to the magistrate's office, Herr Schotzenberger was not there; and the magistrate kept them waiting. It seemed a good while to Abner and he began to rutch around and shuffle his feet. Grandpa frowned, shook his head and said, "Settle!" Abner settled.

"I don't know if I need to tell you or not, Abner," Grandpa said seriously, "but I want you to remember that you are here as an observer only. You are to sit quietly and say nothing. Furthermore, if anything private is said, you are to tell no one. It is not your business and you are to keep out of it. Do you understand? This is another important lesson in life. He turned to Schotzy and added, "I'd be saying the same to you if the shoe were on the other foot."

Schotzy looked puzzled and glanced at his feet. He had on scuffed up shoes that Abner had outgrown.

Grandpa chuckled and explained, "That means, if it were the other way around and you were sitting in on Abner's or anybody else's private business, you shouldn't say anything then, or anything about it later."

"Ya," Schotzy answered, "I get it. It just sounded funny to me."

The magistrate finally came in and Grandpa stood up, motioning for the boys to do likewise. He was a tall, rather dark, heavy-set man with a nose like a hawk. His large, dark eyes were sharp and penetrating, the kind that do not miss a thing. He had a cruel look about him that Abner did not like at all, and he thought, *I wouldn't trust him as far as I could throw him.*

The magistrate looked at each of them, and it seemed to Abner that he was reading each one's mind. It was not a pleasant feeling. The magistrate seated himself and remained quiet for awhile as if thinking, and then he said, "Oh yes, this is the matter concerning trouble between Walter Schotzenberger and Frederick Hartzell. You may sit."

They sat. "Now," he continued, "Herr Schotzenberger awakened me early this morning and demanded that I see him immediately. He said that he had to leave the village because you, Frederick Hartzell, had threatened him and had alienated his grandson. He said that he was afraid to stay in the village. He said that you, Herr Hartzell, want to make his grandson work for you. This will be a hardship for him, and a hardship for Ephraim, too. Because of the way you went about it, threatening him and all, he said that you if you want

Ephraim to work for you, you should have to pay more than the usual fee for a bondservant. What do you have to say about that?"

Grandpa looked so surprised he couldn't say anything. Abner started to interrupt and say that it was a lie, but Grandpa took him by the shoulder and shook his head. It was Schotzy who said very firmly, "That's not true, sir."

"And just exactly who are you?" asked the magistrate.

"I am Ephraim Schotzenberger and Walter Schotzenberger is my grandfather."

The magistrate looked surprised at that news. "So you are Ephraim Schotzenberger. I have been meaning to look you up. I have something here for you. However, back to the business at hand. Which one of you wishes to speak first and tell his side of the story? Remember, you must tell the truth."

Grandpa and Schotzy looked at each other and then Grandpa said, "Schotzy, you should go first."

Abner sat quietly as he had been told and listened to Schotzy's testimony.

"My pappaw, Walter Schotzenberger, hit me on Saturday when I threw up. He called me names, too. He said he was going to bind me out to the first farmer that would take me. Herr Hartzell told him that he shouldn't hit a sick child. He told my pappaw that he would take me, and my pappaw should leave. Herr Hartzell did sound kind of mad."

"Did he sound angry enough that you were afraid of him?"

"Oh, no, sir. Herr Hartzell is the kindest man in the village. I would never be afraid of him." Abner was pleased to hear that Schotzy thought so highly of his grandpa.

"How old are you, Ephraim?" asked the magistrate.

"I'm nine years old, sir, almost ten."

"Did your grandfather hit you often?"

"Ya, pretty often." Abner was surprised to hear this; Schotzy had never mentioned that his pappaw hit him.

"How long has it been that just you and your grandfather have lived together?" continued the magistrate.

"About eight months. My father died late last fall when a tree fell on him. He and my pappaw were woodcutters. My mammaw[*] died just before my father did. She was sick for a long time. My mother died when I was just little and I don't remember her at all."

The magistrate smiled at Schotzy as kindly as his cruel face would permit, and then asked, "Was it a hard winter?"

Schotzy nodded his head and said, "Ya, and it was."

"Would you tell me about it?"

"After my papa died my pappaw didn't talk to me or do anything all winter long, except to look in odd places where my papa or my mammaw may have hidden money. He would ask me if I had any money when he knew I didn't. If he found any, as he did once in awhile, he would go to the biergarten and souff until it was all gone. My papa had got in some carrots, cabbage, turnips, apples, and stuff like that back in the fall. We ate all of that up. All of the food was gone and pappaw still wouldn't go cut wood or do anything to get money. Sometimes I would hear a hen cackle and then I would sneak over and get the gockie if no one was looking. If I asked him what we were going to do, he would just yell at me and hit me if he could catch me.

So that's where the gockies have been disappearing to, thought Abner, *but if they kept Schotzy from starving, I'm glad he took them.*

"On Friday Herr Hartzell asked if I would like to go along to help at Widow Schneider's. I told pappaw about it. He thought on it awhile, and then said that he finally knew what he was going to do, and it wasn't cutting down no trees. He talked about binding me out to a farmer, but he wouldn't say what his own plans were. He just rubbed his hands together and said, 'That's the way to get money. I'm not going to work any more. I've got it figured out.' That's when he told me that he would go along and help at Schneider's the next day."

Schotzy stopped to get a breath and Abner said, "So that's why you kept saying, 'I wonder what that old man is up to.'" Schotzy nodded.

---

[*] mammaw: grandma

The magistrate looked sternly at Abner and said, "You are not being questioned." To Schotzy he said, "Go on, what happened on Saturday?"

"On Saturday my pappaw went along with us to repair Widow Schneider's porch and steps, but I don't think he had a mind to work. I think he put on that he hurt his thumb and went into the house. He stayed in the house most of the time. He and Widow Schneider had been friends when they were young, and he visited with her all morning. I kept hurting myself and having to go into the house to be taken care of. I think my coming in so many times really made him mad, but he didn't let on. I think he wanted to honey up to Widow Schneider and my being there interfered with his plans. That's what made him mad enough to hit me.

"At dinner I made like a hog. The widow just kept piling food on my plate, and piling food on my plate, and I kept fressing it and fressing it, even though I was full. After dinner all of the men, including my pappaw, me, and Abner went outside. I began to mix the mortar, and then I kuttzed into it and ruined it. Then's when my pappaw called me a dumkopf and let me have it. Then he said he was going to bind me out to a farmer as soon as he could; and that's what made Herr Hartzell mad. He told my pappaw that he would take me in and my pappaw must leave. That's all the threat there was."

Abner spoke up, "You forgot to tell him that on Friday we told Grandpa about us going to Pennsylvania, and we both asked him to teach us."

The magistrate frowned at Abner and said, "Young man, you are not to speak until you are asked to do so. If you say one more word, you will be dismissed from the room. Do you understand?" Abner hung his head in embarrassment and said, "Ya, but it's important." He wondered what his Grandpa would say when they got outside.

"Now, Ephraim," the magistrate continued, "is there anything else you want to say?"

"I give Abner right. I did ask Herr Hartzell to teach me on Friday afternoon, but he didn't say he would, but he didn't say he wouldn't either."

"Is that all there is to it?" asked the magistrate.

"No, there's more," said Schotzy. "Saturday afternoon I had a bath at Hartzell's and Abner's mother lent me some clothes because I had puked all over myself. Later Abner and I went to see my pappaw and he'd been souffing down beer. He insulted the Hartzells and told me to go hang with them. On Sunday I went to Sabbath meeting with Hartzells. My pappaw came, too, but he did not talk to me or to them, just Widow Schneider. It was funny that he came because he had never been to there before. I guess he figured it was another way to make up to Widow Schneider.

"Last night Herr Hartzell and I made ourselves over to my house to see him, but he wasn't home. Herr Hartzell had said he wanted to talk and straighten things out. I went into the house and got some things. Herr Hartzell didn't go in. That's all there is to it, except that today, when we were working for her, finishing new stone steps, Widow Schneider was not nice to us. Something's not right because Herr Hartzell, Herr Altland, Abner, and I had worked hard for her for two days and took no money for it. My pappaw must have said something to her that wasn't the truth. He does that sometimes."

"Now tell me, young man," demanded the magistrate. "If you had your choice, would you be willing to be bound out to Herr Hartzell? I don't really have to ask you that, but what are your feelings in the matter? In other words, if you had plenty of money, what would you do?"

Schotzy sat quietly for a bit as if in deep thought, and then he said, "I thought I should stay with my pappaw because he is my family, and I thought he needed me, but he doesn't want me. If I had money, Pappaw would just take it from me and be drunk all of the time, so that wouldn't help. I'd rather stay with Hartzells than be bound out to a farmer I don't know. Herr Hartzell is a good man and I believe he'll teach me if I work for him. Grandma Hartzell, I mean, Frau Hartzell is kind and she likes me, too. I can tell, and she is a good cook. I wouldn't be hungry if I lived there, and I can learn to be a builder. That's a good trade. Herr Hartzell is also teaching me to read and write."

"You are?" The magistrate raised his eyebrows and looked at Grandpa with great surprise. "How did you learn to read and write?"

"It's a long story, too long to tell now," answered Grandpa, "but I assure you that I do know how to read, write and figure and to teach others to do the same. I will teach Ephraim if he works for me and tries hard, but I do not believe in doing something like that for nothing. I believe that people value what they work for."

The magistrate thought for a bit and then he said, "It seems to me that Ephraim will be well off staying with you, and I will allow him to be legally bound to you for the next seven years unless something most unusual should happen." Schotzy looked at Abner, smiled a big smile and Abner smiled back. They both stood up to leave. "Don't leave yet," the magistrate continued. "I'm not finished." He motioned for them to sit back down. "Ephraim, what was your mother's maiden name?"

Schotzy looked at Grandpa, "What does he mean?"

"He means, do you know what your mother's name was before she was married? If you don't, I do. It was Lorelei Slonaker. Her father was Rolf Slonaker."

"That's what I needed to know. Ephraim, your Grandfather Slonaker owned the house you live in and he left it to you. It never belonged to the Schotzenbergers. It's your house. He did not want your father or your Grandfather Schotzenberger to be able to get their hands on any of his money or possessions even after he was dead. Rolf Slonaker did not like the Schotzenbergers. He saw your mother live in poverty and he saw her die. He blamed your father and his father for her early death. He gave me instructions to keep your inheritance until you were of age and not let the Schotzenbergers know that you had it coming to you before then. In the case of your father's death and the appointment of a legal guardian whom I trusted, your inheritance was to be given to him to keep for you. That's what I'm doing now. As for your house, Herr Slonaker stipulated that no Schotzenberger could live there if you weren't there, so your grandfather will have to move out. I suggest that you sell it. It hasn't been well taken care of in these last few years and would take a lot of work to bring it back to what it should be."

Abner looked at Schotzy and Schotzy looked at Abner and they both said, "Ach du lieber!" They both sat with shocked looks on their faces.

Both boys stood up again to leave and the magistrate added with a slight smile and twinkle in his eye, "Don't leave until I dismiss you. I'm not finished." Going to a large wooden cupboard he dug around until he found an old leather bucket with a hinged lid and a sealed clasp on it. He handed it to Schotzy who almost dropped it on the floor.

"It's heavy, really heavy. What's in it?" he asked. Abner craned his neck to look, wondering what could be that heavy.

Schotzy picked it up, set it on his lap, broke the seal, and unfastened the lid. He reached in and brought out a large gold piece, then another and another and another.

As Abner watched his friend's unbelieving face turn to joy, a sudden rage came over him as he remembered how hungry Schotzy had been and how ugly his pappaw had treated him. He stood up and said to the magistrate in an angry voice, "Do you mean to tell me that you had this gold all this time and you let my friend Schotzy nearly starve to death this winter? You never even went to see how he was or anything like that. Was that what his Grandpa Slonaker wanted from you? Who would have got the gold and the house if Schotzy would have died?"

The magistrate's face almost turned purple as he pointed his finger at Abner and said in a coldly controlled voice, "You are a most disrespectful young man. What is your name?"

Abner glanced in Grandpa's direction. He looked very grim. "Abner Hartzell, sir."

"Abner Hartzell," the magistrate repeated. He looked in his desk and found a piece of paper, ink and a quill, and wrote "Abner Hartzell" very carefully. He shook sand over the ink, carefully poured it off and checked to see if the ink was dry. When he was satisfied that it was, he put the paper in his desk drawer and looked up. "Young man, you are impertinent and disrespectful. Furthermore, you implied that I am dishonest. The king appointed me and I have not been here long, so perhaps you do not know my reputation. You will know of it very soon; of that you can be very sure. When you imply that I am dishonest, you imply that the king is dishonest because I am the king's agent. I could fine you a large amount of money because you are slandering the king. How old are you?"

"Almost ten years old," Abner answered in a shaking voice.

"It seems to me that you are old enough to know how to behave yourself in a proper manner. You had better watch yourself because I'll be watching you. You may go now." He pointed to the door.

Abner got up, stood very erect and walked out without looking back. He stood outside the office until Grandpa and Schotzy came out a long time later. *Boy, I'm in a fix** he thought, as he wondered what they were talking about. *What would Grandpa say when he came out? Would he be in disgrace forever? The magistrate just didn't understand how much he cared for Schotzy. What was taking them so long? Papa would let me have it with a paddle if he knew about this. It wonders me what Grandpa will do. This waiting is working on my nerves. I could go home, but I have to face them sooner or later. I guess I better would wait for them and get it over with. A cuppy** more minutes of this and I'm leaving. Ach du lieber, what have I done?*

Abner paced until the door finally opened. Schotzy was carrying the leather bucket, but it was too heavy for him and he handed it to Grandpa. The joy had gone from their faces. Grandpa looked Abner square in the eye and said curtly, "When you make an enemy, you certainly do start at the top. The magistrate is the leading legal officer of this district. If you are involved in any legal matter from now on you can be sure that you will lose. Serious this is. If you are accused of a crime, you won't have a chance; and there won't be

---

* in a fix: in trouble
* cuppy: couple

125

anything that I, or anyone else, will be able to do about it. Furthermore, he debated quite a while before he decided that Schotzy could stay with me, all on account of what you said."

"I'm sorry, Grandpa," said Abner, "it was just..."

"You need to understand that being sorry isn't enough. Proverbs 13:3 says, **'He that keepeth his mouth keepeth his life: but he that openeth wide his lips shall have destruction.'** I've told you before that you should think before you speak. Now you know what I've been talking about. I just hope that the consequences aren't too great. You must know that from now on, you must try very hard to keep out of trouble, and furthermore," Grandpa added, pointing towards the bucket with the gold in it. "You must not mention this to anyone. Not your mother, not your father, not anyone," he emphasized. "Not ever. Do you understand?"

CHAPTER TEN

Abner had never felt worse in his life. His grandpa was disappointed in him, and he had brought who knows what trouble on his own head. Nevertheless, he wasn't ashamed of speaking up for Schotzy because he felt the magistrate was wrong in not watching after Schotzy in the first place. *Grown-ups aren't always right, that was plain to see, but it isn't smart to let them know that's what you think. Dear God, he said to himself, protect me and help me to control my tongue. I know I've prayed that one before. And please don't let Grandpa stay mad at me.*

They walked along the street together, each deep in his own thoughts until Schotzy asked, "Who's going to tell my pappaw that he must get out of the house?"

"The magistrate will do it as soon as he can get around to it, I suppose," Grandpa answered.

"That might take awhile," Abner said sarcastically.

"Abner, you had better learn that you must watch the tone of your voice as well as the words you say," advised Grandpa. "Especially when it comes to that man. Your mouth has a way of getting you in trouble. Do you know that?" Grandpa cocked his head, raised his eyebrows, but he didn't smile as he usually did. Turning to Schotzy he said, "Your pappaw must have known that the house belonged to you. What do you think about all this?"

"Well, sir, it is pretty much to think about. I have to think about the house and what to do with it, and I have to think about what to do about my pappaw. Besides, I cannot imagine where all this gold came from. Grandpa Slonaker never acted like he was rich. Where do you suppose it could it have come from? He was just an ordinary person. He had a truck farm and sold his vegetables here and at market in Kittzheim and Partenbuhl, but a person couldn't get rich from raising and selling vegetables, could he?"

"There has to be some explanation," said Abner. "Maybe when we get into your house we can find some clues. Do the coins have any markings on them?"

"You know, boys, it is dangerous to talk about them even on the street," cautioned Grandpa in a low voice. "Voices carry, people listen, people talk. It is of utmost importance that you say nothing about them to anyone. We must be careful even when we talk amongst ourselves. It is going to be hard. I warn you."

They walked along silently until they got to Grandpa's house when he said, "Would you boys like to have the afternoon off? I have to figure out a place to hide this loot which won't be easy considering that Frau Hartzell cleans every crack and corner of the house."

"What about burying it in the garden?" asked Schotzy. "Frau Hartzell wouldn't dig in there, would she?"

"That's a good idea," said Grandpa, "but first we had better go some place where we can be alone, look at the coins and count them. Then they must be buried where you know where they are in case anything would happen to me. This is a terrible responsibility for me and for you, too, Schotzy. Having riches is a great responsibility."

"Does Schotzy have riches? Is he rich?" asked Abner putting both hands on his head in amazement.

"It looks like it," said Grandpa, "but keep your voice down. Let's go in here to my workshop. I think we will be safe enough. Abner, you stand guard and talk to your grandmother if she should come out. She hardly ever does, but if she should, ask her about little cakes or something. That will distract her."

Abner stood by the door and watched while Schotzy and Grandpa studied the gold coins. After a bit Grandpa motioned for him to come and look, too. "See here," he said excitedly, "They have strange pictures and markings in what might be Latin. Look at them closely. They look freshly minted; and I'm sure no one makes coins like these today. I saw gold coins when I was at court and none of them looked anything like these."

"It's fun to see you excited, Grandpa," said Abner, as he walked back to the door to guard, "and they are beautiful, but they work on my nerves. When are you going to count them? I'll feel better when they are counted and put away."

Grandpa smiled and said, "You are absolutely right. Are you ready to count, Schotzy? Or shall I call you Ephraim?"

Schotzy smiled a big, broad smile and said, "I don't care what you call me, except don't call me that poor little Schotzenberger boy. I've heard that often enough." So they laid them out in piles of ten each and there were five piles.

"Can you count by tens?" asked Grandpa. "Here we go," and they counted together, "ten, twenty, thirty, forty, fifty. Fifty!"

"Ach du lieber," said Abner, "fifty big gold coins."

"Does that make me rich?" asked Schotzy.

"Yes," said Grandpa, "I think it does."

Abner wondered what Schotzy would say next and was surprised when he said, "Let's hide them quick until it's time to go to Pennsylvania." Schotzy took a deep breath and added, "If it's all right with you, sir, let's go on just like we planned unless you want me to pay you to stay here and teach me."

Grandpa patted Schotzy on the back smiled kindly and said, "We'll work things out. You are a good boy and you really want to learn, don't you?" They quickly scooped the gold back into the bucket and Abner sighed in relief when it was out of sight. He wondered what Schotzy would do with all that money. He knew what he'd do. He'd buy himself a horse.

"I'd like to have a dog," said Schotzy, "and I suppose that we will have to spend one of them to fix up my house so that we can sell it, or should we just let it go as it is?"

"As for the dog, we'll see," replied Grandpa. "Fixing up your house would be good practice in learning how to do many things; and business is a little slow now. We could calculate the costs of the materials. All in all, it would be a good project, but it is up to you to decide."

"I'd like to go over there now," said Schotzy. "I should talk to my pappaw. Will you come with me?"

"Actually, I don't feel that I should go with you," replied Grandpa. "I wouldn't feel right about taking the gold with me or leaving it here either, so I'll put it in this tool box under all of these tools, and then I'll put some more tools and things on the top of the box. What do you think?"

"As long as it looks like it usually does, no one would think anything of it," answered Abner, shrugging his shoulders. Grandpa began arranging his tool bench and Abner continued, "I'd like to go along with Schotzy if I may, but first I need to talk to you about something." Grandpa nodded and Abner added, "I don't mean to talk too much and to let my mouth get me in trouble. I've prayed about it and I still do it. Does God hear me or what?"

"God hears every prayer and he answers them in different ways. In letters that St. Paul wrote to Timothy, he tells him to train himself to be godly. He was a young man and he was being trained to be one of the leaders of the church. In the letter St. Paul tells Timothy that leaders of the church should be self-controlled. One of my favorite verses comes from his second letter to Timothy. It says in verse seven, **'For God hath not given us the spirit of fear; but of power, and of love, and of sound mind.'** Which means we can control ourselves; we can discipline ourselves. God will not do everything for us, and God will not make us do anything. We have free will. We make our own decisions. We must be self-disciplined. God gave us the power to do that, but we must want it, and we must work at it. I believe that God wants you to grow up to be a strong, self-controlled man who will be a leader of his people, but now your tongue is like a wild horse without a bridle. An unbridled horse is of no value. Only after it is bridled and under control is it useful."

Abner hung his head and thought about it for a while and then asked earnestly, "Grandpa, will you forgive me for speaking out to the magistrate?"

Grandpa also thought a bit before he answered, and then said, "Of course, I will forgive you, but will the magistrate? That's what counts. You are my flesh and blood and you know how I feel about

130

you, but you mean nothing to him. You had better pray that if you ever have to appear before him, that God will protect you. Is there anything else you want to talk about?"

"No, not really, except, what time should Schotzy be at Widow Schneider's?"

"Perhaps you boys shouldn't go to Schotzy's home before going to Schneider's. It is likely to get late and you shouldn't keep her waiting. Abner, you go on home and Schotzy can find you after he's finished at the widow's."

Abner knew he should go home and change his clothes, but if he did, his mother would find work for him. The chance for free time was too tempting and he decided to take advantage of it. He walked across the bridge to the blacksmith's but it was closed. He wandered around the village, looking into shop windows, and then threw some rocks into the creek. He met a few people, but none were as friendly as usual. That's odd, he thought. He walked down to the lake wishing that he had had something to feed the geese and other water birds. It was a beautiful day and yet he didn't know what to do with himself. He was glad when he saw Schotzy coming down the hill to meet him.

Schotzy was full of news to tell Abner about his fitting with Widow Schneider. "I couldn't believe it," he said. "She wanted to know why I kept hanging with a rowdy like you. She said she could tell that I was a good boy, but if I kept hanging with you, I would turn out bad. She said she saw you with Max, Willy, and Otto on Sunday afternoon, and she thinks you are worse than they are. I asked her why she thought that, and all she would say was, 'I've got my reasons.' I asked her if my pappaw had said anything against you, and she wouldn't answer."

"That's strange," answered Abner. "My wrist is still sore from when Max twisted it on Sunday, and she thinks those rotters* are my friends. I guess we'll find out sometime what it's all about. Let's go to your house now."

---

* rotters: rotten people

131

As they crossed the bridge and walked towards the house, Abner noticed that there was no smoke coming from the chimney and he wondered about it because it was still too cool not to have fire. They walked around to the back porch and up to the back door. There was a broom against it, and Schotzy said, "There's no one home."

"How do you know?" asked Abner.

"Because you couldn't be inside and leave the broom against the door on the outside. My pappaw always left the broom that certain way and when he got back, he knew if anyone had moved it or if anyone was inside. Pappaw said you prop a broom against the door to protect the house from witches."

"More superstitions," said Abner, and shook his head.

Schotzy moved the broom, went in, and Abner followed. It was cold and damp, with a disagreeable musty odor of smoke, unwashed bodies, and the general stench of a place that had not been cleaned and aired out for a long time. Abner left the door open. He would have liked to open a window, but didn't have the nerve. He knew that Schotzy, as homeowner, deserved respect.

"What will we do if your pappaw comes?" asked Abner nervously.

"Ach, no need to worry," answered Schotzy. "What can he do to us? He might holler, but that won't hurt. If he comes after us, we can run."

Schotzy began showing Abner around the house. In general it was neater than Abner had expected. The floors were dirty and there was dust on all of the furniture, but the clutter was limited to the pile of clothes in the corner of one of the rooms that looked like it wasn't used much.

"That's the stuff from Uncle Pete that died," said Schotzy, pointing at the clothes. "We can look at it after I show you the house. Let's go upstairs to my bedroom first."

Abner followed Schotzy and saw that his bed was made but it sloped in the center like a swaybacked horse. Schotzy pulled back the covers and showed Abner that it was a rope bed with a straw mattress. "The ropes needed tightened long already and my mattress wasn't refilled with fresh straw this last fall. That's why it looks like it does. Sometimes I think sleeping on the floor would be more better. Your grandma has a feather mattress on the bed I slept on last night." He smiled with pleasure and added, "It's real nice."

Abner looked at Schotzy's bed and thought about his own. His mother had seen to it that his mattress was made of feathers and his pillow and covers were always clean. It had never occurred to him that his mother worked hard to keep his bed and his room clean. It was a totally new thought to him; that it was a job to keep a house clean and to keep everyone in the family supplied with a clean bed, nice covers and a comfortable mattress. He knew, too, that she would never have let him sleep in such a furrected* bed.

All of a sudden Schotzy laughed, breaking up Abner's thoughts about his own bed. "Did I ever tell you about the last time my mattress was filled with straw? It had been an exciting day, and I wasn't ready to settle down. They told me to go to bed, and stay there, but I kept finding excuses to get up. You know, tell me a story; I need a drink of water; I gotta go potty, until they told me if I got up one more time they would spank me, and I knew that they would. I was trying to go to sleep when I heard something inside my mattress. It was making little chewing noises and moving around." Schotzy shivered just remembering it, and Abner laughed.

"Don't laugh. It really scared me," continued Schotzy. "I imagined it was a rat or a dog or some huge animal that would get me. I couldn't sleep for a long time and when I finally did, I dreamed that there was a dragon in my bed. I woke up screaming, and I ran to my papa's bed. I wouldn't go back, so Papa let me stay with him. Pappaw and mammaw said it would spoil me rotten. The next morning I insisted that there was something in there, and Mammaw took up for me. She opened up the mattress, rattled the straw, and a little, tiny mouse came out, not much bigger than my thumb. It was more scared than I was."

"I wouldn't like to have a mouse in my bed either," laughed Abner.

---

* furrected: worn out, out of shape or broken

133

Schotzy showed him the rest of the house, a third floor, an attic and a full basement. The plastered walls were thick and the windows had deep windowsills. It was, all in all, a good, sturdy house that painted, repaired and furnished right, would be a very nice place to live. Schotzy opened the doors and showed him every room but one on the second floor. That one, he explained, had never been opened in his whole life. No one had a key to the lock and as there were many other rooms, nobody ever bothered with it.

"You will have to open it before you sell the house," said Abner. "You have to know what's in it. There might be more treasure. Grandpa will know how to open it." The smell was getting to Abner and he said, "It's getting late. I'd like to look at your Uncle Pete's stuff but I have chores to do. I know we must do the work next to Widow Schneider's tomorrow and no doubt we'll come here after that."

"You go on home," said Schotzy. "I'll poke around here for awhile and see you in the morning."

That night was very cold with a killing frost. Abner got up in the night, put the window down and pulled on more covers. He lay there, cold, thinking of all sorts of things and unable to get back to sleep. That business with Widow Schneider worried him. *What could be the reason she felt as she did? Was it just something that Herr Schotzenberger had said, or was there more to it?* It occurred to him that he had not prayed about it. He did so, and then he went back to sleep only to be awakened in no time at all.

The day settled into a routine of breakfast, chores, lessons, and work. When Abner told Grandma that he had forgotten the basket again, she said, "That's all right, I won't be baking today anyways." She didn't act as if she felt very well, but Grandpa and the boys went to work anyway.

At the house next to Schneider's, Grandpa showed the boys the properties of different kinds of stones. "The stones in these steps were harder than the ones in Schneider's," he said. "That's the reason they haven't worn down like those did."

Abner looked at them closely and asked, "How can you tell which ones are harder?"

"The ones that are harder will scratch the ones that are softer. See that pile of stone over there at the back of Widow Schneider's lot? Those are the ones we took out. Go get a several different kinds and colors and I'll show you."

Abner ran over and was picking some up, when Widow Schneider came out onto her porch and screamed, "GET OFF MY PROPERTY, YOU LITTLE THIEF!"

Abner was so startled, he couldn't move; but Grandpa and Schotzy dropped everything they were doing and ran over to her. Grandpa demanded, "What is this all about? I sent him to get stones from the pile we put there on Saturday. Why do you think my grandson is a thief? I told him to do it. I didn't think it would matter. I was going to haul them away for you in a couple of days. I can't believe you want a pile of stones in your back yard."

"Well, he shouldn't be taking anything from anybody's property without the owner's permission," she said defensively. "Besides, he is a thief, because he took the pfennig that I always keep on my windowsill for good luck."

"Just exactly when was this pfennig missing?" Grandpa demanded.

"After dinner on Saturday, after all of you left. That's when I noticed that it was gone." she answered.

"Which windowsill was it on?" Grandpa asked.

"The one back of the table next to the china closet."

"If you think about it, Frau Schneider," Grandpa continued, "you will remember that Abner sat on the front side of the table and never was near that windowsill."

"Ach," she said.

"And just exactly who sat at the back of the table near that windowsill?" demanded Schotzy, glaring at her hard, "and who had no money to buy food on Friday, but had money to get drunk on Saturday night?"

"Not Walter," she gasped.

"Yes, Walter, my pappaw, Walter," said Schotzy rather sharply. "He wasn't home all day yesterday or last night. Do you have any idea where he might be?"

Widow Schneider became very flustered, wringing her hands and turning red. After a bit she said, "He came over on Sunday night and said that he had an idea for a business. He said that it was sure to make money and we could get married right away. I gave him all of my money. He went down the mountain on Monday morning to invest it. You don't really think he took my good luck pfennig, too, do you?"

"Yes, I do, and I know that Abner wouldn't have," Schotzy replied. With a worried look he turned to Grandpa and said, "I must go find him. I know how he is in by now. Maybe I can get some of the money back. Will you go along with me?"

"Of course, we'll leave right away." Turning to Widow Schneider, he asked, "Are you going to apologize to my grandson?"

She lifted her nose up in the air, turned on her heel and went inside as fast as she could.

When they reached Grandpa's house, they discovered that Grandma was really quite ill. She had chills, her head felt hot, and she had gone to bed. Abner ran to get his mother, but he couldn't find her. One of the neighbor ladies said that she had seen her with Trudy and it looked as if they were going for a walk up towards the mountains. Abner thanked her and ran back to his grandparents' as fast as he could. When he got there Grandpa was bathing Grandma's face with cool water.

"Abner," said Grandpa, "I'm sorry, but I can't go with Schotzy to find his pappaw. Your grandma is too sick for me to leave her, but you can go. You are both sensible boys and you'll be all right. I gave Schotzy some money and told him to rent a cart to bring him back in. If he isn't in Partenbuhl, the first village, go to the next one, which is Kittzheim. I can't imagine that he would have gone any farther than that. I'll tell your mother where you've gone, and I'll get Trudy to help her with the chores if you aren't home until late. One more thing, go to the kitchen and pack a lunch. You can have whatever you can find." He placed one hand on each of their heads and said, "May God send his ministering angels to protect you."

Abner peeked in at Grandma, but she was sleeping, so while Schotzy went to the outhouse, he went to the cupboard and got some bread and cheese, and then to a crock and dug out two nice pieces of meat that were left from Sunday dinner. There was a bowl of apples on the table and he took two of them. He found two pieces of cloth on one of the shelves, wrapped the food in two bundles and tied them to two walking sticks that were in the workshop. Abner and Schotzy put the sticks over their shoulders and they were ready to go.

The cold morning had turned into a perfect day for an adventure, nice and warm in the sun, but cool in the shade. Schotzy was obviously too concerned about his pappaw to enjoy it. He kept saying, "That silly woman. Imagine giving my pappaw all of her money. That silly woman! By now he is so drunk he can't walk. That silly woman!" He shook his head in disbelief. "How could anyone be that silly?"

Every once in a while, Abner would stop and look around, commenting on how their village looked from a distance, how big the church spire Partenbuhl was, how much clearer the castle was becoming, or just how beautiful everything looked. Once he stopped to examine a hedgehog. They weren't common and Abner hadn't seen very many.

"Come on and quit gawksing* around," said Schotzy, becoming a little aggravated with his friend. "It's getting late and we may have a long way to go yet."

"I'm sorry," said Abner as he looked at Schotzy and realized that he genuinely loved his pappaw even though he was what he was. Abner loved his own grandfather as much or more than he loved anyone else, but that was because he was so special. Frederick Hartzell was wise, smart, kind, good, and nice looking besides. Walter Schotzenberger had none of these characteristics; yet Schotzy loved him. *I don't really like anyone who doesn't like me, and I*

---

* gawksing: gawking, staring, wasting time by looking around

don't like anyone who is not likable, he thought. *That makes Schotzy a better person than I am.* Abner shook his head in wonder.

Going downhill was easy and they walked quickly. Some of the trees along the way were in full leaf and some were just budding. The mixture of sun and shade was refreshing and enjoyable, and after about an hour they came to Partenbuhl. "I believe that Pappaw was wearing the royal blue outfit with gold buttons and the plumed hat," said Schotzy. "I didn't see it in the house last night. When we get to the first biergarten* I'll go in and ask if anyone saw him, but let's eat something first."

"That's all right with me," said Abner. "Let's sit in the shade of that tree over there. It's level and looks like a good spot."

As they sat on the ground eating their dinner, Schotzy looked down the street and spotted sign with a beer mug on it. "Already I see a biergarten down there. Do you see the sign with the mug on it?"

Abner could see a number of signs, and he finally picked out he right one. "Ya, I see it now, halfway down the street. I've never been in a biergarten before, have you?"

"Ya," Schotzy answered grimly. "It's no fun." They finished eating and headed toward the biergarten. Schotzy walked in confidently and asked if anyone had seen a man who fit his pappaw's description. No one had seen or remembered him in the first, second, or in any of the biergartens in Partenbuhl, so the boys knew they must go on down to Kittzsheim.

As they left the village, Abner gazed at the church spire that he could see from his home. "I can't believe how tall that spire is. It's the tallest thing I've ever seen, Schotzy. Can you imagine all of the work that went into making it?"

"Ya, it took a lot of work," Schotzy answered without paying much attention. Abner could see that he wasn't interested in anything except finding his pappaw.

Kittzsheim was more than a two hour walk from Partenbuhl and a much bigger place than Abner had ever seen. It was a real town

---

* biergarten: beer hall, saloon (bier sounds like beer)

and Abner really wanted to look around a bit, but he restrained himself and kept his mind on the task at hand. They stopped at the first biergarten and the bartender did remember seeing Herr Schotzenberger. He told them that a man in the fancy suit had money, and that he had drunk beer until he could drink no more. Then he had left, barely able to walk. The bartender had no idea where he may have gone.

Schotzy frantically asked people on the street and the proprietor of the nearest inn about him. No luck. It seemed to Abner that Schotzy asked more people than lived in all of Rittendorf. Finally, a man who looked as if he frequented biergartens said that he believed he'd seen a man in a fancy suit and hat go into Wildasin's Livery Stable the evening before.

The stable was nearby and there was someone in it. "Excuse me, sir," said Schotzy politely. "Have you seen a stranger who may have slept in your barn last night? He was probably wearing a fancy blue suit and a fancy hat with a long feather."

Abner was surprised as the man knelt down, put his arm around Schotzy and asked kindly, "Do you have a grown-up with you?"

"No sir," answered Schotzy. "It's just me and my friend. We've come looking for my pappaw."

The man took a deep breath said in a kind voice, "I hate to tell you this, and I sure hope it's not your grandfather, but there is a body in the hay. It doesn't have on a blue suit, though, just underwear."

"I hope not, too," Schotzy gasped, "but I have a feeling." He put his hand to his mouth and walked bravely to the back part of the barn where the body lay. Abner followed. Schotzy looked at the body and said, "Ya, sir, that is my pappaw. It looks like someone has stolen everything, even his boots." Schotzy wiped his eyes, composed himself and asked, "Do you know of anyone with a horse and cart who would take us back up to our village? We live in Rittendorf."

The man answered without hesitating, "You're a brave boy and I'll be glad to help you. I am, in fact, the wagonmaster, and my name is Pete Wildasin. I will do it for two marks."

"All right, said Schotzy, "We'll give you one now and one when we get to our village. Do you have a blanket to cover him?"

When the wagonmaster went to hitch up the horse and to tell his wife where he was going, Abner put his arm around Schotzy and gave him a hug. "I'm sorry about your pappaw. I know you cared for him." He gave him another hug and said, "I can't get over the way you handle yourself. You really sound grown up."

Schotzy stood erect and said with dignity, "Thank you, but you see, I've got to. I'm the man of the family now." Even though he sounded brave, Abner could see how tired and upset he was. Abner decided to ask the wagonmaster's wife for another blanket, just in case it was needed.

Frau Wildasin brought out the blankets. Herr Wildasin lifted Schotzy's pappaw, put him gently into the cart, covered him with one blanket, and they all headed back up the hill toward Rittendorf. While Abner and Herr Wildasin talked about the care and feeding of horses, Schotzy crawled under the second blanket and went to sleep.

It was very late when the boys arrived back at the village. Grandpa greeted them with a smile and then told them to go on into the house and let the wagonmaster explain what had happened. Abner was very glad to hear him say, "I will take care of everything. You boys just go in and eat the food that is warm on the hearth. Your mother prepared it, Abner, so you are to eat before you go home. Your grandmother is sleeping and you can see her in the morning. Don't concern yourselves about studies tomorrow. We've decided to let both of you sleep as late as you want."

"I'm almost too tired to eat," said Abner, but he managed to put away chicken potpie, buttered turnips, a piece of black walnut cake and a mug of milk before heading for home. Schotzy went to sleep while he was eating and Grandpa carried him upstairs and put him to bed.

As tired as he was, Abner could not sleep immediately. He couldn't get over Herr Schotzenberger's sudden death. It could

140

happen to anyone. It could happen to him. "Dear God," he prayed. "I'm not ready. Help me to get ready, and help Schotzy to get ready, too. Am I too young to be baptized? I think I want to be baptized as soon as possible. Then I'll always belong to You. Elder Wentz said he'd baptize people on Sunday. Yes, I've decided. I want to be baptized on Sunday. Thank you, Father, that we found Herr Schotzenberger and managed to get him back up here with no trouble. I ask you to watch after Schotzy every way you can, and I also ask for a good night's rest. In Jesus' name. Amen."

With that, he went to sleep.

CHAPTER ELEVEN

When he awoke Abner could tell that half the morning had passed. He had not slept this late for a long time. A late spring storm had moved in. The wind was blowing fiercely, and there was a light sprinkling of snow on the ground. Abner breathed a prayer of thanks that he and Schotzy hadn't had to walk down the mountain on a day like this. Even though he could take his time, it was too cold to do so. He dressed quickly, eager to tell his mother all that had happened and that he had decided to be baptized on Sunday.

Rachel was in the creamery, serving customers milk, cheese and butter. He tried to get her attention, but she shook her head in annoyance, and said, "Not now. Can't you I'm busy?"

I guess she doesn't know what I have to say is important, but I know Grandpa will listen to me. He went back upstairs, ate some smiercase and apple butter on toastbread, and then trotted over to talk to his grandpa and to see how his grandma and Schotzy were doing.

As Abner was going in the back door, Grandpa was going out. "Grandpa, don't go yet, I have something important to say to you. Where's Schotzy?"

"He's gone to Widow Schneider's. She and Trudy sewed for him yesterday afternoon and much of the night. They have some of his clothes nearly ready, and he went over for a final fitting. He also felt that he should tell them what happened to his pappaw. What do you want to talk to me about?"

"I'll be ten years old next week, and I want to be baptized on Sunday."

Grandpa sat down and put his arms around his grandson. "This a very important decision. Are you sure you are ready, or is it just because someone died suddenly?"

"I know that Herr Schotzenberger died suddenly, and I thought about not being ready, but that's not all of it. Tell me, what must I believe to be saved and go to heaven?"

"First, let me ask you some questions, and then I'll know what to tell you. Do you really believe that Jesus is the Son of God?"

"Ya, I do."

"Do you know that you are a sinner and that only the blood of Jesus can save you from your sins?"

Abner nodded his head thoughtfully, "Ya, I do," he said

"Are you sorry for your sins?"

"Ya, I sure am."

"Do you want God to forgive you and to help you to be a better person?"

"Ya, I do."

"Do you really feel that God is calling you to be baptized and become a member of the church?"

"I really do."

"Abner, the next step is to ask Jesus to come into your heart and dedicate your life to him," said Grandpa seriously. "Then ask Him to send the Holy Spirit to you to show you what your life work will be, and to help you every step of the way. Are you ready to do that?" Abner nodded his head very seriously. "Well then, it sounds to me as if you are ready. I'll see Pastor Wentz and arrange it for Sunday."

"Thank you, I'd be pleased to be baptized as soon as possible."

Grandpa got up and said, "Now I must see the minister of the Protestant church and make arrangements for Herr Schotzenberger's funeral. I hope it can be done tomorrow."

Abner heard his grandma coughing and wheezing even before he got to the kitchen. "How are you doing, Grandma?" he asked. "That is a pretty bad cough. You don't smell like onions. I thought that you are supposed to wear an onion poultice when you have a bad cough. Why aren't you wearing one?"

"Because the onions are all," she replied, with a wheeze.

"Well, what about those little bitty ones that are out in a basket by the workbench?" he persisted.

"Those are onion sets," she explained. "You never use onion sets except for planting. They are the seeds for this year's crop. If you used them for anything else, you wouldn't have any more onions. That would never do. No doubt your grandpa will plant them in a day or two."

"Well then, why don't you use your goose grease? Papa got three geese last fall with his slingshot. You should have plenty still."

"It's all, too. I gave it to the sexton's wife for their children last winter when all of them had the croup.[*]"

"Why did you do that?" he asked indignantly. "They don't even go to our church."

Grandma looked at him as if she could not believe what she had just heard. "Abner, Jesus said that we are to love our neighbor as we love ourselves. Ya, I do need it now, but they needed it then. As a Christian, it was my duty to give it to them when they needed it. Do you understand?"

Abner felt as if he had never loved his grandma more in his life than he did right then. "I'll tell you what," he said, "The geese were down at the lake yesterday. I'll get my papa's old slingshot off the wall in the workroom and see if I can get one. I never have, but I might be able to."

"That's a good idea, you..." Grandma began, only to have another coughing spell. When she finally stopped coughing and got her breath, she put her hand to her chest and said, "Hexen schuz."[*]

"What do you mean by that, Grandma?"

"A witch is shooting me. She gives me pain and makes me cough. I can't get rid of her."

Abner didn't want to say anything about superstition when she was so out of fix,[*] so he said, "I'll get you a drink of cold water. Cold water usually helps me."

---

[*] croup: a deep persistent cough (rhymes with soup)
[*] hexen schuz: literally, a witch is shooting me; casting a spell (schuz sounds like shoots)

While she sipped the water, he told her about the walk down to Kitzsheim, about finding Herr Schotzenberger, and about bringing him back.

Grandma sat quietly for a while and then said, "Every time someone dies, it always wonders me who will be next. Sometimes it's just one at a time, but if two die close together, a third will die soon, because what gives two, gives three."

This was too much for Abner to believe, and he blurted out, "Grandma, are you sure that's not just one of your superstitions?"

"You don't have to believe me, but you just wait and see," she insisted. "Anyways, I have something for you. Does the palm of your hand itch? It should, because I found something in the bottom of my drawer that I want to give to you. Besides that, I've been wanting to tell you what itches mean. If your palm itches it means you are going to get money. If someone keeps scratching his fingers, watch out for him. It means that person is a thief, and either has stolen something or is thinking about stealing something. If your ears itch, someone is talking about you, and if your feet itch, it means that you are going some place."

"My mother says that if my feet itch it means that they need to washed," laughed Abner.

"That might be so." Grandma smiled and then she remembered what she had been going to do. She opened a cupboard, picked up five pfennig and handed them to him.

Abner looked at the money in surprise, gave her a hug and said, "Thank you, Grandma, thank you very much. I had eight pfennig and five more makes. . ."

He began counting on his fingers, but Grandma interrupted, "Oh, no, that will never do."

"What will never do?" asked Grandpa, who had returned for money to pay the gravedigger.

"Abner can't have thirteen pfennig," she answered. "I gave him five pfennig and he has eight pfennig, and that's all I have.

(..continued)
* out of fix: sick, poorly; in the case of machinery, not working right

145

Frederick, you must give him one. Thirteen is just too unlucky. He can't have just thirteen pfennig; it will never do."

"Bertl, I don't have an extra one handy, and I don't have time right now to hunt one. Now just forget it. I'll give him one as soon as I get one." Grandpa got the money that he needed and went out again.

Grandma looked at Abner sadly and said, "You now have thirteen pfennig, and I don't have any more to give you."

"Well, here, take one back."

"I can't do that either. Whatever is going to happen, is going to happen."

Without meaning to, Abner looked in the direction of the one on the windowsill. She took notice and said, "That's my lucky pfennig. I always put a new pfennig on my windowsill on New Year's Day. That way I will have good luck all year, and I will never be without money." She coughed, then sighed a deep sigh, and said, "Well, I guess it's better not to have good luck than to be assured that you're going to have bad luck."

Abner looked confused. "I'm ferhuddled. How's that again?"

"It's simple. If I give you my lucky pfennig, I may not have good luck, but if I don't give you my lucky pfennig, you will have bad luck. I would never forgive myself if I caused something bad to happen to you. So if I give you one more pfennig and how many will you have?"

"Oh Grandma, you are too much," Abner laughed, "Thirteen and one more makes fourteen, and eight plus five is thirteen. I shall remember that all of my life. But really, I do not believe that your giving me five pfennig so that I have thirteen pfennig could possibly cause you to bring bad luck on me, but thank you very much anyways. Is there anything else that I can do for you?"

"No, dear little mansly,* you just go play. I'm going to rest my eyes a little bit." Abner was a little worried about his grandmother, because, like his mother, she was generally busy all of the time. She began coughing again as he went out the door.

---

* mansly: little man

Abner got the slingshot and headed for the lake, but there were no geese there. *They must have all gone north*, he thought. *The miserable things! They were here yesterday.* He felt bad about not being able to get a goose when one was needed, but there was nothing he could do about it. He walked back and put the slingshot where it belonged because he remembered, having been told nearly every day of his life, *There is a place for everything and everything belongs in its place.*

The rest of the day went quickly. He did what he always did when there was no work for him to do and he had no one to play with. He went to the blacksmith shop and watched the smith. He loved to see him heat the metal, pound it and shape it into something useful. Besides, it was a warm place on a cold day. The smith liked Abner and sometimes asked him to lend a hand. Today he was shoeing a high strung horse. He had put a sling under it and using a ratchet, had lifted it off the ground.

After Abner had been there awhile, Herr Schmidt, the blacksmith, who was filing the horse's hoof, spoke to him. "I just took notice of you, lad. Will you hand me a couple of nails? In that bin near the corner," he said, pointing with his chin.

Abner found the nails, handed them to him and asked, "Where did you get them, the nails? My grandpa hasn't been able to get any lately, and it's hard for him to do his work without them."

"I make them myself. Sometime when I'm not so busy, I'll show you."

"Grandpa says that the king gets all of the nails in the kingdom."

"He doesn't get the ones I make for myself to use on horses. It's true, though that he wants them all."

"Grandpa would be mighty pleased to get some. I've got money. How many nails will you let me have for two pfennig?"

"They all are supposed to go to the king, my nails."

"My grandpa really needs some. You know my grandpa, Frederick Hartzell. He needs nails to make another coffin and for other things, too. It's hard to do the things he needs to do without nails." Abner pulled five pfennig from his pocket and showed them to the smith. "How many nails for five pfennig? I think I should get at least fifty." He started to walk away as he had seen his papa do in similar situations.

"All right, boy, ten nails for a pfennig. I might have given you twelve."

"You are pulling my leg and I know it," laughed Abner. "I'll give you two pfennig now and the rest when I get the nails. I trust that will be soon."

The smith finished shoeing the horse, and then he rooted around in the nail bin. "Here lad, count them out and be sure you get straight ones. Take one of those pieces of rag and make a toot* unless you want to carry them so.* Can you count to fifty?"

"Ya, I can," he said, as he made five piles of ten each. He laughed to himself. *Schotzy has five piles of ten each and so do I. I'll give these to Grandpa. They may not be worth as much as Schotzy's but they will be useful, and Grandpa will be pleased.*

"Make sure you don't tell a soul that I gave those nails to you," said the blacksmith as Abner gave him the five pfennig and prepared to go back out into the cold. "If anyone finds out, I can get into real trouble and so can you."

It was still cold, windy, and overcast the next noonday when the funeral was held at in the Protestant Church. Abner wanted to ask about the stained glass windows and the water basin at the front, "What's that all about?" he whispered. Grandpa clamped his lips together and shook his head. Talking was not allowed.

Abner looked around. There weren't many people there. Rachel couldn't come because she had to stay with Grandma who had taken a turn for the worse. Trudy had come; but Widow Schneider had not. As the bells began to toll fifty-six times for the years of Walter Schotzenberger's life, they did not go Clang! Clang! Clang! Clang! as they usually did. Instead, they went Clump, Clump, Clump, Clang!

---

* toot: bag or pouch, (rhymes with foot)
* carry them so: as they are

148

Everyone looked around to see what the problem was, but Abner knew immediately what Max, Willy, and Otto had been up to when they wanted him to help. They had climbed into the bell tower and tied rags around all of the clappers, except the littlest at the top. Abner, being smaller, could have climbed up into the narrow spot and reached it, to tie rags around it; but they could not. That was why the small one at the top sounded with its high pitched clang, and the rest went clump.

The minister, a short, stocky man with flashing black eyes and gray hair that came down to his collar, was obviously very upset and angry. For the funeral, he read out of a book and occasionally sang or chanted. Schotzy, as the chief mourner, sat on the front pew all by himself. Abner could see that he was crying and hoped that the service would be cut short, but it went on and on.

He looked at the coffin. He knew it was well made because Grandpa had made it and Grandma had lined it. That was one thing that they did on the side to make a little money. He usually had three coffins on hand, a small one for babies and little children, a medium sized one for women and older children and a larger one for men. Grandpa had dovetailed the corners because he had no nails. It took longer but it made a nice looking coffin. It was odd, looking at the coffins in the workshop, wondering who would need the next one. Would it be an old person or a young one, a man, a woman or a child? Some men made their own, but mostly the villagers bought or bartered for them from Grandpa. Abner knew that he would be working on another one soon, but at least he would have some nails and that would make the job easier. He hadn't given him the nails yet. He would keep them until the right time.

Thinking about making coffins gave him the shivers, and he tried to think about something else. He hoped he would never have to sit up there in the mourner's seat, but then again, that meant that he would die first, not a good solution. He shivered again and then he remembered that whenever anyone shivered, Grandma would always say, "That means someone is walking on your grave."

The service was finally over and the funeral procession followed the minister and Schotzy to the burying ground. The wind was bitey* and there was no sign of the sun. Abner was glad that his mother had given Schotzy his last year's good winter coat because it fit him perfectly and was still a very good coat. *This is a miserable day for a funeral*, Abner thought, *but then again, no day is a good day for a funeral. I wonder what fer* trouble will come next.* He was off in a world of his own when he took notice that the minister turned around and glared at him and Grandpa several times. Schotzy stood bravely by the graveside and Abner was proud of the way he behaved, thinking, *a royal prince could not have had more dignity.*

After Herr Schotzenberger was laid to rest, the minister turned to Grandpa and shaking his finger in his face, said menacingly, "You and your sect will be sorry for what happened today. You desecrated the bells. You interrupted a funeral, a ceremony that many people consider sacred. How dare you come to this church after arranging such a travesty?" He was seething with anger, and as he spoke the spit flew out of his mouth. "You have much nerve, but we will see how much nerve you have before I'm finished with you. As I said, you will be sorry. The bishop will hear about this and so will the king." He was muttering as he stalked away, his black robe flapping in the wind.

Grandpa looked sad as he stood quietly shaking his head. "I believe it was Max, Willy, and Otto that did it," whispered Abner.

"Whoever did it, it wasn't such a smart trick," answered Grandpa grimly.

They walked over to Schotzy, who was still by the new grave. After a while, he went to the old grave of his mother, and the recent graves of his papa and mammaw. "Goodbye," he said sadly, "I'm not going to be buried with you. I'm going to Pennsylvania."

He took Grandpa's hand and greeted the other mourners, asking them if they would like to come to Hartzell's for a meal, as was the

---

* bitey: bitter
* what fer: what kind of

custom. Trudy was the only one who accepted. Schotzy took her hand, and the four of them headed for home.

Rachel, who had prepared enough to feed twenty-five people said, "Well, it looks as if the six of us will have enough to eat."

"Yes," said Abner, "for days and days and days."

After everyone had finished eating, Schotzy gave Trudy and Rachel each a nice toot of food to take home and also asked if he could take some to Elder Wentz and his family. Abner realized that it was probably the first time in his life that Schotzy had had the opportunity to be generous and that he loved it. Abner looked fondly at his friend. *He'll do all right,* he thought.

As Trudy was about to leave, Abner saw Schotzy take her aside and heard him say, "I'm sorry that my pappaw took all of your mother's money. I hate to tell you, but he was robbed and there wasn't anything left when we found him."

Trudy, turned pale, sat down quickly and gasped, "What?"

Schotzy started to repeat what he had said, but she said with a shaky voice, "I heard you, but this is such a shock. I didn't know she had given him her money. No wonder she's been in such a state. I thought it was just because your pappaw had passed away." Trudy stared at Schotzy for a few seconds and then asked, "How do you know she gave him all of her money?"

"She told us so on Monday when we were working at your neighbor's. That's why we went looking for him."

Trudy shook her head in disbelief. "She had enough money to keep her the rest of her life," she said. "Now she has nothing. No wonder she's so upset." She shook her head again. "What is she going to do?" she asked softly.

"I'll make it up to her," said Schotzy. "I've got. . ."

Grandpa came over quickly, put his hand on Schotzy's shoulder and interrupted him, saying, "She is an excellent seamstress and cook. I'm sure she will be able to earn enough to keep herself, especially if she goes along to Pennsylvania with you and Jake."

"She won't like that," said Trudy.

151

"Well," said Grandpa, "there's a saying that goes, 'It's not what you want, it's what you get that makes you fat."

"But she's always been so proud."

"And you know what goes before a fall," he added.

"Yes, I know, but it's not going to be easy." With a worried look, Trudy thanked Schotzy for the food and hurried out the door.

Abner saw Schotzy look at Grandpa with a puzzled look on his face and say, "I wanted to tell her that I would give her the money when we sold the house."

"I didn't know what you were going to say, but whatever it was, I figured that it would do the widow good to stew awhile," said Grandpa, with a grin and a twinkle in his eye. When he saw that look on Grandpa's face, Abner thought, *Grownups are hard to figure sometimes, but I understand how he feels.*

"Herr Hartzell," Schotzy said, "How do people keep track of their money? I need to know."

"You need a ledger. That's a sheet of paper or a book in which you write down everything you take in and everything you spend," answered Grandpa. "I'll make one up for you tomorrow."

"I really would like to make up a ledger right now," Schotzy said. "I want it written down so I'll know how much you spent for me, sir. I really appreciate your doing this and I want to be sure you get paid back."

Grandpa got out his ledger, found an empty page near the back and wrote on it: *Ephraim Schotzenberger's Expenses, April 25, 1734.* Abner and Schotzy watched as he wrote the amount for the wagonmaster and the coffin, the cost of the funeral, the gravedigger, the food for the meal, and the offering for the minister.

"I also want to pay Widow Schneider for making my clothes," he insisted. "I don't want anything from anyone who would treat my friend so ugly for no good reason."

Abner didn't blame him a bit, but Grandpa cautioned him against becoming proud. "Schotzy, I just said to Trudy 'You know what goes before a fall.' Do you know what goes before a fall?"

"No, sir, I don't."

"It's pride. Pride goes before a fall. I respect your feelings, but I want you to remember that God put all of us on earth to worship him, to do his will and his work. Pride interferes with our ability to do that. We worked hard for Frau Schneider and she was not grateful. It will do her good to make your clothes as a favor for us. We must look at this situation and every situation and learn whatever we can from it."

"I'll try, sir," answered Schotzy. "I've never had anything and I must not let this go to my head. Is that what you mean?"

"That's about it, young man, and I know you are going to do all right. Speaking of doing all right, I believe that we can get to work on your house this afternoon or tomorrow at the latest. Is there anything in particular that will need to be tended to first?"

Abner, who was listening, had to put his mouth in. "Grandpa," he interrupted, "did Schotzy tell you about the door in his house that hasn't been opened for years? We could go over and have you look at it and maybe you could figure out how to get into the room behind the door. He can't sell the house unless he knows what's in the room." Abner's eyes sparkled and he added, "It's a mystery and it just might be full of treasure."

"That's not likely, but you are right. You can't sell a house without knowing what's in it," said Grandpa smiling. "Let me see if our neighbor lady, Frau Hoke, will sit with your grandmother awhile. After I talk to her, I'll go to your place, Schotzy, and look it over. I'll check on what all needs to be done to the house, and especially what can be done about getting the door open. After that, I must get started on another coffin. I also want to show you two how to dovetail boards. Both of you boys change into work clothes and I'll meet you at the house shortly."

"I must bid 'Goodbye,' to Grandma and tell her I hope she feels better soon," said Abner. "I keep forgetting to bring back her basket. I must tell her that she must get well so she can make me some more little cakes."

As Abner and his mother walked home together he told her about the minister being so angry that he spit. It seemed funny to him and he laughed.

"It is no laughing matter," said Rachel with a worried look. "Whoever played such a foolish trick had no idea of what could happen as a result. We could be driven from our homes."

"Do you really think that could happen?"

"Yes, son, it could. You just never know. You just wait. No doubt something bad will come from all of this."

There she goes again; something bad is going to happen, Abner thought. *That is the way she thinks, but then again, she may be right. The minister was very angry and Klaus said that the king wants to rid the country of people who worship the way we do. This may be the excuse he has been looking for. Now she's got me worrying.* He prayed silently: *Dear God, I know that your Word says that whatever happens and wherever we go, You will be with us. Help me to remember that and put my trust in You.*

Rachel was quiet for awhile and then said, "I think I'll look over our belongings and get together bundles of things that we would need if we have to make a quick get away. One for you, one for me, and one for your papa. I have a feeling. . ."

"Oh, Mama, you are such a worrywart, but if it would make you feel better, go ahead and do it."

She laughed, smacked him on his butt and said, "You nix-nooks. You sound just like your father." Abner saw it coming, tried to dodge and couldn't. He caught her hand, pulled her to him and gave her a hug. It felt good.

All of a sudden he was crying. "I'm glad I'm not an orphan like Schotzy," he sobbed. Rachel held him close and kissed him on the forehead. She was crying, too. He blew his nose, wiped his eyes, and regaining his dignity said, "Grandpa and Schotzy are going over to his house to see if they can get a door open that hasn't been opened for years and years. I'd like to go along to learn how to open a door that can't be opened."

Putting her hand over her heart, Rachel smiled at him tenderly, and said, "I think you already know."

CHAPTER TWELVE

Abner changed his clothes quickly and headed for Schotzy's. It had not warmed up much and the wind was still blowing hard. As he approached the house he saw that the back door was open and he walked in. Someone had started a fire, but the house was still cold. He wrinkled his nose in distaste even though it did not smell quite as bad as it had before. Even so, he was glad the door was open.

Evidently Grandpa and Schotzy were already there, although they were nowhere in sight. Abner walked around in the rooms on the first floor looking at the rickety chairs, the trestle table, the chipped dishes, the dry sink, the wooden buckets, the corner cupboard and all of the things that go to make up a home. He wondered what Schotzy would keep, what he would sell, what he would give away, and what he would throw away. He was glad that he didn't have to make those decisions because it would be hard for him. All of his possessions were precious to him and he hated to get rid of anything. He had often heard his papa say that a person never, ever knew what he might need, and when he might need it. The very thing that he had thrown away yesterday he would undoubtedly need tomorrow. It always worked that way. As soon as he'd thrown something away, he'd need it, even though he had had it for a long time and had never needed it before. Grandpa said the same thing.

As he looked around he saw on a shelf in the corner, a small, wooden shepherd dog. It was old, and looked as if it had been handled a lot. Abner picked it up to look at it closely. It was really nice. Heavy footsteps told him that someone was near, and looking up, he expected to see his grandpa. However, it was the magistrate, swooping down on him like a hawk.

"Ah, Abner Hartzell, come to see what you could steal, I see." Abner was so startled that he dropped the dog and its tail broke off. He reached down and picked it up, as the magistrate continued, "I told you I would check up on you and keep an eye on you! Do you want to know what I have learned?" His voice was cruel and his eyes were evil.

Abner couldn't think of anything to say, and didn't answer. He looked down because he couldn't stand to look at him.

The magistrate continued in the same malevolent voice, "I have discovered that you were one the boys who desecrated the bells. You were seen running on the Sabbath and you were seen with the boys that are known to have done it. I heard also that you stole something from Widow Schneider's house on Saturday and from her backyard on Monday."

Abner knew what a small bird felt like when a hawk came after it. He couldn't defend himself, and he couldn't get away.

The magistrate went on with his accusations. "You have never been to the true church and you have never been baptized. All of this, combined with your actions at the hearing on Monday, makes you a very undesirable person. As an officer of the court, I suggest that you and your people move out of this village immediately."

Abner stood still with his mouth open, but no words would come. Grandpa, hearing the voice, came down the stairs to investigate and heard only the last few words. "What is this all about?" he demanded.

Thereupon, the magistrate proceeded to repeat his so-called evidence against Abner.

"But he is just a child, and all of it can be explained," said Grandpa in a very calm voice. "I'm sure he will keep out of trouble from now on. He is really a very good boy."

"We shall see what we shall see," answered the magistrate, "All I can say is, he better not get into any more trouble because if he does, I may be forced to remove Ephraim from your custody. We wouldn't want Ephraim to be contaminated by Abner's bad behavior." The magistrate paused and added ominously. "As he is your grandson, it seems to me that it would be bound to happen."

Schotzy, who had come downstairs, too, looked at Abner and shook his head as if he could not believe what he was hearing. "Sir," he said very politely, "Abner is the best friend a boy ever had."

The magistrate, twisting every word, rolled his eyes and said sarcastically, "Listen to that. The poor soul doesn't even know any better." Grandpa shook his head, hoping that the boys wouldn't say anything and they didn't.

Turning to Schotzy with a false smile, the magistrate said, "The reason that I came here today was to offer to buy your house. Right now, as is."

"Oh, I couldn't do that, sir," answered Schotzy without hesitating. "I need to look it over and decide some things. Next week or the next or even next month will be time enough, I think. There aren't any empty houses in the village, and it shouldn't be hard to sell."

"You, you little…" The magistrate raised his arm and opened his hand as if he were going to slap him. "You'll be sorry, too," he hissed, as he clumped out the door and down the steps.

"I wonder who else will be mad at us," said Abner. "You know, there is one thing I've learned from this. When I get to Pennsylvania, I am going to buy as much land as I can, and I am going to live in the middle of it. I swear I am never going to live in a village. You can't even go to the outhouse without everybody knowing about it."

The magistrate stuck his head back in the door. Looking at Grandpa he asked, "Don't you think it strange that Herr Schotzenberger was found dead the day after he said that he was afraid that you would do him harm? I'm going to look into this." He clumped back across the porch and down the steps.

Abner looked at his grandpa and knew that this was not happening. It wasn't possible for anyone to accuse his grandpa of doing wrong. All Grandpa said was, "Don't say a word." Then motioning for the boys to sit down, he said, "I've been telling you boys, especially Abner, to watch your tongues and not to lose your tempers, but I lost my temper and did not speak kindly to Schotzy's grandfather on Saturday. I am sorry, because things may have turned out differently had I acted in the way Jesus would have wanted me to act. I am also sorry because now I can never apologize to Herr Schotzenberger and ask his forgiveness. I should have apologized to you boys sooner, too, because here I was acting as if I am perfect, and I'm not, definitely not! Please forgive me. Tempers have a way of getting a person into trouble, not just children, but grown-ups, too."

While Abner hugged his grandpa, Schotzy put out his hand to shake and said, "That's all right, Herr Hartzell, I understand." Smiling broadly he added, "It pleases me that you took up for me. Let's go upstairs and look at the door."

Grandpa had a bunch of keys in his pocket. He inserted them into the keyhole one by one, but none of them fit. Abner went into the next room and noticed that the window had no lock. With considerable pushing and huffing he was able to push the bottom part up. Schotzy came in while Abner was looking out. They both looked out the window and Abner said, "It's a long way to the ground."

Grandpa came in, looked down and said, "You're right; it is a long way to the ground; but do I believe that your father's extension ladder will reach. We won't get it now, because it's getting late. We'll get to it in the morning after lessons, but first I want to talk about something else."

Abner picked up his ears because usually when Grandpa spoke in that tone of voice, he was about to say something interesting.

"Schotzy," he said, "I was thinking about what you said about your Grandpa Slonaker not acting like he was a rich man, even though he had all that gold; and I remembered a story I heard when I was a boy that might explain it. I guess that the reason I didn't think of it right away was that has been so long since I heard it. It is about something that took place many years before I was born, and is about the Slonaker family.

"There was a beautiful young girl who lived in this village. I don't know her first name, but her last name was Slonaker. She fell in love with a boy from the village who had a habit of getting into trouble. Her father objected to her choice and ran him off. The boy's troubles caught up with him and he was about to be arrested when he asked the girl to elope with him. She agreed and off they went; but her father took out after them, found them, and brought her back, but the boy kept on going. The rumor was that he had become a pirate or joined a band of robbers. Several years later he came back just as the girl was about to marry someone else. According to the story, he had a wagonload of loot with him, and he offered all of it to the girl; but she told him she was marrying someone else and refused to listen to him. That made him very angry. He put a curse on all of the Slonakers, saying that no one by that name would ever benefit from what he had brought, that it would always weigh them down so that they could not stand upright. I remember that the Slonakers never stood up straight, do you?"

"Ya," said Schotzy, nodding his head. "I remember Grandpa Slonaker was really bent over but I always thought that was because he worked so much in his garden."

"But Grandpa, I thought you said that there was nothing to superstition," said Abner.

"It's true that there is nothing to superstition if you don't accept it, but if you do accept it, you can be bound by it," answered Grandpa, somewhat irritated with the interruption. "Gardening might be the reason he was bent over, but whatever it was, this is the story. Do you want to hear the rest of it, or not?"

"Ya, sure, sorry," answered Abner, surprised to be asked.

"All right then, I'll go on. If I remember it right, the curse also was for anyone who took the loot who had no right to it, or tried to use it before every Slonaker who lived in Rittendorf was dead. The young man had no more than finished saying that, when he died." Grandpa snapped his fingers, "Just like that!"

"Ach!" exclaimed Abner, "that would get your attention."

"After that," continued Grandpa, "members of his robber band came looking for him and the loot, but just as they arrived, they died too. They all had the plague. Then the girl died and so did more than half the people of this village, and more than half the people in all of Europe for that matter. The loot disappeared; and that was the last I heard of it until the gold turned up on Monday. Schotzy, have you ever heard anything like that?"

"Never have, sir," he answered, shaking his head. "Do you suppose that's the reason the magistrate wanted to buy my house today?"

"It could be," answered Grandpa. "You just never know." He sighed a deep sigh as he usually did when he said, "You just never know," and added, "Now I think it's time for us to go home."

As they walked together toward the town square, Grandpa, ever the teacher, asked if they knew the names of the trees. When they came to a pine tree, he showed them that pine needles always grow in bunches, and then compared them to the needles on spruce trees grow around the branch. "Do you think you will remember that?" Then pointing to the rocks in the water, he asked, "Do you remember the lesson on stones? What kind are those?"

Abner looked at Schotzy, and Schotzy looked at Abner. They shrugged their shoulders, shook their heads and said, "Don't know."

"Wet ones," he laughed. "I got you on that one."

Schotzy grinned and said, "That one was a good one."

"Grandpa, you got us good," laughed Abner, as he slapped his knee.

At the square they parted, Abner going uphill, Grandpa and Schotzy downhill. "Goodnight," he called, "I'll see you in the morning."

When Abner went to bed that night, he spent a long time praying for his grandmother, for Schotzy, for Trudy, for his papa and for Cousin Jake. "Help us all, Father, help us all, and help me do what you want me to do."

Friday dawned clear and bright. Springtime weather had returned and it was a glorious morning. It was easy to get up. He looked out his window and saw the spires and the castle. *I know where those places are,* he thought. *Someday I'll walk through them and keep right on going until I get to Pennsylvania.* He began to sing, *Iss des net ein Schnitzelbenk? Ya des iss ein Schitzelbenk. Iss des net en Kaz und lang? Ya des iss en Kas en lang,* but then he remembered his grandma's saying, 'Sing before breakfast, cry before night.' *I don't like that saying,* he thought, *and I don't believe it.* Nevertheless, he stopped singing.

160

He could hear Grandma coughing as he rounded the corner. As soon as he heard her coughing, he thought, *She's won't be out to enjoy this nice day. The tulips blooming aside* * *my house might cheer her up.* He ran back and picked a bunch for her. He took notice when he handed them to her that she looked pale and her hand shook. He could hear her trying to catch her breath as she cleaned up the breakfast dishes.

"You never give up, do you, Grandma? Can I help?" Abner found a vase, put the tulips in it, then took the dishrag and wiped off the table. He tried to think of something that would cheer her up and finally came up with an idea. "Winter is over and we should celebrate," he said. "We should have a family party like we had last year at this time. What do you think?"

"No, Abner, I just don't feel up to it. It hurts to breathe and that's not good."

"Grandma, don't talk that way. I went down to the lake to get a goose, but they had all left. Maybe someone in the village has some goose grease. I'll find out."

"That's good of you to want to try to find some, but I'm afraid the Lord is about to call me home."

"Now that sounds like you are giving up. What did the doctor say?"

"He said to drink chamomile* tea, and put an onion poultice on my chest, but you know there are no onions. He said to stay in bed, but I can't stay in bed, there's too much work to do."

"Please do what the doctor says," Abner begged. "You are too precious to us for you to take chances. Now, if he said that you are to go to bed, I am going to walk you into this little room back of the kitchen and take off your shoes. I might even hide them. I'd nail them to the floor if I had any nails with me. Now, come on!"

Grandma did what he said and then, looking up from her pillow, asked, "Will you get the powwow doctor for me?"

---

* aside: beside
* chamomile: a small aromatic plant used in Europe for healing even in the 21st century (pronounced kam uh mile)

After thinking about it, Abner answered, "No, Grandma, I can't. Grandpa wouldn't like it. Besides, if you rest and do as the regular doctor says, I'm sure you'll get better. I've been praying about it."

"Before you go, will you please open the little window up in the corner? I'd like to have it open."

Abner got a chair, climbed up and as he opened it, he asked, "Why do you want this open? I've never seen it open before."

"That window is called a soulenfenster.[*] You need it open when a sick person is in this room, so that if that person dies, his or her soul can escape through the window and go straight to heaven. Otherwise, that person's soul might be trapped and then it would have to become a spook."[*]

Abner raised his eyebrows, shook his head and said, "You rest now; I must go study my lessons."

When lessons were finished Grandpa checked on Grandma and saw that she was sleeping. Then he and the boys went to Abner's house to get the ladder. It was a double long ladder. They struggled to get it off the hooks on the wall and struggled to carry it. As they walked up the hill and across the bridge, Abner could feel the sweat break out, and wondered how he could keep on doing his part, it was that heavy. He figured that Schotzy must be feeling the same or worse. They were about halfway to Schotzy's when they felt the ladder lighten. The strange little man who had been at their Sabbath meeting had put his hand on the ladder and was helping to carry it.

When they got to Schotzy's the little man pointed to himself and said, "Antonio Eby."

Grandpa introduced himself and the boys, and then Antonio helped Grandpa set the ladder up against the wall and pull up the extension. He seemed to be very strong for a little man. He and the boys watched while Grandpa climbed up and opened the window. It was easy to see that Grandpa was too big to crawl through, so he came back down, and then Schotzy climbed up and went in with no trouble.

---

[*] soulenfenster: soul window (soulen rhymes with stolen)
[*] spook: ghost or lost spirit (rhymes with cook)

He stuck his head out of the window and cried excitedly, "There's a lot of stuff in here. Wait 'til you see! What do you want me to do about the door?"

"The hinge pins have to be taken out," shouted Grandpa. "Can you do that?"

"I don't have any idea how to do it," answered Schotzy.

"You take hold of them and pull them out."

Abner, who couldn't wait to get inside, climbed up, crawled in the window, checked on the hinges and reported, "The hinge pins are rusty or corroded or something, and it looks like it will take a tool to pry them loose."

Grandpa produced a sturdy old knife from his tool apron. Antonio took it, climbed the up the ladder, crawled in the window, pried loose the hinge pins and pulled them out.

"They're out, Herr Hartzell," Schotzy called out the window; and Grandpa went around the house and up the steps to the door. He pushed it with all of his might and the door refused to budge. He kept banging it with his shoulder until Antonio crawled out the window, went around the house, went up the steps and joined his strength to Grandpa's. The door finally opened but not without breaking the doorjamb.

Grandpa and the boys shook Antonio's hand and thanked him, and then all of them looked to see what was in the room. The first thing Abner saw was a sword that was covered with dust. Schotzy picked it up, wiped it off with his hand and wiped his hand on his shirt. Grandpa watched him, but didn't say anything.

"This must be the loot!" cried Abner, jumping up and down in excitement; "and look at that sword! That's gold on the handle, but what is that black stuff?"

"That's silver. It just needs* polished," answered Grandpa. "Silver tarnishes, but gold never does."

Antonio looked at the sword and said, "Romano!"

Schotzy picked up the sword and pretended that he was fighting with it.

---

* needs polished: the infinitive to be is generally left out

163

"Careful," said Grandpa.

"Here's a helmet," cried Schotzy as he put it on his head.

"Romano," said Antonio, "Si,* Romano." He pointed to himself. "Romano."

"He means that he is from Rome, and the sword is from Rome," said Grandpa. He nodded his head, pointed to Antonio and said, "Romano."

Antonio smiled the biggest smile imaginable and said, "Si, Romano."

Grandpa made the sign of the cross and said, "Christian." Antonio did the same. Both men nodded and looked pleased with themselves.

The most interesting thing in the room was an elaborately carved chest, which Schotzy immediately opened. It was full, and on the top was something made of silk, probably a dress because there was lace around what appeared to be the neck. Abner looked at Schotzy's dirty hands and said, "You better wouldn't touch anything. We won't be able to tell what else is in the chest until our hands are clean."

Schotzy looked at the dress and asked, "Do you think Fraulein Trudy would like it for her wedding dress? It's really pretty. Let's go wash our hands. Then we can come back up and root around and see what all's in there."

Abner looked over at Grandpa and saw that he and Antonio were working together replacing the hinge pins and rehanging the door. "Good idea," he said, "They don't need us."

As the boys were going down the steps, Abner he heard Grandpa say, "If I had some nails, I could repair this doorjamb. Someone sealed the door shut with paint. That's why it was just about impossible to open."

Abner remembered the nails and shouted up to Grandpa, "I have a surprise for you and I've been waiting for the right time to give it to you. I must go home now and get it."

As they raced along the street Abner told Schotzy about the nails, forgetting that he had been warned by the blacksmith not to tell

---

* si: yes (sounds like see)

anyone about them. When they were almost to the bakery; they saw Trudy going in.

"You stay here and catch her when she comes out," Abner said, "and I'll get my surprise for Grandpa." He ran as fast as he could to his house and got back just as Trudy came out with a loaf of bread.

"Greetings, boys, what are you two up to today?"

"Fraulein Trudy, this is the day for surprises and this is a nice one," Schotzy said. "If you come along with us to my house, I will show you something; and if you want it, you can have it."

"Ya, we're full of surprises," laughed Abner. "Come on, Fraulein Trudy, you would never guess what it is, but first I must give something to Grandpa."

Trudy joined them and they walked back to Schotzy's. They went upstairs and Abner handed Grandpa the toot of nails. "You'd never guess what this is, so I will give it to you without guessing," he said.

"Well, this is a surprise," said Grandpa with a big smile. "Thank you very much. Where did you get them?"

"It is a secret and I can't tell. I promised I'd never tell. Aren't surprises fun?"

"Ya, surprises can be fun," replied Grandpa giving his a hug. "I hope that all of your surprises are good ones." Abner had no foreboding that before long he would get a surprise that would be anything but fun.

Just then a honeybee flew in through the window. Antonio pointed to the bee and then to himself. Next, he spoke gently to the bee and shooed it outside. He smiled and said something that Abner didn't understand, and then he pointed to himself and said "Apiarist."

"What do you think he's talking about?" asked Abner.

"If I remember my Latin, apiarie refers to bees and that means that an apiarist would be a beekeeper," answered Grandpa. "He wants us to know that he is a beekeeper. I imagine he wants to take bees to America and he probably has a queen bee in the box that he

165

carried. Would you like to help him find a beetree and rob it of the honey?"

"I'm not sure if I would or not, but I think maybe not," said Abner. "How about you, Schotzy?"

Schotzy jumped up and down with excitement and said, "I like robbing bees. I helped my papa already, and I know where there's a bee tree up in the woods. My papa found it last summer; and there's netting around here some place to cover ourselves so we won't get stung." Schotzy went over to Antonio and waving his hand in the air, said, "Buzzz." Then he pointed towards the forest and made a motion towards his mouth as if he were eating. "Mmmmm."

Antonio smiled, nodded his head and said, "Si."

"Schotzy, you are... I don't know what you are, but look at that, Grandpa, Antonio understands. Talk about surprises," said Abner.

"Now it's Fraulein Trudy's turn," said Schotzy. "There's this old stuff up in a room that's been locked for years. Come and see." They went into the room, walked over to the beautiful chest, and Schotzy opened the lid. He waved his arm with a theatrical gesture and said, "Take notice of this!"

Trudy took one look and said, "Ach du lieber, it is so beautiful! May I touch it?"

Schotzy smiled and said, "Ya, you can touch it. I said that you could have it, didn't I?"

Trudy lifted it up and it was a dress. She looked at it in wonder and said, "It's hard to believe, this dress. I've never seen anything like it in my life. I never even ever dreamed that there was anything so beautiful." She held it against herself and checked to see if it would fit. She looked at it again, rubbed her hand over it and began to cry.

The boys looked at her dumbfounded, not knowing what to say or do. Abner wrung his hands and Schotzy scratched his head. Finally Abner asked, "What is the matter? Don't you like it?"

Trudy wiped her eyes, laid the dress carefully back into the chest and put her arms around both boys. "I love it, and this has made me the happiest person on this earth," she said. "I prayed all night about what to do, whether to marry Jake or stay here with my mother.

Then toward morning, I asked God for a sign, and here it is! A wedding dress! I can't get over it; it is hard to believe." She rubbed her hands together, smiled again and asked, "Will you boys come to my wedding?"

"You couldn't keep us from it, could she, Schotzy?" said Abner.

"We'll help any way we can," agreed Schotzy, "I'll be the best man and Abner will be the flower girl."

"I'll get you for that," said Abner, and gave him a shove.

"Boys!" laughed Trudy. "We'll find appropriate jobs for both of you. Now let's look to see what else is in the chest. Do you want to help?"

Both boys laughed and said, "We forgot to wash our hands."

Trudy lifted things up and Abner saw that under the dress was a quilt, appliqued with birds, flowers, and geometric designs; and under that was other bedding and table linens.

"This had to have been some girl's hope chest,"* said Trudy. "Isn't it beautiful? I wonder whose it was."

"I don't think we'll ever know who it belonged to, but this much I do know, you can have it for your wedding," said Schotzy, grinning. "All of it. Happy wedding, or whatever you're supposed to say."

"Thank you, Schotzy, thank you very much, but I can't take it all."

"Why not?"

"Well, it might be greedy. Everything is so lovely and I'd feel selfish taking all of it."

"Fraulein Trudy," said Abner. "I heard Klaus say that your father did not want you to marry, not ever, so he would not even let you have a hope chest to get things together, in case you did get married. Is that true?"

Trudy's flushed a bright red and then an angry look came over her face and she said, "Ya."

---

* hope chest: a chest full of things that a girl makes or accumulates in hope that she will get married

"After your father died, did your mother ever let you start saving stuff?"

"No, she always told me that I was too old, and I wasn't pretty, and no one would ever want me, so why bother?"

"Ach, Fraulein Trudy, that's awful," said Abner. "I think that you are pretty and nice, and I'd marry you myself if I were old enough and had more than nine pfennig."

"I would, too," added Schotzy very seriously.

Trudy had to laugh. "My goodness, three proposals of marriage all in one week, and I thought I would die an old maid for sure."

"Let us believe that this is God's way of making it up to you for the way your parents have treated you," said Abner. "This is perfect for you. It's an answer to your prayer. Grandpa says that God often gives us more than we ask for, and more than we can even imagine. Here is an example!"

"Well, I still don't know," Trudy answered.

"Well, look at it this way, what in the world would Schotzy do with all of this stuff? Besides, if he ever gets a wife; she will be talented and have stuff every bit as nice as this." Abner had to laugh at his own cleverness.

Trudy reached out and hugged the boys again. "My mother might think that you two are nix-nookses, but I know you are angels," she said. "Pennsylvania will never be the same after you get there. We'll have to see if Jake can take it."

She started to remove some of the bedding, when Schotzy interrupted her and said, "You are to take the chest, too."

"No, I can't do that. I think you had better sell it when you sell the house. It is really very nice and you will get a good bit for it. You will need all of the money you can get to go to Pennsylvania and get started."

"Don't worry about Schotzy, not having enough money, Fraulein Trudy," said Abner. "He has a pile of gold." Realizing what he had said, Abner put his hand to his mouth, turned red, and said, "I'm sorry, Schotzy. I'm sorry. I can't believe I said that. Fraulein Trudy, don't tell anybody. It's a secret."

"Not any more," said Schotzy. "Fraulein Trudy, you may as well tell the neighborhood gossip or shout it from the top of the chimney as to tell him to keep anything a secret. I know you didn't mean to tell, Abner, but you got diarrhea of the mouth. My pappaw would say you couldn't stop it up with a cork." Schotzy looked disgusted.

"I won't tell," said Trudy. "I promise you, I didn't hear a thing. I'll be glad to have the hope chest if Jake can take it along. I'll keep it until Schotzy gets married and has a daughter. Is that a bargain? Jake will be surprised. How will we get it downstairs and to my house?"

"I'll go get Grandpa and he'll figure something out." Abner left the room, feeling as if he were in disgrace. It was then that he remembered that he had told Schotzy about getting the nails from the blacksmith after promising never to mention to anyone where he got them. *I am hopeless,* he thought, *completely hopeless.* He was so ashamed he couldn't look at anybody. Trudy, pretending nothing happened, took her bread and the dress and went home looking as if she were on top of the world; and Schotzy kept happily poking around in the room, trying to see everything that was there. Abner left the room not knowing what to do just as the church bells announced that it was midday. "It's dinnertime," he said. "I'm gona go home and eat."

CHAPTER THIRTEEN

On his way home Abner could not shake a feeling of apprehension. It seemed as if people were looking at him strangely. *No,* he thought, *it's just because I can't keep a secret, and I feel guilty about it.* But the feeling wouldn't go away. He shook his head as if it would clear his thinking. *But no, something is definitely working on my nerves, and it is worse than it was a bit ago. What is it?* He looked around. *Nobody's around. This really wonders me.* He scratched his head and looked around again. He tried to think of someone who would want to harm him, but he couldn't think of anybody who had it in for him. Never before had he ever felt so uncomfortable in his own village. Suddenly the hair on the back of his neck raised up and a sense of horror came over him. He looked at his arm and he could see goose bumps and he felt tingly all over. *What could it be?*

He walked faster, continually looking around to see who might be out. Then he saw someone duck behind a bush. Zing! Past his head flew a stone. He scrunched down and ran with all his might. Zing! There flew another second stone, barely missing him. The third stone grazed his foot; and he made it home in record time.

He burst into the kitchen, huffing and puffing, only to be scolded by his mother who was on her hands and knees with a bucket of soapy water and a rag in her hand. "Why are you running so hard and coming into the house without wiping your feet? Can't you see what I'm doing? Do you think I stand down and scrub the floor just for the fun of it? Any dumkopf could see that it's still wet, and here you come tracking in more dirt."

His nerves were wild and the tone of his mother's voice scratched a raw spot. *The nerve of that woman expecting me to wipe my feet when someone out there is trying to kill me,* he thought. *I swear I'm never going to tell her anything.*

Rachel got up and said, "Just stay where you are until the floor is dry. I have some chicken soup ready for your grandmother. I'll put it in a crock, the soup, and you can take it while it's hot still. It'll make her feel better for sure. Nothing is better than chicken soup when you have a cough and cold. Are you ready to take it to her? It will be ready when you get back, your dinner."

"You–you–you want me to take the sa-soup ra-right now?"

"Ya, right now, not tomorrow. It's dinnertime and you're to take your grandma the soup right now. She needs something hot to eat."

Abner thought fast. "I must go first," he hollered over his shoulder as he ran out the door. He went through the barn, looked both ways and ran to the safety of the outhouse. *Oh, my, what am I going to do now? I'm going to stay here awhile, that's for sure. This place stinks bad, but being here beats getting hit by rocks. I should have put lime down the hole long already. It's one of my chores and I've not done it. I guess sitting in here and taking in the stench is what I get for not doing my job.*

It hadn't warmed since morning and wind was still blowing so it didn't take long until his heinie[*] was freezing, but he stayed there until his feet had gone to sleep and he couldn't stand it any longer. He hesitated about leaving, but he knew he had to take the soup to Grandma. *I best go,* he thought, *maybe whoever was after me has left now.* He ran for the barn and then slowly made his way to the kitchen.

"I thought you'd fallen in," scolded Rachel. "The soup has cooled and I must replace it with hot." She poured the cold soup into another container and ladled up another crockful.

He took the soup and headed for the door. "Dear God protect me," he said as he stepped outside. He ran as carefully as he could on the cobble stone street until zing! a stone whizzed by his head. He stumbled and fell, breaking the crock and spilling the soup. He scrambled to his feet and tore back to the house.

---

[*] heinie: bottom

"Now what's got into you?" demanded Rachel angrily. "How could anyone be so doppy?* Now what is your grandma going to have for lunch? I guess she will eat yours and you will go without."

"But, Mama . . ."

"No buts." She quickly found another crock, ladled up more soup, and handed it to him.

Well, he thought as he walked out the door, *like Queen Esther said, 'If I die, I die.'* He walked as quickly and as carefully as he could, watching his feet to be sure he wouldn't fall. He didn't look around, but once in awhile he zigged or zagged to the left or right. His adversary must have given up, or decided Abner wasn't crazy enough to come out again, because he made it to Grandma's and delivered the soup safely. She was up trying to make dinner, and was happy to see him.

"Grandma, you sit down and eat it awhile.* It is still hot, the soup. I'll stir up the fire and do whatever you tell me to do to make dinner for Grandpa and Schotzy." He found some potpie in the cold cellar and was putting it over the fire to warm when they walked in. Schotzy was wearing the Roman helmet and carrying the sword. They were laughing and Abner knew that they had not encountered any trouble. "Your grandpa asked me a riddle and I knew the answer. Do you? Which candle burns longer, a tallow candle or a wax candle?"

"Wax candles always burn longer."

"No, no, no," said Schotzy very seriously. "I thought that any dumkopf would know that all candles burn shorter, not longer." He and Grandpa laughed, but not Abner, who could laugh and joke with the best of them. This was the second time today that someone called him a dumkopf, and he didn't think it was funny.

"Where's Antonio?" he asked, without cracking a smile.

"He went to the inn to eat, but he'll be back." said Grandpa, "He's a good worker, and Schotzy thinks it would be a good idea to

---

* doppy: or doppich, clumsy, awkward (rhymes with sloppy)
* awhile: The use of awhile is an idiom that defies explanation. It probably means at this time.

172

have him help us until Jake gets back." Abner nodded and stirred the potpie without saying a word. Grandpa, assuming that Abner had eaten at home, did not ask him if he wanted anything, so Abner served them the food and didn't eat.

Schotzy looked at his friend curiously and asked, "What's the matter with you? Do you think that I am still mad at you for running at the mouth?"

Grandpa raised an eyebrow and looked at him questioningly. Abner felt his face get red and he ran out the door. He sat on the bench in the sun and petted Princess for a bit, wondering what to do next. His stomach growled with hunger, and he thought of one of Grandma's sayings: *My stomach thought my throat was cut.* He remembered the apples and turnips in the cold cellar at home. *I'll go get one of each. I can't sit here like a scaredy cat forever.* "Off you go Princess," he said as he gently put the cat down. He walked to the corner cautiously, looked both ways, and then ran hill the hill up as fast as he could. He was halfway home when zing! A stone hit him squarely on the back of the head and down he went, out cold.

Abner had no idea how long he lay there, but when he regained consciousness, he was lying on the bed in the little room off the kitchen that Schotzy had been in the week before. His head was on his mother's lap; and Rachel was wiping his face and her tears with a cool, damp cloth. "Oh, Abby, my son, oh, Abby, my son," she cried, over and over again. "I'm sorry. I'm sorry. You tried to tell me and I wouldn't let you. Oh, Abby, my son, my only son."

Abner was still in a daze, but he looked up and saw that the little soulenfenster was still open. *I guess I didn't die yet,* he thought, and then he heard Grandpa say, "Rachel, the doctor is here to look at your wrist. I fear that it is broken."

"No, no, he must look after Abner first. My son is hurt."

"I know that he is hurt, but he is not hurt as much as you are. There's probably a bump on the back of his head, and he'll be all right in a day or so, but your wrist must be set."

Rachel was determined. "No," she said. "The doctor must tend to Abner before he tends to me."

Grandpa was right about Abner's head. There was a big bump on the back and another on the front. He must have pitched forward and landed on his forehead. The doctor said that he should stay quiet for a few days, and he added that the bruise on the forehead would probably drain down giving a him a black eye. For now, he needed cold compresses and some chamomile tea.

"Abner took care of me when I needed it and now I'll take care of him," said Schotzy. Abner watched him get a rag and a basin of cold water. He dipped the rag into the water, wrung it out, folded it into a square and applied it gently to one bump and then the other.

"That feels good," said Abner. Schotzy changed the compress often and did not let it get warm.

"Get some wine for your daughter-in-law," said the doctor. "It will ease the pain of setting her wrist, and then make some feverfew[*] tea for Abner. It will help keep his head from aching."

When Grandpa gave the tea to Abner, he made a face as he drank it. "Ach," he said, "this stuff is not so pretty good."

Abner wiped his mouth and watched as the doctor began setting his mother's wrist. He could see that she was very brave, gritting her teeth and holding still, while the sweat stood out on her forehead. "You are a brave woman," the doctor said. "I'm going to put on some knitbone[*] and a splint. Then I'll give you a sling to support your arm. It will take six weeks to heal."

"It can't take six weeks! Who will milk my cows?"

"I don't know, madam, who will milk your cows; but if you try to do it, you will be crippled for the rest of your life. The charge today will be seven pfennig."

"I'll pay you, Herr Doctor, as soon as I can go home and get some money."

"Madam, I don't think you will be going home for awhile. I saw people going in and coming out of your house, carrying away many of your belongings."

---

[*] feverfew: an herb with healing properties
[*] knitbone: an herb, comfrey, used as an aid to promote healing bones

"Oh, no! They can't do that, those swine! I'm going home and stop them." Rachel cried. She stood up and headed for the door.

"Rachel, you can't," said Grandpa, putting his arms around her to restrain her. "Now settle. If you would go over there now, they would turn on you and do you more harm. You must stay here. There is nothing you can do about it. No doubt the magistrate will send for the militia."

Abner saw that his mother was not about to give up without a struggle.

"Rachel," said Grandpa, holding her tightly. "I do not want to hurt you; but you are not going anywhere!"

"Give her some more wine," said the doctor, as he took hold of her good arm. "Make her lie down. You may as well give her chamomile tea. I'm going to look in on Frau Hartzell while I am here. You have your hands full, Herr Hartzell. Just try to keep all of your patients quiet and don't let your daughter-in-law go home."

Abner watched Grandpa help his mother upstairs to one of the bedrooms; and when he came down, he asked him for something to eat. He ate bread, butter and cheese, and then slept. Later that day he awoke with a fierce headache and Grandpa gave him more feverfew tea that tasted so bad he had to gag it down. For supper they all ate leftovers from the funeral luncheon.

On Saturday morning when Abner awoke, he announced, "Today is Friday. On Sunday I am going to be baptized."

Schotzy looked at him funny and said, "No, Abner, today is Saturday; and you are not going to be baptized tomorrow, because you have to stay in bed."

"Yes, I am going to be baptized on Sunday. Today is Friday and I am going to be baptized on Sunday."

"No," insisted Schotzy. "This is…"

"It's no use arguing with him," interrupted Grandpa. "He has a concussion. That means that his brain swelled up and he can't think right. That's why he must rest. He'll be all right in a few days. Would you like some oatmeal? I'm making a big potful. That's one thing I know how to cook. I'll make enough for everybody."

"I'm not sneaky,"* said Schotzy. "I eat anything. My pappaw knew how to make oatmeal, too, sir." After breakfast he asked, "Would it be all right for me to go with Antonio and rob the bees? Some honey would sure taste good to me on oatmeal or anything else. I wish Abner could go along."

"Abner can go another time, if he wants to," said Grandpa, "but I don't think he's much for robbing bees. I'm sure, though, that he'll be glad to eat the honey. We all will. Do you have a smoker and rags? I heard you say you had netting."

"Yes, sir, I have everything I need, and I think robbing bees is great fun. I'm glad Antonio knows how to do it." Schotzy hurried out.

Abner had just finished his oatmeal when Rachel came down. He thought that she looked worse than he had ever seen her. She wore the same clothes she had worn the day before; she had big circles under her eyes, and her hair was hardly combed. She came in to see him and said, "You don't look so good."

Abner decided not to say that she didn't look so good either. He remembered another saying, *If you can't say anything nice, don't say anything, especially to a lady. Who used to say that?* He couldn't think.

"Why did we stay here last night, Mama? I sleep better in my own bed."

"Oh, Abner," said his mother taking a deep breath. "It's hard to tell you. It's hard to talk about." Her face was so serious he knew something bad had happened. She took another breath and began, "You were hit on the head with a rock and were knocked out. When I heard about it, I ran to help you and I was hit, too. I started to fall and I put my hand out to catch myself, and I broke my wrist. We were both lying on the street until your grandpa came out and carried you here. I wanted to go home, but he said that it was too dangerous. I must give him right, because it would have been."

Abner's head hurt horribly, and he couldn't take it all in, but still, he had to know. "Do you mean to tell me that it was dangerous to

---

* sneaky: persnickety, picky about food, hard to please

176

stay in our own house? I always felt safe in our house, even with Papa away."

Rachel looked at him sadly and replied, "Our neighbors went in and looted and vandalized our house. Can you imagine that? I always minded my own business, but I guess that wasn't enough for these people. I don't understand it myself, and I have no idea how long we will have to stay here. Your grandpa said that he is the head of the family and that we must stay until it is safe for us to return home. The decision is his, not mine, so you may as well rest. I'll get some more feverfew tea for you. I can tell that your head aches and it's good for that. The chamomile tea seems to help your grandma feel better, too. She hasn't been coughing as much." He had heard Grandma coughing through the night, but it all seemed like a bad dream. Abner drank the tea with difficulty, closed his eyes and slept almost all morning.

Just before dinner, Schotzy stuck his head into the little room. Seeing that Abner was awake, he said softly, "You gotta see the honey. We got a nice tubful. Antonio is a real expert. He even captured another queen bee that he hopes to take to America." Schotzy got excited talking about Antonio and began to talk louder. "He must be some kind of a saint because the bees don't even sting him. He told me to bring you some honeycomb to chew on. He says it is really good for what ails you."

"Please don't talk so loud," said Abner, holding his head. He took the spoon that Schotzy held out to him and put it in his mouth. He thought of the Bible verse, *'Taste and see that the Lord is good.'* * He crushed the wax between his teeth, and enjoyed the sweetness as it broke out of the cells. He swallowed the honey and chewed on the honeycomb that was left. "That is really good. Will you ask my mother if I can have some butterbread with honey on it, and some milk, too?"

After he had eaten his snack, Abner said to Schotzy, "I don't know why I'm here in bed. It's Friday and I'm going to be baptized on Sunday. I'm going to get up and go home."

---

* Psalms 34:8

Schotzy shook his head and answered, "No, Abner, you must stay in bed. It may not do any good for me to tell you, but today is Saturday and you can't go home. Yesterday was Friday and you were hit on the head with a rock. Your neighbors looted your house. They stole milk, butter, cheese, and most of your hens and peeps. Some boys, probably the ones who threw the rocks, went into your house and tore up the place. They broke dishes, tore down curtains, overturned furniture, cut up pillows and scattered feathers all over the place."

"Why would anybody do this to us?" asked Abner, holding his head. "We never did anything to hurt anybody. It must be a mess."

"It would have been worse if Antonio hadn't been walking by," answered Schotzy. "Here is the big surprise: Antonio used to be a priest. When he saw what was happening, he spoke to the mob like a priest would, and everyone understood what he was saying. He told me that he took authority in the name of Jesus, and that he ordered them to stop what they were doing, and to go home. Everyone in the village is talking about. Many believe that it is a miracle because those people listened* to him and did what he said."

"Antonio did that? Little Antonio?" Abner found it hard to believe.

"Ya and he did!" continued Schotzy, "and then he walked into the house and ordered those boys to redd up. He told them that they should be ashamed, and besides that, they should be sorry for their sins and ask for God's forgiveness. He told me that they laughed and said that they had nothing to worry about. All they had to do was to pray and God would forgive them, that was all they needed."

"And what did Antonio say about that? I know what Grandpa would say."

"Antonio really lit into them and told them God doesn't work that way. He made them redd up before they could leave. Can you believe it?" Schotzy's voice kept getting louder. "It's amazing! Little Antonio controlled the whole mob. Many of the men and boys were bigger than he is, and I can't even tell you how many were

---

* listened: paid attention

there. I asked Antonio about it, and he said that he was not a hero. He said that the name of Jesus did it all because Jesus' name has great power to convict a person of his sin. You want to know something else that is strange? I couldn't hardly understand Antonio yesterday and today, I could. There is something strange going on around here."

"Thanks for letting me know about it," said Abner, still holding his head. "I am tired of staying in bed. Maybe I can be up some this afternoon."

"I hope so. I best go see if I can help your mom make dinner. I know her wrist hurts. After dinner I'm going to see Trudy and get my new clothes."

"Do you think anybody would try to get me if I went out a bit after dinner? This being cooped up all of the time is awful."

Schotzy shook his head. "Things have calmed down, but you better wouldn't even think about it. No doubt it will be safe after the soldiers come."

Abner lay in bed thinking about his house and the looting that had taken place. *It wonders me if they took our money. Mine was in my pillowcase. It wasn't much, but it was all I had. Let me see, I had eight pfennig, and Grandma gave me five pfennig, plus one more, and I spent five on the nails. Oh, my head. If they took them all, what difference does it make? Mama keeps hers in a little hidey-hole behind a rock, under the water that cools the milk and cream. I doubt that they found it. I hope not.*

Abner was allowed to get up and dress for dinner. Afterwards he wandered around the house and visited Grandma. She was breathing hard and coughing now and then, and she didn't look so good. "When are you going to be better, Grandma?" he asked.

"Soon, I hope, what are you up to? I see you have a blackeye. Were you in a fight?"

"If I was, I lost," he replied. "I'll let you rest." *The tulips I brought her are nice still, but when they wither,* he thought, *will I be able to go get her more?*

He wandered out into the kitchen and talked to his mother. "Who's milking the cows? Who's feeding the pig and gathering the eggs? Who's making the cheese and selling the milk?" He spoke mindlessly and didn't wait for answers until he thought about being at his grandparents'. "Why are we here? I think we should go home."

"We'll go home as soon as we can." replied Rachel patiently. "Grandpa, Trudy, and Schotzy milk the cows. They set some of it out for the cream to rise, and fed the rest to the pig. Schotzy wants to learn everything he can, and he says he will make butter this afternoon when he gets back from Schneider's. He is a good boy. I never realized it before."

"He's my best friend," replied Abner, "and he always will be."

"I told your grandpa where I hid my money, and he went and got it last night. Those thieves hadn't found it, even though they overturned all of the crocks, kettles, sieves and buckets in their search."

"Did he find mine?"

"You didn't tell him where you had it hidden."

Later that afternoon, Schotzy brought the cream and churn, and Rachel showed him how to make butter. He churned and churned and churned but the butter wouldn't come. "Sometimes it acts like that and you must sing to it," said Rachel. "Come butter, come butter, come butter, come," she crooned.

Schotzy kept on churning and the cream still didn't turn to butter. Abner heard Grandma say something, so he went in and asked her what she had said.

"Take the poker," she replied softly while breathing with difficulty. "Make it hot in the fire, plunge it into the cream and say, 'Raus mit du, hex.'* After you do that, the butter will come."

Abner went back to the kitchen and said, "It's probably just one of Grandma's superstitions, but this is what she says to do to make the butter to come."

---

* raus mit du, hex: get out witch or evil spirit

Schotzy continued to churn while Abner got the poker. Rachel didn't say anything, so Abner heated it in the fire, plunged it into the churn, and said, "Raus mit du, hex!" The cream sputtered and sizzled from the heat; and after a few more churns the cream began to clot. Before long the butter separated from the buttermilk.

"I don't believe there was an evil spirit in the cream," said Schotzy.

"Me either," replied Abner. "Maybe it was just too cold, and the poker warmed it up enough."

"You are probably right," answered Schotzy. "This much I know. This is going to be the best butter I've ever made."

Rachel showed Schotzy how to gather the butter together with the butter paddle, rinse it, salt it, and form it into a ball. It was finished when Abner called out, "Of course, it's the best butter you ever made. It's the first butter you ever made."

"It wondered me how long it was going to take you to catch on," laughed Schotzy.

CHAPTER FOURTEEN

On Sunday morning the church bells awakened Abner as usual, ringing just as loud or maybe louder than they did at home. He was confused because he didn't know where he was. He looked out and could not see the mountains as he would have had he been looking out his own window at home. *Where fer am I? What fer am I doing here? I must think on this, but I'm all ferhuddled. Ya, now I know, I'm at Grandpa's and there is the little window that lets a person's soul out when he dies. It seems like it's Friday, but it must be Sunday.* He tried to sort it all out. *If today is Sunday, am I going to be baptized?* He heard someone in the kitchen and went to see who it was. Grandpa had just come in with a big bucket of milk and was standing by the fire.

"Well, good morning, Grandson," he said. "You look like you feel better but you have a beauty of a shiner.* It's purple like one of the tulips you brought Grandma."

Abner looked in the mirror that hung on the wall, "It's something, all right. I can't see out of it; it's that swelled up."

"Can you see that it's a beautiful morning?" Grandpa asked. "It's warmer than yesterday, but the floor is cold. You better would put your shoes and stockings on, since you have no slippers here."

Abner smiled and asked in a hopeful voice, "Does that mean that I can get dressed and go along with you to church this morning?"

Grandpa smiled, and then said seriously, "Don't put words in my mouth. I think you may get dressed, but I don't think that you should leave the house. It would be too much of a strain on you. You can eat your breakfast and then just lie around. You can read the Bible to Grandma, if you feel up to it. How is your head?"

"It's still there."

Grandpa laughed. "What kind of an answer is that?"

---

* shiner: blackeye

"I mean I think I'll live. It's better than it was but not as good as it should be. Where is Schotzy? Did he help milk and do the chores?"

"I decided to let him sleep because I thought that some extra rest would do him good. If you want to get him up now, you may."

"I'll roust* him out all right," Abner said rubbing his hands together. "It'll be a pleasure." Abner put on his stockings, went upstairs, banged on his door, and hollered, "Hey, you lazybones, it's time to get up. Didn't you hear the bells? I'm surprised at you! I had no idea you were so lazy."

Rachel opened her door. "Are you talking to me, Son?"

"No, Mama, I wasn't even thinking about you. Grandpa said to get Schotzy up."

"One of these days you will think before you make so much racket, I hope."

"Sorry, Mama."

Schotzy came out of his room dressed for going to work in the barn. "Good morning, friend," said Abner. "Grandpa beat you to it and has all of the chores done. He's making breakfast now."

"He'll spoil me, if he doesn't watch out," said Schotzy with a smile, "but I don't mind."

"Ach du lieber," said Grandpa when all of them came down for breakfast. "Last night was Saturday night and I forgot to have you boys take a bath. How could I have forgotten such a thing?" He looked at both of them. "Why didn't you remind me?"

They both laughed and Schotzy said, "I thought about it, but I figured if you wanted me to have one, you'd say something."

Grandpa smiled and said, "You nix-nooks! After breakfast, you get a basin of warm water, a washrag and soap, and scrub up in the room Abner's been sleeping in. Then get ready for church."

Grandma was sitting up in bed eating her oatmeal when Abner walked into her room. "Grandpa said that I could get his Bible and read to you if you want me to," he said.

"That would be nice, whenever I'm done eating."

---

* roust him out: make him get up

"You finish your breakfast, I'll choose something good." Abner got the Bible down and started paging through. He thought about the twenty-third Psalm. *Ya, Grandma would like that. There is something in Isaiah about the trees clapping their hands with joy that always tickled him. The idea of such a thing! There it is, Isaiah 55. He would read that first.* After Grandpa, Rachel, and Schotzy left to go to Sabbath meeting, Abner began reading. When he got to verse 12, he said, "Now listen Grandma, this is the part that I like best in this whole chapter, *'For ye shall go out with joy, and be led forth in peace; the mountains and hills shall break forth before you into singing, and all the trees of the field shall clap their hands.'* Do you get the picture Grandma? All of the mountains and hills singing, and all of the trees clapping their hands for the joy of the Lord!"

"That is some picture all right," she smiled. "I've heard that the joy of the Lord is your strength," said Grandma, "but I guess I haven't had enough joy lately, because my strength is draining away fast. Maybe I'll sleep now." She lay back, however she but didn't sleep, because all of a sudden there was yelling and screaming outside. She sat up suddenly and asked, "What fer racket is it, Abner?"

Abner ran to the window and saw Max Bosserman running as fast as his fat legs could carry him, but it wasn't fast enough for him to get away from a roaring mob of young men who were chasing him. One of them caught up to him, tackled him, and brought him down, whereupon all of the others started to kick and pommel him.

"What is it?" asked Grandma.

Oh no, thought Abner, *I can't tell her how horrible this is. If they don't stop, they're going to kill him. Should I go out and help him? No, it wouldn't do any good. There are too many of them and they'd kill me, too.*

"What is it?" Grandma asked again.

"Just some young rascals carrying on," he answered.

"On a Sabbath morning?" Grandma was shocked. "Have they no shame?"

When Max didn't move any more, one of his attackers gave him one more hard kick, and all of them began to scatter. Abner stepped back from the window because he didn't want them to see him. Then he saw a number of men forcing Elder Wentz to go with them down the street toward the lake. Behind them was Grandpa, followed by the rest of the members of the church. Abner watched as the men took ropes and tied Elder Wentz so that he stood in back of a horse. Then they whipped the horse and it ran wildly down the road and across the fields, dragging Elder Wentz behind it as far as Abner could see. He put his hands over his eyes and tried not to say anything that would upset Grandma.

"What is it? What is it?" she cried, staining to get up and look.

"You don't want to know," he answered. "Please, Grandma, don't get up. You don't want to know," he repeated.

After a bit he glanced out of the window and saw that Grandpa was bringing the congregation to his house, except for several men who went to see about Max and Elder Wentz, and Widow Schneider who kept right on going towards her home. Abner met them at the door. "Why didn't you fight them, Grandpa?" he demanded. "I don't understand."

"I'll explain as soon as I get these people in and settled. First we must pray. Jesus is the Prince of Peace – let your minds dwell on him." Everyone was very quiet, except for an occasional sob. Abner and Schotzy helped everyone find a place to sit and then there was silent prayer.

Following prayer, Grandpa got up to speak. "In the absence of the senior elder, I, as second elder, will conduct the service. My grandson wants to know why we did not fight back, and why didn't we? We did not fight back because we do not believe in fighting back and we don't believe in getting even. It is one of the tenets of our faith. Jesus turned the other cheek and so do we. God is in control. It may not look like it, but rest assured that He is. When we got to our meeting place and those young men were in it, it was plain to see that they were looking for trouble. You see, for some reason, the Protestants feel threatened by us. Everyone should have left immediately. Instead, Max, Otto, and Willy went in and tried to argue with them. This is contrary to what we believe and teach.

"Nearly two hundred years ago, Martin Luther nailed his ninety-five theses on the door of the church at Wittenberg. This list described ninety-five practices of the Roman Catholic Church that Luther felt were wrong. Luther was a Catholic priest and did not want to break away from the Catholic Church; he merely wanted changes to be made. Later however, other believers who followed Luther were determined to break away from the Roman Catholic Church and to worship the way that they believed was right. The leaders of the Roman Catholic Church were determined that the Protestants, as they came to be called, would not break away, but would obey the church and follow its teachings. The Protestants were sincere. To them, it was a matter of what was right. To the Catholics it may have been what they thought was right, but it was also a matter of political power. Can you believe that a war began to decide how to worship and what to believe? It not only began, it lasted thirty years. Other countries got involved. The country was ruined and half of the people were dead. Something had to be done.

"As you know, each section of this country is called a principality and is ruled by a prince. There is one king over all of them. The Treaty of Westphalia in 1648 provided the solution. Let each prince decide whether his principality would be Roman Catholic, Lutheran or Reformed. The Reformed church was made up of followers of Zwingli, Calvin and Hus. In general the princes of the southern part were Catholic and the princes of the northern part were Protestant, but any principality could be changed any time with death of one prince and the succession of another. The Brethren were left out completely.

"Sensible people could see that fighting and wars only bring great hardship and suffering to everyone, and then someone, while reading the Bible, rediscovered that Jesus did not believe in fighting back. Anyone who truly follows Jesus does not fight. He said that if anyone slaps you on one cheek, you turn the other cheek and let him slap you again. If everyone did that, there would be no wars. That is how our sect began. We follow the leading of the Holy Spirit and we do not fight under any circumstances.

"Now, nearly one hundred years later, we want to worship our way, and we should be able to, but whoever is in power is always fiercely jealous of his power and his territory. It might not be so bad if one prince would live a long time and there would be some stability, but this part of the country has had several different princes in the last few years. Every one of them wanted us to worship different from the last. Sometimes the prince belonged to the Lutheran Church and we're supposed to follow Luther's teachings. Sometimes the prince belonged to the Reformed Church and we're supposed to follow its teachings. Sometimes the prince was Roman Catholic and we were supposed to go back to the old ways. The people are so confused they don't know what to believe. Each prince wants everyone to worship his way, and is willing to do anything to achieve that goal.

"We have other beliefs that are different from the Protestants and Catholics. We do not believe in infant baptism, but in believer's baptism. As you know, it is against the law for us to baptize adults by immersion; many early believers were given life sentences as galley slaves. Another belief that we hold to is that everyone should dress plain. Why that bothers anybody is more than I can guess, but this much I do know: when this is all over, we will see how God's hand was in it, and we will be amazed." Abner listened closely because he knew Grandpa was saying all of this for his benefit.

After a prayer of thanksgiving and praise, Grandpa asked for God's protection for the people, and they were dismissed to go home. Only then did the men who had checked on Max and Elder Wentz report that both of them were dead and the building where they had held Sabbath services was on fire.

"There's really nothing we can do about the fire," said Grandpa. "Perhaps we weren't meant to have a church. We can always meet in the homes of our members."

Trudy stayed to help make dinner for the Hartzells and Abner heard her say, "I don't know what my mother is going to do, but I

187

am going to marry Jake, no matter what she does." *Good for her*, he thought.

Grandpa had invited Antonio to stay. Abner liked Antonio and was glad to see Grandpa, who understood a little Latin, communicating with him and becoming his friend.

Abner thought that it was going to be a long day because he was told to go back to bed and stay there, except to use the pot. Poor Schotzy had to empty it and that struck Abner as funny, but he didn't let on.

"Ach, I'm so schushlig,"[*] Grandma said as she shuffled to the table. She had got out of bed for dinner, but was very weak. Abner thought about the basket that he had never brought back, and he was sure that he would return it first thing after he was allowed to go home. He watched his mother trying to do her part of making the dinner, and he could tell she was in pain. Worse yet, she hated being there; she needed her own space. She had grown used to being an independent woman and returning to being a dependent one was hard. He wondered how it would be when his papa came home. No one spoke of what had had happened that morning. It was too much and too soon to talk about it.

The afternoon passed much more quickly than Abner expected it would because he slept. Schotzy, Trudy, Rachel, and Antonio worked with Grandpa on a reading lesson from the Bible until it was time to milk the cows and do the chores. While they were gone, Grandma called out and Abner went to see what she wanted.

"Ach, Matthias," she said, "I always wanted to give you brothers and sisters, but I never did."

Abner was confused at first, but then he realized that she thought he was his papa, when he was a boy. "You've missed having a big family," she said in a strange voice. "I came from a big family, twelve brothers and sisters, but maybe it's not too late. Maybe it'll give another baby."[*]

---

[*] schushlig: uncoordinated, shaky (rhymes with push pig)
[*] give another baby: I'll have another baby.

Abner knew that he should keep her calm because she was not right, so he said, "Grandma, it's all right. We don't need any more babies."

"Why do you call me Grandma, Matthias? That's not funny. Don't do it any more. I'm not a grandma. I'm only twenty-seven years old." With that, she drifted off to sleep, and Abner sat holding her hand until the others returned.

It had been a long hard day and everyone went to bed early. Abner tried to think of all of the things that he should pray about, but his ability to think was still not there. He went to sleep, only to dream that the magistrate was after him.

The next day was partly cloudy and cool, and Abner awoke thinking about going outside and running until he could run no more. "Please, God, let me get outside," he prayed, not realizing that before long he'd be outside, wishing he could be back in.

Elder Wentz and Max were buried early Monday morning and Grandpa conducted both services. The coffin that Grandpa had on hand fit Max, and Pastor Wentz had made his own several years before. That left only a baby-sized one.

"How is Grandpa going to do all he needs to do?" Abner asked Schotzy, who had just returned from doing Abner's chores.

"He is busier than a one-armed paperhanger," he answered.

Abner laughed because he'd never heard that saying before. "It feels good to laugh," he said. "It seems like a long time."

"I'm glad that made you laugh," answered Schotzy, "because this won't. The soldiers came this morning. The first thing they did was move into your house and slaughter your pig. They are having a pig roast."

"What did you say?" asked Rachel who had just come to the kitchen from Grandma's room.

"I said that the soldiers have moved into your house and are roasting your pig."

"Those swine, those dirty, rotten, low-down, stinking swine," screamed Rachel. She stamped her feet, clenched her fists and had a fit as she vented her anger. "Those lazy louts, those thieving hogs, stealing my pig and slaughtering it in my own house! I am going over there and give them a piece of my mind. They'll know what I think of them!" She started for the door.

"Mama, you can't. Mama, you mustn't," said Abner, as he tried to stop her.

"Get away from me," she said as she gave him a shove. He fell to the floor and banged his head.

Abner lay on the floor saying, "Oh God, help us." Schotzy ran to the workshop to get Grandpa.

"Rachel, in the name of Jesus, peace be unto you." Grandpa said as he rushed in. He touched her gently on her good shoulder and said, "I'm not going to let you go anywhere. I don't know why we are going through this, but it will all turn out to be a blessing. God asks us only that we have faith in him. Cursing gets you nowhere. The first Christians were persecuted in Rome and then driven out. The result was that Christianity spread very rapidly throughout the Roman Empire. We are in the same situation as those early Christians were, and we are blessed because God has chosen us to do his mission. St. Peter wrote to the believers that if you are insulted because of Christ, you are blessed, for the spirit of the glory of God rests on you."

Abner sat up and listened to their conversation. He could see that his mother was embarrassed that someone else had seen her lose her temper and talk so ugly. He heard her say, "I'm sorry I spoke the way I did, sir. Matthias always hated for me to lose my temper, but sometimes it just boils up out of me. Please forgive me." She put her hand over her face and cried. "I don't know what I'm going to do. This can't go on much longer."

"God will be with us, no matter how long it takes," said Grandpa.

"You have more faith than I do," she replied.

"God will work things out. Just trust him. Our ways aren't his ways. Nevertheless, I do believe that you and Abner had best get ready to leave here as soon as possible. These people are all riled up and it isn't safe for you to stay."

"But, Papa." It was the first time that Rachel had ever called him Papa. "How can we go? Abner isn't well yet, and Grandma isn't fit to travel. As for me, I couldn't carry much."

"I can't go, but I'll let Schotzy go with you."

"How can I care for another child? It would be too much."

"Rachel, Schotzy would be more of a blessing than you could ever conceive of, and I'll ask Antonio to show you the way over the pass into Switzerland. You will be safe there."

Abner was pleased to hear his mother answer, "All right, if you insist."

"I didn't get a chance to tell you," said Schotzy, as he came in the back door, "I saw Klaus and he talked to me after all. He told me to tell you that he would help us all he could. He said we ought to leave soon, but I told him that Abner got hit on the head with a rock and is all ferdudst;* that Rachel's wrist is broken; and that Frau Hartzell has pneumonia and is dying."

Abner gasped, "It can't be!" No one had mentioned that Grandma might be dying. Her family knew she was very sick, but pneumonia was incurable so they had refused to face it.

"It's all right, Abner," Grandma said from the other room. "Come and sit with me." Abner got up off the floor and went to her. He sat down beside her and held her hand. "I know I'm going to go soon. I'm ready, and I'm not afraid anymore," she sighed. "All of my life, I've been afraid. All those superstitions! And now that the time has come, I'm not afraid at all. I can hear the angels sing." She coughed a deep cough and then said, "Please Frederick, take me to the room where Abner's been sleeping. Then my soul will be able to go out the soulenfenster and straight to heaven. You will be going to Pennsylvania in body, and I will go along in spirit. I'll be in heaven watching over you and praying for you." Grandpa half carried her into the small room and Abner sat with her until she went to sleep.

Grandpa, Abner, Rachel and Schotzy sat quietly for a long while and then Schotzy said, "Trudy is bringing dinner. Klaus managed to

---

* ferdudst: not right in the head; all ferdudst means completely bewildered, much worse off that being ferhuddled

save a piece of pig meat and she put it to sauerkraut and noodles for us."

"That is very nice of Trudy," said Rachel. "We'll have to figure some way to pay her back. We don't want to be eating Widow Schneider's food when she may not have much for herself. What did she decide about going to Pennsylvania?"

"Trudy's mother said that she is not going," continued Schotzy. "She says her home is here, and if she would go there, she would not have a home. She says if she stays here, she can take in boarders, or sewing, or something, and get along until Klaus gets out of the army."

Grandpa looked concerned. "What about the church?"

"She says she'll go back to the other church before she'll leave here. She says it can't make that much difference."

"She has the right to make up her own mind," said Grandpa. "Going to new country will be very difficult for some people. Conquering a new land and bringing God's word to it! It's an exciting and challenging task. I'm going to go sit with my wife and pray for guidance." Grandpa went into the little room and closed the door. Everyone just sat around awhile thinking his own thoughts.

The quiet was broken by a knock on the back door. It was Trudy bringing supper, all ready to eat. She also brought something special, a hog maw.* "Klaus saved it," she said. "I've cleaned it for you since I knew you couldn't. If you get the filling, I'll prepare it for you. Then you can bake it tomorrow."

"Thank you, very much," said Rachel, "I was so hungry for hog maw, I could almost taste it, and I thought those lazy, rotten louts threw it out. I couldn't imagine them cleaning a hog maw, much less preparing and baking one. It takes work and soldiers don't want to work; they just want other people to feed them."

"When did the soldiers come?" asked Abner. "I don't remember them coming."

"They came today, which is Monday," said Schotzy.

---

* hog maw: pig's stomach cleaned, filled with diced potatoes and sausage, sewed shut and baked

"How could today be Monday? Today is Friday and I'm going to be baptized on Sunday." said Abner, shaking his head.

"Just trust me, friend, today is Monday, Sunday is over, and tomorrow you will be better. The doctor said so. I asked Klaus if he had seen your papa or your Cousin Jake, and he said that he had not."

Just then there was a strange sound in the room where Grandma lay and all of them got up to see what it was. Grandpa was sitting beside her, holding her hand. Even though tears were flowing down his cheeks, the glory of God shone on his face.

"The heavenly messenger was here," he said. "He came to get Bertl and to tell me that I was to lead my people across the ocean and across a wide river to a place that God has set aside for us. It is to be a special land where truth will prevail, and people will be free to worship in spirit and in truth according to God's word. More martyrs will die before the new land is settled because the seeds of a new kind of government are being germinated in martyrs' blood.

CHAPTER FIFTEEN

"Trudy," said Grandpa, "instead of working on the hog-maw, would you be so kind as to prepare my wife for burial? I must make a coffin for her. Then we must have her service and leave as soon as possible. I know we thought we had more time, but I am afraid that we don't. It is too dangerous to stay any longer. Are you ready?"

"I'm about ready, sir, and yes, I'll be glad to prepare Frau Hartzell. It's an honor to be asked. Can I help with the coffin? What do you have to line it with?"

"We'll line it with the dress she was married in thirty-four years ago," he answered. Rachel had gone into the room, closed Grandma's eyes and straightened her body as best she could. Grandpa measured her and called Schotzy. Then, seeing Abner sitting on the bed so forlorn, he went to him, took him on his lap and cradled him like a baby.

"It's hard, especially when you've prayed earnestly for someone to be healed and they're not. But God's ways are not our ways. This journey that we must take would have been very hard on your grandma. Had you noticed how fussed up she had been getting lately? We must trust God. He knows what's best for all of us."

"Yes, sir," cried Abner, "but I never brought her basket back."

Schotzy was crying, too. "I just lost another grandma."

Grandpa put an arm around Schotzy, too, and said in the kindest most compassionate voice Abner had ever heard, "Oh, Schotzy, you have gone through a lot, and this is one more blow; but it's bound to get better. Your name Ephraim means fruitful in a suffering land. Don't ever forget that. In the Bible, Joseph named one of his sons Ephraim. He suffered a lot, but God was there with him, and he was fruitful in a suffering land. We will take your name to be a promise. You will be fruitful. It is God's promise to you. You are a good boy. I'm glad that you are now part of our family and are going along with us to Pennsylvania." The three of them consoled each other until Grandpa asked Schotzy, "Do you think it is safe for you to be out on the streets?"

"I think so, sir. I don't see why not. They don't see me as worth bothering about, the people."

"Do you suppose you could find Willy?"

"Ya," Schotzy answered. "I know where he lives and I don't think he will be out roaming the streets after all this fussing around."

"Will you please find him and tell him that I need to see him immediately. The soldiers are here and I believe he will be safe if he moves fast. After you find Willy, go to the brethren of our church and tell them to come here because we need to meet together as soon as possible. Tell the first one you see to go tell others in all directions until everyone has the word."

Abner sat on his bed feeling useless. "Please, isn't there anything I can do to help? I'm not sick or anything, I'm just ferdutzed, much better than yesterday."

"If you could get blankets or quilts together for bedrolls for yourself, your mother, Schotzy and me, that would be helpful. But I do not want you to exert yourself. It is important that you are as strong as possible when we leave here."

"The other day Mama said that she was going to get things together in case we had to leave in a hurry," said Abner. "I wonder if any of it is still at our house."

"Probably not, so you may as well take bedding from here. Also, look through your grandmother's things and if there is anything that you would like that was hers, you may have it; but remember, you may have to carry it. Tell your mother I would like her to take all of the jewelry and anything she thinks your father would like to have."

Abner looked around the house, then walked up the steps and looked at things up there. He glanced out the window and saw Willy running around the corner toward the back of Grandpa's house. His curiosity got the better of him and he headed for the workshop where Grandpa had gone to work on Grandma's coffin. He got there just as Willy was telling Grandpa that he was sorry.

"Willy," said Grandpa, "I'm glad you are sorry, but as I told Abner just recently, being sorry isn't enough. You must determine to control yourself from now on. You can control yourself with God's help. You know you're are in great danger, don't you? In fact; we all are."

"Ach. I know," answered Willy, twisting his fingers nervously. "Did you send for me to tell me that?"

"No, I sent for you to see if you would be willing to go to Kittzheim and ask Herr Wildasin, the wagonmaster, to come here as fast as he possibly can."

Willy nodded.

"Good. Now I think you should go home, fix a bedroll, and not come back to Rittendorf if that's all right with your papa. The soldiers can't keep an eye on everyone all of the time. If you get away once, you'd best not come back."

"I understand, sir. Would it be all right for Otto to go along with?"

"If you can promise me that you two won't get into any trouble or try to play any tricks that backfire, it will be all right with me. You will be responsible for your own safety, you know. How old are you?"

"Fourteen."

"I hope you've learned your lesson."

"Yes, sir, I have. I feel awful bad about Max. He was the leader, and we just did whatever he said. Now I think Otto and I have had enough tricks to last us our whole lives. I'm truly sorry."

"I'll give you money to pay the wagonmaster. I do hope he can come right away. May I suggest that you pack your dinner and carry it along."

When Grandpa went to get the money, Willy turned and saw Abner. He looked ashamed and said, "I'm sorry you got in trouble on account of us. We didn't think. How is your head?"

Abner put his hand on the back of his head. "The lump's still there, and I'm not sure what day it is, and everyone tells me my shiner is beautiful, all purple and getting yellow around the edges, but I'll be all right."

"If I can ever do anything for you to make up for it, I will, and that's a promise," said Willy as he put out his hand. Abner extended his, and they shook hands like men.

Grandpa came back, gave Willy the money and as he left Grandpa said, "May God's angels watch over you."

Grandpa immediately got back to the task of making Grandma's coffin. Abner watched a couple of minutes, then reached out and helped hold the board steady and then asked, "Wouldn't you be able to make the coffin faster, if I held the boards for you?" Grandpa smiled, nodded and kept on working. He had sawed the headboard and the footboard first, and now he was working on the sides and bottom. He did not make a tapered coffin as usual, because it would take much more time to mitre the sides and fit them together properly. When the sawing was finished, he fit the boards together and hammered in the nails one by one.

"I really appreciate these nails," Grandpa said. "Did you find them among your papa's things?"

"Grandpa, I told you that it was a secret, now don't ask me, because I'll never tell. I'm trying hard to keep a secret." Abner shook his finger at him and said in a teasing voice, "You ought to be ashamed of yourself for trying to worm it out of me." Grandpa laughed for the first time that day.

The brethren of the church and their families were gathered before the coffin was finished; and Grandpa went into the house to address them. "Our senior elder is gone and it is time to draw lots for a new leader. It is biblical to draw lots. We trust that the one who the Lord wants to be the leader will be the one who will be chosen. We must have at least three names."

Someone called out, "Frederick Hartzell." No one else was nominated.

"In this case every man's name must be must be placed in a basket. Abner, go get a basket and some paper, ink and a quill." Grandpa wrote every man's name on a piece of paper. Schotzy cut the names apart, put them in the basket and stirred them around. A small child drew out one piece of paper, and on it was written: "Frederick Hartzell."

Grandpa bowed his head and prayed, "Father, I know that being a leader is an awesome responsibility. I ask you to give me your strength, wisdom, and courage. *'Let the words of my mouth and the meditation of my heart be acceptable in your sight, O Lord my strength and my redeemer.'* [*] Help us to know your will and to do your will. We ask that you will give us protection as we leave this place and go to another place that you have prepared for us. We ask this in Jesus name." Most of the people said, "Amen."

Abner was surprised when a man spoke up, "My wife and I think that you and Elder Wentz blew this thing all out of proportion. If we just sit back and mind our own business, and let things cool off, everything will be all right. If we move to America, we will lose our house here and we will have no home there. I can't see that that's going to benefit us. We're staying right here." *He wasn't hit on the head with a rock like I was, or killed like Pastor Wentz,* Abner thought.

"We're not going either," stated another man. "It will blow over. We'd lose too much if we go. If all of these homes go on the market at once, no one will get anywhere near the value of any of them."

"You're right," another man called out. "We won't get nothing for our homes. The minute we move out someone will squat in them, and we will never be paid for them. You know that's true."

"My parents are too old to move, and there would be no one to take care of them if I go," said another.

"I'm afraid," said a woman. "What about those Indians? I know Herr Altland said that the Indians are friendly, but I don't trust them, and I don't really know him. How do I know that he's telling the truth?"

Grandpa held up his hand for quiet. "No one has to go who doesn't want to, but my family and I are going as soon as possible. You may or may not know that my wife died earlier this afternoon. We will have a service for her as soon as the coffin is finished and

---

[*] Psalm 19:14

the hole is dug. I really do not want to leave here either, but I had a visitor from heaven earlier today who told me that we had best leave immediately. He said that the Lord wanted me to lead you people to the new Promised Land across the ocean and across a wide river. I was chosen to be your leader in confirmation of his visit and message. God wants this new country to be settled by godly people who will form a new kind of government with no kings."

"That's a little too much for me to swallow," said a man as he stood up to leave. "How could any country get along without a king? It's unheard of. Come on, wife. We've wasted too much time already."

"But I want to go to Pennsylvania," she objected. "If we stay here, we'll have to go back to the other church. How can we do that, believing as we do?"

The man took her roughly by the arm and said, "We've had enough of this nonsense."

"No," she said defiantly.

In an ugly tone of voice he said "You're coming with me," and he dragged her from the room. Abner heard her crying as they left and he felt bad about it, but he knew that no one should interfere between a man and his wife.

"Will the rest of you please hear me out?" pleaded Grandpa. He waited for them to settle and then continued, "When the angel told Joseph to take Mary and Jesus and go to Egypt, did Joseph say, 'It doesn't suit me to go this year; I'll go next year after I've sold my house, otherwise I'll lose a lot of money?' Thousands of baby boys were killed that time, and thousands of people in other parts of Europe have been killed this time. What makes you think you're safe? All that I can say is, anyone who wants to go with us should get ready now, and come back here as soon as possible. We may not be able to leave today but certainly by tomorrow. To the rest of you, I wish you the best."

Abner and Schotzy followed Grandpa back to the workbench where he was putting the finishing touches to the coffin. As he pounded in the last nail, the magistrate and the Protestant minister came bursting in. "We've had reports that you were pounding nails, and we came to investigate," the magistrate stated. With a devilish look on his face, he continued, "And look what we discovered! We've caught you in the act of using nails. You know that all nails in this country, except those used to shoe horses, belong to the king. We know that you have been out of nails for awhile. Where did you get the ones you were using?"

"I can't tell you," answered Grandpa.

"Then we are placing you under arrest."

Looking first at Abner and then at Schotzy, Grandpa said to them very calmly, "This is not about nails. Get yourselves ready. Keep the faith and keep quiet. I will not be hurt. I do not know how God will work this out, but he will." Turning to the magistrate and the minister, he asked, "May I please be given time to bury my wife?"

"No! You are under arrest for heresy against the church, for suspicion in the death of Herr Schotzenberger, and for stealing the king's nails," said the magistrate. "You are much too dangerous to be released."

Abner started to say, "But I'm the..."

He was interrupted by Grandpa who said very sternly, "Don't say a word, and do as I say. Find someone to put your grandma to rest. I know that I will be all right. I know that God will protect me."

"That's what you think," sneered the magistrate. "You had better get someone to dig two graves instead of just one." He took hold of one of Grandpa's arms. The minister took hold of the other, and they led him away. The boys stood there stunned by the speed of the events.

"We'd best do what Grandpa told us to do," said Abner.

"Well," said Schotzy, "I don't think it is safe for you to be on the street, besides you might not be well enough." He laughed, "Sometimes you seem to be right in the head, and sometimes you're all ferdudzt." He stopped laughing. "All right, I'll get serious. I'll do the errands; just tell me what to do."

"Have I been all ferdudzt these last few days?"

"Yes, you haven't known what day it is since Friday and today is Monday. Now tell me what I should do."

"I think that Herr Hoke, you know, the husband of the neighbor lady that watched after Grandma, I think that he would be the one to ask to dig the grave and to see about the burial. If you happen to see Klaus, tell him what's going on. What else did he say? What else did Grandpa say?"

"He said for us to get ready to leave here. How should we do that?"

"Get whatever you want from your house. We promised Trudy we'd get someone to carry down the chest for her. I hope we can take it. I'll try to make up the bedrolls, and then I'll help my mother. I wish I could do more."

Abner tried to stay calm, but he was very agitated when he went into the house. His mother, looking at him asked, "What is the matter? Are you sick again? You look like a pan of sour milk."

"Mama," he said, trying not to cry. "The magistrate and the minister have arrested Grandpa; but he said that he knew that he would be all right. He said to get ready. We'll leave as soon as we can. He didn't seem afraid, but I am. I'm really scared."

"Ach," she said putting her arms around him. "This is too much. You go ahead and cry if you want to. Just too much has happened, and we're supposed to get ready to leave. How can we do everything that needs to be done with my broken wrist and you not as strong as you usually are? God is going to have to perform a miracle for us to get out alive."

Abner stood up, wiped his eyes, blew his nose and said, "After Schotzy's pappaw died I told him that he was very brave, and he said that he had to be brave because he was the man of the family now." He straightened himself up, smiled a weak smile, and said, "If Schotzy can do it, I can do it."

Rachel looked at her son tenderly, "I'm proud of you, and I'm sorry I knocked you down," she said. "We'll get out of this somehow, with God's help."

"If we want a miracle, Mama, we'd best pray for one."

"You're right, son. Isn't it funny that we can be in such a bad situation and not even think about praying? I am afraid, too. I'll admit that. I never wanted to move to this village, but now that I know that I have to leave it, I don't want to do that either. Isn't it strange, too, that people we've known for a long time can suddenly turn on us? Yes, we must pray. Abner, you begin."

Abner looked shyly at his mother. He took a deep breath, thought a bit and began, "Father in Heaven, I ask you to protect us and especially Grandpa. In Jesus' name, Amen."

"Aren't you going to thank him for anything?"

Abner looked at her in surprise, "What is there to thank him for? We're being driven from our homes and our village. Papa's away. Your wrist is broken. Grandma is dead and so is Elder Wentz, not to mention Max. Grandpa's been arrested. They burned down our meeting place. Soldiers are in our house. They killed our pig, and I'm all ferdudzt and I have a black eye. So what's to thank him for?"

"You can thank him that you and I weren't killed the other day," she said . "And we, you and I, made it through the winter." Rachel paused and thought, and then added, "And you and I have broken through some kind of a barrier that kept us apart. That's something to thank the Lord for."

Abner bowed his head again and prayed, "Lord, I'm sorry I couldn't think of anything to thank you for. Thank you for watching over us and protecting us and thank you for giving me the mother that you gave me." He looked up again.

Rachel said gently, "Jesus said to pray for your enemies."

"What?" Abner became angry just thinking about it. "You expect me to pray for those rotten eggs who hit me on the head with a rock, and made you break your wrist? You mean to say that I'm supposed to pray for those miserable men who took Grandpa, and the soldiers who took Papa, and the people who broke into our house and stole our stuff? I'd just as soon cuss 'em all out."

"I understand," said Rachel with a smile. "You can believe I understand, but that's a habit that's better not to get into. Let's get back to what we were talking about. There has to be a good reason for Jesus to have said that we should pray for our enemies. I know I was angry, but that didn't solve anything, did it? Right now, your grandfather is in the hands of two unscrupulous men who will show no mercy. We need a miracle in order for him to be released and for all of us to leave the country safely. I know that it's hard to pray for your enemies, but we must pray according to God's will, and that means we must pray for our enemies."

"All right, Mama, what shall we say?"

"Let's think about it. The minister never does these things himself. He gets the people to do them for him. He knows that he will have to stir the people up before they will do any harm to your grandfather."

"That's right, Grandpa is the kindest man in the world. He has done favors for nearly everyone in the village. Everybody knows that."

Rachel nodded in assent. "Ever since I came here, and long before that, he always spent one whole day every two weeks working for needy people. He never charged them because he said that it was part of his tithe. I used to say to your papa, 'That old man is crazy working like that for people who don't appreciate him,' and your papa would say, 'That's his way of showing real Christian love.' Now we'll see if the people remember or not." Abner and Rachel began reciting the good things Grandpa had done:

"He fixed their broken furniture, and repaired their roofs and porches and mended their fences."

"He listened whenever they wanted someone to talk to, gave them good advice and helped them whenever they were in trouble."

"He wrote letters for them and read letters to those who couldn't read."

"He gave food to the hungry and took in people who had no place to stay."

"He either loaned them money or gave them money for emergencies when there was no one else to turn to."

"He watched after the older children in a family while Grandma was helping to bring a new baby into the world."

"He always helps put things to rights every year after the Hallowe'eners come up from Kittzheim to cause all the devilment they could, tipping over outhouses, breaking down fences, soaping up people's windows, putting cows in a pig pen and any other trouble they could get away with."

Abner stopped and thought a bit then added, "You know, Mama, it seemed like there was more damage this last fall than most years, and that odd one that acted strange and talks funny wasn't along with them."

Rachel laughed, "Do you mean to tell me that you never guessed that the odd one was your father? He always dressed up in old clothes and tried to keep some of the hellions from doing so much harm, especially to old people's property."

Abner shook his head unbelievingly. "No," he said, "I never would've guessed that was my papa. He's a good actor, ain't?"

"Ya, he's a good actor and a good man, just like your grandpa."

"If the people of this village think about how good Grandpa is, how can they hurt him?"

"I think now we know how to pray," said Rachel. "I think that we should pray that God will bring to everyone's mind all good deeds your grandfather has done. Then we'll ask God to put it in their hearts not to harm him in any way."

"Yes, Mama, that's what we will do." Both of them bowed their heads and prayed silently.

After they had prayed awhile, Abner looked up and said, "This is funny, but it's like God spoke to me and said that we were still praying for Grandpa, not for our enemies."

Rachel raised her eyebrows and thought a bit, and said, "It's true. So now what should we pray?"

"Last week one day, something came up and Grandpa said, *'Ye shall know the truth and the truth shall make you free.'*[*] So I asked him what it meant, and he said that God's word is the truth; and when you know what is in the Bible you know the truth. So I asked him what it freed you from, and he said that truth would free you from any bondage. He said that Grandma refused to believe that, and she was in bondage to superstition all of her life."

---

[*] John 8: 32

"All right, that makes sense," said Rachel. "So we'll pray that the people of this village will know the truth, that the truth will set them free, and that they will be blessed because of this day, including the magistrate, the minister and the ones who broke into our house."

After they had prayed for their enemies Abner asked, "What else we should pray about?"

"We need help. Trudy had to go home. Someone came and told her that her mother fell and hurt herself so badly that she couldn't get up. Someone had to lift her off the floor and put her in bed. Trudy left immediately."

"I'll pray that this doesn't keep Trudy from going."

"How about Widow Schneider? She's the one who's hurt. Don't you think you should pray for her?"

"She's another one that I'd just as soon not pray for, but I will if you say so."

Rachel smiled. "You know what's right." She reached over, mussed his hair, and then became serious. "Trudy left before she finished with your grandma. She needs to be taken care of and I can't do it. Besides that, I can't lift anything heavy or move things around to get ready. It's good to take time out to pray."

"I'll do whatever I can to help; but if I get too tired, I get all ferhuddled. Schotzy says I'm all ferdudst, but I'm not that bad, am I?"

Rachel had to laugh, "You're funny, and I know you'd help, but there are some things that are just too heavy for you. I hope we can go to our house before we have to leave here. There are things there that we need to take, but it's not safe for us to go out on the street in order to get them." They prayed again and while they were praying, there was a knock on the door.

It was Antonio. "I will help," he said. Abner took him out to get the coffin; and Antonio carried it into the house. He proceeded to do everything that remained to be done to prepare Grandma for burial. When he was finished he came out of the bedroom, nodded seriously, and pointed towards the door.

CHAPTER SIXTEEN

Abner and Rachel went into the room together. "She was the best Grandma anybody ever had," he said as he looked at her sweet face.

"And she was a good mother to me, too," said Rachel, wiping her eyes. "I learned a lot from her, and I could have learned more if I hadn't been so bullheaded."

They walked to the window that overlooked the street and stood looking out. Abner was thinking about the good times he had had in this house and the great love that his grandma had always shown him. *We're going to leave here and we'll never see this place or Grandma again.* He wiped his tears on his sleeve and said, "Grandpa told me that I could have anything of hers that I wanted and that you should take all of her jewelry." He looked around the room and spotted a beautiful patchwork quilt that she had just finished. I think I'll take that quilt and keep it until I'm grown up."

Rachel found the jewelry. It was quite old and Grandma had not worn it for years; not since they had joined the Brethren movement and the elders had said it was not biblical for women to wear jewelry. Rachel looked at it longingly. "I know I can't wear it," she said, "but I won't sell it unless I have to. I'm not sure how to hide it. It should be sewn inside my clothes, and I can't sew with my wrist broken."

Abner took the quilt and rolled it up inside an older one. As he finished, he looked out the window again and saw a mob of noisy people coming down the street. In the front the mob was Grandpa, accompanied by the minister and the magistrate.

"Stand back from the window," whispered Rachel, as if they could hear her for all of the racket. "You must not let them see you. This is a dangerous situation."

When the minister reached the front of the house, he stopped, began to shout. Abner could hear every word. "This is the home of

206

the villainous heretic who stands before you. He slanders our church and our people and he teaches others his heretical views. I asked him if he would renounce his evil ways and return to our church. I asked him if he would obey the king's ruling, the ruling that has kept people in this country from religious warfare for many, many years. He refused. DID YOU HEAR THAT? HE REFUSED!" The minister stopped shouting and looked around, pleased with the way things were going.

"Frederick Hartzell is also guilty of taking part in the death of Walter Schotzenberger," shouted the magistrate. "He threatened Herr Schotzenberger the last time he was seen in this village. Two days later he was found dead. That's not all. We saw him using nails this very afternoon. Now it is well known that he has been out of nails for quite some time. Where did he get them? He won't tell. No doubt he made a pact with the devil to get them, or stole them from the blacksmith. There is enough evidence here for the death penalty, but that is too easy. First, he should be given thirty-nine lashes with a whip."

The minister motioned to the sexton who was holding the whip and ordered, "Begin!"

Abner had edged up to the window so he could see. The sexton stood still, not lifting the whip. "Oh God," prayed Abner. "Now is the time for the miracle. You can do it. Please make the sexton remember the many times Grandpa took food from his garden to him, his wife, and his seven children. Please make him remember how Grandpa mended his fence and dug his garden around when he'd hurt his back, and please make him remember how Grandma helped bring his babies into the world."

The sexton looked around for a way out, but the minister insisted. The sexton tried to lift his arm, but he couldn't. Then he began to shake until he slumped to the ground and could not move.

The minister took the whip from the sexton and handed it to another man. Abner knew that Grandpa had taken food and clothing to this man's family. He remembered also that Grandpa had repaired a window in his house that one of his children had broken.

It had been in the wintertime and very cold. Grandpa had even supplied the pane because the man had no money to pay for it. This man reluctantly took the whip, but he, too, shook until he fell to the ground. The minister handed the whip to another man and then another. Each man who took the whip shook until he could no longer stand, and down he went.

After five men had fallen, and all of them lay quiet, a great fear came over the mob. They didn't know if the men on the ground were dead or alive, but everyone backed away from the minister as fast as possible because no one wanted to be handed the whip. Someone in the back of the mob shouted, "He's a good man. Let him go." Another in the back shouted, "Let him bury his wife." Someone else called out; "We won't let anyone harm you, Herr Hartzell."

Just then the soldiers rode up on their horses. Abner could see the sergeant talking to the minister and heard him say, "Give me the whip, I'll take care of any yellow dog heretic, just as the king has commanded." He took the whip, shook and fell over, too. This left Klaus in command of the soldiers.

Klaus faced the mob, held up his hand for quiet and ordered, "All right, everyone, go home." To the minister and the magistrate, he said, "Turn Herr Hartzell loose."

"You have no authority over me," the magistrate answered. "You are only a corporal in the king's army. If you insist on turning this heretic loose, I will most assuredly let the king know of your conduct. You know that he wants all heretics burned at the stake, drowned, or driven out of this country. You are a soldier and letting this man go is disobeying a direct order. Is it worth your life to let Frederick Hartzell go? You know that the king will have you hanged or sent off to become a galley slave."

Klaus did not hesitate. "Turn him loose!"

The minister screamed to his parishioners, "GATHER WOOD, GET A STAKE AND A ROPE! WE'LL TAKE CARE OF THIS TROUBLEMAKER FOR GOOD!" Several men went to carry out the minister's orders. The minister and the magistrate began to lead

208

Grandpa to the village burn pile, when both of them began to shake, and then they fell over, too.

"Look at that! Look at that!" shouted Abner jumping up and down excitedly. "God's knocking them down right and left. They're dropping like flies. Grandpa's free and he's praying."

"Praise God," said Rachel, bowing her head. "Now we know that the Lord will see us through."

Schotzy ran in, followed by a smiling Grandpa. "I told you God would help us!" he said.

Abner glanced out the window and saw Klaus tying up the minister, the magistrate, and sergeant with the rope the minister had ordered. "Men!" he shouted to the soldiers. "These people need help to escape. We must help them in every way we can. You saw what happened to anyone who tried to harm Herr Hartzell. That is God's doing. The sergeant is incapable of carrying out his duties therefore I am now in charge. I take full responsibility. Private Eshbaugh and Private Heiner, go with Schotzy and do whatever he asks of you. He will show you what he wants from his house. Private Brubaker and Private Lauer, go to Pastor Wentz's widow and help her. The rest should patrol the streets to keep order. Do not touch these men on the ground and don't let anyone else touch them either."

Klaus knocked on Hartzell's back door and when Rachel answered, he stepped into the house. He looked around to see who was there, and then he spoke softly, "I must go along with you, but don't let on. I must go help Trudy to get ready."

"Don't you know that your mother fell and hurt herself badly?" asked Rachel. "She couldn't even get up. Trudy said that she can't go. She must stay and care for your mother."

Klaus squinted his eyes and looked disgusted. "That's just like my mother," he said. "She would do anything to get her own way. I saw her pull that trick more than once. She'd put a dried pea in her shoe so that she would remember to limp on the same foot. I put the pea in the other shoe when she wasn't looking; and when she put the her shoes on, and she limped on the other foot. I'll take care of her.

She'll come along if I have to hog-tie her. She is not going to stop Trudy from going along and getting married if she wants to." He turned to Grandpa and said, "You go ahead and bury your wife. The grace of God is on you, and I am sure you will be safe, but I'd feel better if you hurried."

Grandpa went to the coffin to take one last look at his wife before the final closing. "If anyone wishes to view the body, please come now," he said softly. "Isn't she beautiful? She always was so beautiful," he added with a sob.

As they all crowded around to say goodbye, Abner heard the back door open. He looked around and there were his papa and Cousin Jake! Hanging back, far behind them was a girl about Abner's size.

"What's going on here?" asked Matthias in a booming voice, and then, as his eyes became adjusted to the inside, he put his hand to his mouth and said, "Oh."

Abner and Rachel rushed to Matthias and put their arms around him.

"Much has happened since you left," said Grandpa. "Your mother passed on this morning from pneumonia. We must bury her and leave here as soon as possible. I am so glad that you are here. She's not been sick long, your mother, and she died peacefully just as this other business came to a head."

Abner could see that his father was stunned and couldn't speak. Matthias walked over, viewed his mother, and left the room without saying anything.

Grandpa closed the coffin, nailed it shut; and along with Cousin Jake, Schotzy, and Abner, began carrying it out. When they got to the door, Antonio, Matthias, and Herr Hoke joined them. Rachel, and Frau Hoke followed. It wasn't far to the cemetery and the service was a simple one.

Schotzy reached out and patted the coffin just before it was lowered into the ground and the wart on his hand fell off. He showed it to Abner and said, "Now ain't that something!"

When they got back to Grandpa's house, Abner's papa pulled him close, looked at him and said, "You've grown and almost become a man while I've been gone. It is so good to see you and know you are all right, well, almost all right." He hugged him and kissed him on both cheeks, carefully avoiding the black eye.

"You can't believe how much we missed you and how glad we are that you are here," Abner relied. "But how come you're here? How did you get away?"

"God's hand was in it. Jake showed up in just at the right time," said Matthias. "I was going to be sent to Italy today. Jake showed up three days ago. He didn't let on that he knew me; and I didn't let on either. That Jake, he's something! He's got his tricks! He pretended that he was a big shot in charge of the project; and he told the workers, soldiers, and guards that he would throw a big party before we had to go to Italy. We had worked hard, he said, and the king appreciated it. He got food, and beer, a lot of beer, and the party began. Then he said he didn't think there was enough beer and he needed a volunteer to go with him to get it, so I volunteered. Of course, he chose me and it was then that I discovered he even had a horse for me. Was I ever glad to see that horse! We stopped at a brewery, ordered more beer, and Jake told them where to deliver it. We kept right on going, and got here as fast as we could. We had a great sense of urgency. Like I said, God's hand was in it."

"Papa," said Abner, "that's just one of many miracles that have taken place around here lately. Wait 'til we tell you."

Matthias patted Abner on the head, mussed his hair, and said, "That black-eye! I wish I could hear all about it and everything else, but we must get moving. So, what is everybody going to do now?"

"I'm going to go see Trudy," said Cousin Jake. "I wonder what she'll say. Can you tell me what she has decided?

Rachel smiled. "It's not up to me to tell you whether or not she'll marry you," she teased.

Cousin Jake started to leave when he remembered the little girl. "Ach, I'm a fine one," he sputtered. "I forgot about your little niece here. That's what thinking about Trudy does to me. She leaves me all ferhuddled." He motioned to the girl and said, "Minnie, dear, come here wunst." She had been out on the bench, petting Princess,

211

and Abner heard him say, "I didn't mean to forget you, little one." Cousin Jake put his arm around her and brought her into the kitchen. "Minnie, this is your Aunt Rachel, and your cousin Abner. Abner, I want you to meet your cousin, Minnie Ness."

Abner saw a skinny girl who needed to comb her reddish brown hair, wash her dirty face, and put on a clean dress. "How do you do, Minnie Mess."

She scowled at Abner and said firmly, "That's Minnie Ness and don't you forget it." She turned on her heel and went outside without looking back.

Cousin Jake began explaining to Rachel why he had brought Minnie. "Your sister is not good at all, and the rest of the family was talking about binding Minnie out. I knew how you felt about girls being bound out, so I brought her along. I knew she would be welcome, but I had no idea of how it was here. There really was no one else for Minnie to stay with."

Cousin Jake lowered his voice, and Abner strained to hear him. "Actually nobody wanted her because she can be a difficult child. I thought that she might be of help to you, though; and that you could handle her. She can cook, clean, milk cows, make cheese, garden, and whatever else you would want her to do. All you have to do is figure out how to get her to do it." Abner stayed very still, pretending that he had not heard.

Rachel went to the door, called Minnie and when she came, Rachel put her good arm around her. She looked her full in the face, smiled and said, "I want to welcome you, Minnie. I'm sure we can get along together. Can you sew?"

"Some."

"Come, I needed a girl just like you to help me. I'll show you what I'd like you to do. You are an answer to prayer."

Abner watched them head upstairs and asked, "Who all is going to our house now? I want to go along."

Rachel turned around, looked at him and said, "I know you want to, but you really must rest. Tell your papa what you want and where it's at, and then you must lie down."

"Oh, Mama, must I?" Abner almost cried, but he held back because he couldn't cry in front of a girl. "I'm never going to see my house again and there are so many things I want, I won't be able to remember to tell him all of them."

"I know, but you couldn't take all you want anyway. I'm sorry, but you have been through a lot, you are going through a lot more, and you really must rest. We'll probably be up all night."

Abner sighed a deep sigh of defeat and said, "Oh, all right." Actually he was so tired he couldn't think of what he wanted to take along anyhow, except the money in his pillowcase.

Abner lay in bed, looked up at the soulenfenster and thought, *Well, little window, my soul won't escape through you. I wonder whose soul will be the next to go through. This much I know; it won't be a Hartzell, because we're leaving.* He was too wound up to sleep and he began wondering about Minnie. He knew that girls could be trouble. *I've never been around girls much,* he thought. *We got along without one for all these years, and I don't see why we have to have one now. I'll have to think up some good tricks to play on her. It wonders me if she'll be a good sport or if she'll brutz. Ach, she'll brutz! I know she will. Well, if she does, she does. Schotzy and I will have fun with her.*

He still couldn't sleep, and he thought, *It wonders me who will go along. The woman whose husband dragged her out of the meeting, Frau Bentzel, she's nice, and I hope they go. I know she wants to. They rent their house from the magistrate, so they wouldn't lose any property if they did leave. Max's parents, I'm sure they'll go. They have lots of children and are very poor. All of them will no doubt have to become bondservants. Cousin Jake says it's a chance for a better life. I wonder if I'll have to be a bondservant. One thing's for sure, Schotzy won't have to. The blacksmith, he doesn't go to our church, but he sounded disgusted with the king. It would be good if he went. A blacksmith is always needed wherever he goes.* He tried to think of others, but he dozed off, and seemed like no time at all until his mother awakened him.

"Wake up, we must go," said Rachel. "Everything and everybody is ready except you. Your papa I found nine pfennig and this little dog in your room and brought them along. I thought you would want them."

"Thanks, Mama, the money is mine and the dog is Schotzy's. I accidentally broke off its tail. Do you think Papa can fix it?"

"I'm sure he'll try, but you must hurry. Here's your coat and hat. Go to the outhouse, get a drink of water; and I'll get some bread and cheese for you. You'll have to carry this bag of apple snitz. Just think, we'll be on the road tomorrow for your birthday. Except for the last nine months, these ten years have gone by fast."

When Abner went outside, he saw the minister, the magistrate, the sergeant, and the other men still lying on the ground, and asked Grandpa, "What's going to happen to them?"

"No doubt they will come to after we are safely on our way."

Abner looked around. No one was close so he whispered, "Did you get the gold?"

Grandpa nodded, "Ya."

"Did you hide it good?"

"Ya," Grandpa whispered. "It's inside the horses' saddles on the cart."

Abner looked again, the two horses that Cousin Jake and his papa had ridden were hitched up to two small carts and the cows were tethered to the back. The carts were loaded with Trudy's chest, bedrolls, clothing, food, and tools. Everyone, including the little children, was carrying something. Antonio had his precious box with the queen bees. *That's good*, thought Abner; *Antonio kept bees in his country and he would keep them in Pennsylvania, too.*

The neighbor lady, Frau Hoke and her husband were there. So Max's whole family, as well as Willy's and Otto's. There were Elder Wentz's wife and children; and Klaus was wearing Elder Wentz's clothes. They were a little tight, and he looked a lot different from when he was in uniform. His mother stood beside him. Trudy and Jake were standing together and they looked like people should look when they are in love. The blacksmith, his wife and five children brought up the rear, riding on a wagon with his

214

anvil and everything he used in his trade. The Bentzels weren't there. *That's too bad,* he thought; *they'll be sorry before it's all over with.*

There was a strange-looking person, standing near his mother that he didn't recognize. The man was rough shaven and had on ragged clothes. He was bent over like Schotzy's Grandpa Slonaker used to be; and he stood, moved, and acted as if he weren't quite right. *Who can that person be? It's odd to have such a person join us now.* The stranger motioned for him to come closer, but Abner hesitated.

"He wants to talk to you," said Grandpa. "It's all right, he's not as strange as he looks."

In a rough ugly voice, the stranger asked, "How old you be, boy?"

"Ten years old tomorrow," answered Abner nervously.

"You'll never forget it, this birthday. Here, I made a present for you."

Abner took the present. It was a ball, made of the pig's bladder and stuffed with sawdust. He took it, looked at it and smiled with pleasure. Then he looked at the stranger closely, and gasped, "You cut off your beard. You're my papa!"

Matthias grinned, put his finger to his lips, and whispered, "You don't know me. This is in case the soldiers come looking for me. I figured if you didn't recognize me, they wouldn't either."

"You fooled me. I never saw you before without a beard," whispered Abner. "Thanks for the ball. It was the nicest thing you could have given me. Except for your coming back."

"I figured you deserved something for all of the times you fed that pig." Matthias looked around and added, "I think we are about ready to go. Just don't hang around me very much. I'd just as soon nobody knows me."

Abner nodded his head and walked to where Schotzy was standing. "How did Klaus get his mother to come?" he asked.

Schotzy laughed. "Jake told her that there lots of unmarried men in Pennsylvania, young and old, rich and poor, many men with nice houses and no wife to live in them. He told her that no doubt she could have her pick. When she saw that Trudy was determined to go, she got right out of bed and got ready as fast as she could. She decided that she had best come along. That Jake could talk anybody into anything. Look how he talked your mother into taking in Minnie."

"So you've met Minnie Mess," said Abner.

Minnie, who was near, heard him. She walked over close to Abner, looked at him straight in the eye and punched him in the gut as hard as she could. "I told you not to mess with a Ness," she said as she walked away.

Abner was surprised and hurt, but he didn't want to let on.* "Don't anybody go without me," he shouted. "I have to get Princess." He handed Schotzy the ball and the apple snitz, ran back around the barn and doubled over with pain. He stood there for a few seconds catching his breath and then called, "Kitty, kitty, kitty. Come here, Princess." *That blasted cat is always under foot when you don't want her.*

As he looked for the cat he took notice that people were fighting over who would move into Grandpa's house and Hoke's house. He shook his head thinking, *Those greedy people can't even wait until we're gone.* He looked around the village and up the street toward his house, and thought, *Goodbye my village, goodbye my house. I wonder who'll be sleeping in my bed tonight. Tomorrow is my birthday, and I will be ten years old. I've lived here every day of my life and now I'll probably never live here again.*

Princess emerged from the barn, yawning and stretching. "Come on, kitty," Abner said, as he scooped her up and ran back to the others just as the sun went down.

Grandpa held up his hand. "We must ask God's blessing on this trip. We will walk down to the Rhine River, catch a boat to the ocean, and then get on a ship for Philadelphia, Pennsylvania. Jake and Karl say it is a dangerous journey. There are thieves and bounty hunters who would get a reward for turning us in. If this were

---

* let on: let it be known, act as if it bothered him

216

summer or fall we would go through the mountain pass into Switzerland. It would be quicker and safer then but you know that springtime is avalanche season and Antonio says there is a great amount of snow that could come down on us. Whichever way we go there is danger, but God will be with us. Let us pray. 'Father, we ask for your continuing care and we thank you for it. In Jesus' name. Amen.'" He looked up and said, "Before we leave, I want to ask Jake about the wide river that we will cross before we get to our Promised Land. What is the name of it?"

Cousin Jake looked up, smiled and called out, "It's called the Susquehanna."

THE END

Characters:

Abner Hartzell
Schotzy, Ephraim Schotzenberger
Frederick Hartzell, Grandpa
Bertl Hartzell, Grandma
Rachel Hartzell, Abner's mother
Matthias Hartzell, Abner's papa
Jacob Altland, Penn's land agent and Rachel's cousin
Walter Schotzenberger, Schotzy's pappaw
Widow Schneider, member of their sect that other members care for
Trudy Schneider, Widow Schneider's daughter
Klaus Schneider, corporal in the king's guard and Widow Schneider's son
The Magistrate (no name)
Protestant minister (no name)
Herr Hoke and Frau Hoke, the neighbor lady and her husband
Elder Wentz, elder (leader) of the Brethren
Herr Kessler, powwow doctor
Antonio Eby, a refugee from the south and a beekeeper
Otto Schwartz, Max Bosserman and Willy Gruver, boys who cause trouble
Pete Wildasin, wagonmaster, owner of the livery stable in Partenbuhl
Herr Schmitt, the blacksmith
Private Brubaker
Private Eshbaugh
Private Heiner
Private Lauer
Dolly, Beppy and Gretel, the cows

GLOSSARY

A
ach du lieber: good heavens
air going: breeze blowing
all: all gone
apple snitz: dried apple slices
aside: beside
awhile: The use of awhile is an idiom that defies explanation. It probably means at this time.

B
be dear: are expensive
be-ins: due to the fact that
believe so half: think so, but not completely sure
beppy: baby
better would: had better
better wouldn't: had better not
biergarten: saloon or beer hall
big-feeling: pompous, arrogant, acting as if one is more important than he is
bitey: bitter
brutz: to whine or cry (rhymes with puts)
brutzich: whining or crying; brutz is the verb (rhymes with put stick)
butterbread: buttered bread; bread with jelly is jellybread; bread with honey is honeybread.

C
cakes: soft cookies
carry them so: as they are

chamomile: a small aromatic plant used for healing even in the 21st century (pronounced kam uh mile)

cluck: setting hen (rhymes with look)

cold cellar: a deep cellar with a ground floor, where vegetables and fruits are kept

croup: deep persistent cough (rhymes with soup)

cuppy: couple

D

daresn't: we dare not; we should not

defrocked: removed from the priesthood

dig it around: turn the ground over with a shovel and prepare it for planting

dippy egg: toast dipped in a soft boiled or sunny-side-up egg

doppy or doppich: clumsy, awkward (rhymes with sloppy)

drysink: a wooden sink without plumbing

dumkopf: dumb-head, stupid person

Dunkards: members of he Brethren Church, because they baptize by full immersion; from dunk, to dip, thus mocking their baptism

Dutcher: Pennsylvania Dutchman, a person from the Deutchland

E

Englisher: A person from England

ess: eat

excommunicated: thrown out of the Catholic Church

F

fastnachts: heavy fried doughnuts traditionally eaten on the day before Lent

fer: for

ferdudst: not right in the head (dud rhymes with stood)   All ferdudst means completely bewildered, much worse off than being ferhuddled.

ferhuddled: confused, bewildered (hud rhymes with stood)

fetch-me's: fetching whatever is needed

feverfew: an herb with healing properties; good for headaches

filling: dressing or stuffing for a bird

fix: see in a fix and out of fix

fress: to gobble, eat like an animal

freundschaft: any blood relative up to second or third cousins and even beyond (rhymes with find loft)

furrected: worn out, out of shape, broken

fussed up: nervous and worried

G

gasthaus: inn (sounds like gast house)

gawksing: gawking, wasting time by looking around

get legs: walk off by itself

give another baby: have another baby

give you right: admit you're right

gockies: eggs; hens cackle gock, gock, gock after they lay an egg;

greistlich: ugly, disgusting (rhymes with spiced pig)

grex: fuss and moan

growling: grumbling, complaining

gut: good (rhymes with boot)

guten appetit: enjoy your meal literally, good appetite

guten morgen: good morning

H

hairs: hair

hex: curse or evil spirit

hexen schuz: literally, a witch is shooting me, casting a spell (schuz sounds like shoots) heinie: bottom

hog maw:

hope chest: a chest full of things that a girl makes or accumulates in hope that she will get married

hummy: calf

I

in a fix: in trouble

It wonders me: I wonder.

K

knitbone: an herb comfrey, used as an aid to promote healing

kruttzy: dirt encrusted, filthy, scabby (rhymes with muttsy)

kumm ess: come eat; when a human eats, the word used is 'ess,' but when an animal eats, the word used is 'fress' unless it implies that the human is eating like a pig. (kumm rhymes with doom)

kuttzed: vomited, puked (rhymes with mutts)

L

lederhosen: short leather dress pants (rhymes with raider chosen)

left: let, allowed

let: leave

let on: act as if something bothered you

listened: paid attention

little cakes: soft cookies

long already: awhile back, a long time ago

M

make down: rain

mansly: little man

N

nein: no (same as nine)

needs polished: needs to be polished, the infinitive to be is generally left out

nix-nooks: a young mischievous trickster, a bad boy (nooks rhymes with books)

O

ooey-kuttz: oh, puke (rhymes with dewy cuts)

old maid: a woman who has never married

out of fix: sick, poorly; in the case of machinery, not working right

P

panhas: scrapple, finely chopped pork and broth, thickened with meal, cooled, sliced and fried crisp (sounds like pun hoss)

peeps: baby chicks; from the fact that they go, "Peep, peep, peep," all of the time

pelthy: withered or spongy (rhymes with healthy)

poor souls: persons who are slow or can't help themselves

powwow: Rituals that have their roots in both Christianity and superstition. The word itself may have been borrowed from the Indians, but such rituals were practiced in the old world.

pressing: involuntary servitude, forcing one to work or join the army against his will

R

raus mit du: get out (raus rhymes with mouse)

raus mit du, hex: get out witch or evil spirit

rathaus: town hall (sounds like rot house)

red beet eggs: boiled eggs pickled in beet juice and vinegar

redd up: clean and straighten

rotters: rotten people

roust him out: make him get up

rutch: wiggle or squirm (rhymes with butch)

S

schmutz: kiss (rhymes with puts)

schmutzich: kissing or smearing; slobbery kisses, anything smeared such as cake icing (rhymes with puts pig)

schushlich: uncoordinated, shaky (rhymes with push pig)

si: yes (sounds like see)

shiner: blackeye

smiercase: cottage cheese (sounds like smear case)

sneaky: persnickety, picky about food; hard to please; choicy: picky about other things such as clothing

souffing: drinking, often hard liquor; a souffer is a drunk (ou in souf sounds like ou in south)

soulenfenster: soul window (soulen rhymes with stolen)

speck or schpeck: the fatty part of ham or bacon; any animal fat

spook: ghost or lost spirit (rhymes with cook)

spritz: to sprinkle or rain lightly

stand down: do something distasteful or difficult

strublich: windblown, uncombed (sort of rhymes with bubbly, sexcept the u has the same sound as oo in good)

T

the takeoff: one of the healing rituals in powwowing, a mixture of superstition and Christian doctrine

take notice: notice, pay close attention, study

toot: bag, pouch, (rhymes with foot)

W

wasn't so good: wasn't feeling well

what fer: what kind of

where the king walks: down the middle

wonderful good: wonderfully
worked up: stirred up, worried, in a nervous state
wunderbar: wonderful (pronounced voonderbar)
wunst: at once; or as an idiom: sometime, as in: Come see me
wunst.

Y
ya: yes

BIBLIOGRAPHY

Bittinger, Emmert, F. *Heritage and Promise, Perspectives on the Church of the Brethren,* The Church of the Brethren General Board, 1970

Freeman, Margaret B. *Herbs for the Mediaevil Household,* The Metropolitan Museum of Art, 1943

Heistand, Esther May Longenecker A *Pitchforks and Pitchpipes, A Portrait of a Lancaster County Mennonite Family,* Heistand Publishers, Marietta, Pennsylvania, 1990

Klees, Frederic *The Pennsylvania Dutch,* The Macmillan Co., New York, New York 1950

About the Author

Louise Coffman was born in Turlock, California, in 1924, and raised on a dairy farm in the San Joaquin Valley, a descendant of pioneers. After graduating from Modesto Junior College in 1944, she taught school for one year. She married Dean Coffman, a sailor from the Pennsylvania Dutch Country, and accompanied him there when world War II was over. Culture shock! She had never gone to a school without indoor plumbing and the school in Abbottstown, where they moved, had an outhouse. The people had customs, superstitions and ways of speaking that were strange but intriguing. When she was amused, confused, or appalled; she tried not to show it, knowing that she was just as strange to them.

In 1952, wanting a better school for their son and two daughters, they bought a wooded lot near York, lived in the garage, and spent five years building a house with the help of Dean's family. Louise became a Den Mother and a Brownie leader. Dean worked at Nabisco Pretzel Bakery. When the house was finished, he joined the Naval Reserve; and she began teaching elementary school while taking classes toward a Bachelor's Degree at Millersville University. She graduated in 1961 and earned a Master of Education Degree from Western Maryland College in 1966.

In the 50 plus years since moving east, she has learned to love the beauty of York County and respect the Pennsylvania Dutch of York County. They are different from the Lancaster Pennsylvania Dutch in that there are no Amish riding around in buggies, no one wearing 17th century costumes, and no homes without electricity. Nevertheless, she found that York Countians are products of the same Germanic culture and difficult to know. Still, as a person inside a Dutch family, she learned their ways, their speech, their food preparation and their secrets in a way no one else could.

In 1979 Louise began to free-lance for the *York-Lancaster Sunday News* and was asked to write a weekly column. *Notes from the Country* was a regular feature for nearly ten years. She retired from teaching in 1984 and became active at church, traveled and enjoyed being a grandmother to six grandchildren and two great-grandchildren. To help celebrate York County's 250th Anniversary in 1999 she wrote *Abner's Story*, to tell the reason some of the Pennsylvania Dutch left Germany in the first place.